Combating Plagiarism

Combating Plagiarism

A HANDS-ON GUIDE FOR LIBRARIANS, TEACHERS, AND STUDENTS

Terry Darr

LIBRARIES UNLIMITED®

An Imprint of ABC-CLIO, LLC

Santa Barbara, California • Denver, Colorado

Library of Congress Cataloging-in-Publication Data

Names: Darr, Terry, author.
Title: Combating plagiarism : a hands-on guide for librarians, teachers, and students / Terry Darr.
Description: Santa Barbara, California : Libraries Unlimited, an imprint of ABC-CLIO, LLC, [2019] | Includes bibliographical references and index.
Identifiers: LCCN 2019020786 (print) | LCCN 2019980586 (ebook) | ISBN 9781440865466 | ISBN 9781440865473 (ebook)
Subjects: LCSH: Plagiarism—Prevention. | Authorship—Study and teaching. | Bibliographical citations—Study and teaching. | Information literacy—Study and teaching.
Classification: LCC PN167 .D36 2019 (print) | LCC PN167 (ebook) | DDC 808.02/5—dc23
LC record available at https://lccn.loc.gov/2019020786
LC ebook record available at https://lccn.loc.gov/2019980586

ISBN: 978-1-4408-6546-6 (paperback)
     978-1-4408-6547-3 (ebook)

23 22 21 20 19   1 2 3 4 5

This book is also available as an eBook.

Libraries Unlimited
An Imprint of ABC-CLIO, LLC

ABC-CLIO, LLC
147 Castilian Drive
Santa Barbara, California 93117
www.abc-clio.com

This book is printed on acid-free paper ∞

Manufactured in the United States of America

Contents

Acknowledgments

This book is a dream come true. I am indebted to Jessica Gribble of Libraries Unlimited for an opportunity of a lifetime. Thank you to everyone at ABC-CLIO for making this book possible, especially Michelle Scott. Thank you to the hundreds of boys at Loyola Blakefield since 2009 who patiently sat through the various iterations of this instruction until I got it right. I am the librarian I am today because of all of you.

Thank you to the following people for your advice and support: Deborah Allen, Dr. Patrick Brugh, Tom Durkin, Vonda Duncan, Carolyn Fitzpatrick, Bernie Frank-Bishoff, Suzanne French-Levine, Mary Gombert, Leandra Laird, Desi Lukanova, Sherry Miles, Brian Plunkett, Kristi Skinner, Mike Skinner, Cynthia Sprehe, Dorothy Stoltz, Paula Wichmann, and Elizabeth Wise. No words will ever be able to express my appreciation to Patricia Kammer. You showed me the way.

Ultimately, this book would not have been possible without two people. Thank you to my original collaborator, Jack Crawford. Coach, we knew that we were right. Dr. Vincent Fitzpatrick: Your confidence in me made this book a reality. Thank you, sir.

Caroline Darr, this book is for you.

Introduction

Plagiarism prevention and education have never been more important than they are right now. Print books, with a definitive publication process, are no longer the mainstay of academic research for high school and college students. Digital information, now immediately and infinitely available, appears abstractly on computer screens, often without a firm connection to the authorship and publication of the source. This means a dramatic increase in the number of complex variables by which someone can unintentionally plagiarize.

This book provides a proactive, practical pedagogy for middle school, high school, community college, and university teachers and librarians to reduce plagiarism in the classroom. The digital information explosion mandates getting to know sources in a new way to respect authors and use information ethically. This instruction, when combined with information literacy, has the potential to improve student writing and research. For schools with Turnitin.com or other plagiarism checkers, this book has the resources that students and teachers need to correct plagiarism errors.

Avoiding plagiarism is a skill set. Along with numerous citation examples throughout the book, there are citation guides and an extensive student reference section. These examples are meant for illustrative purposes, *not* to be a substitute for consulting with official style manuals. The citation conventions for digital resources are in a continual state of flux; a deeper understanding of the parts of sources through the examples in this book will add context to sources seen only on a computer screen.

The reasons why students plagiarize have been discussed in the professional literature for decades. This book focuses on how to help students stop through practical information.

Here are a few of the premises found in this book:

- Citation instruction, along with a review of sources, is necessary for students, even when online citation tools are used. Now that digital sources dominate research instead of books, understanding the parameters of authorship, titles, and publication is no longer intuitive.

- Information analysis skills matter. Teaching students about relevance, common knowledge, facts, opinions, and ethical paraphrasing is an essential information skill set for every educational level and professional life.

- Talking about plagiarism changes everything. Whether the conversation is in the classroom, the library reference desk, or the writing center, students improve unintentional plagiarism through a practical learning process, which allows them to move past incorrect misperceptions through practice and discussion.

Plagiarism education is a good investment of time. Classroom instruction, along with feedback, creates a culture of academic integrity. This skill-building process reduces plagiarism without threats. The resulting confidence from this mastery can set students up for long-term academic success and good personal decision-making. Students move beyond passive reliance on citation machines and plagiarism checkers and take proactive control over their writing. They understand how to use information ethically, creating better research and writing products.

The lesson plans and exercises found in this book are designed for teachers and librarians to present as classroom instruction, classwork or homework. Students greatly benefit when librarians and teachers collaborate on plagiarism education. This instruction is also recommended for writing center staff members. It can be delivered to students during the research process, after incidents of plagiarism, or anytime during the school year. For college-bound high school students, community college students, and first-year college students, the micro-paraphrasing lesson should be repeated if time permits. After instruction and use of these practical exercises, school administrators and teachers can feel more comfortable applying consequences for plagiarism when appropriate. Education before punishment levels the playing field for students at every level.

1

The State of Plagiarism Today

The Internet is the most amazing information equalizer of our time. We are creating more information and viewing more digital information than ever before. It has created a drastic change for research, which has not been fully addressed by teachers and librarians. There is a dramatic difference between walking into a library to check out a book for research and reading a website for a similar purpose. Authorship and publication exist indefinitely in a stable, fixed format for published books. Anyone with a device and Internet connection has immediate and continuous access from anywhere to large amounts of information on many different topics through websites. This has changed the idea of authorship and publication forever. Students view so much digital information through phones and other personal devices that it all can "read" the same, even when the information is from very different source types. Authorship and publication boundaries begin to blur when these digital sources are consumed in large quantities with unrestricted access.

Consistent instruction for the ethical use of this information has been missing from the pedagogy we use to teach students. Digital information lives on a computer screen. This abstract quality creates so many variables to consider that instruction is now essential in order to reduce plagiarism.

THE ONLINE COMMUNITY

The Internet has created a global community of information seekers. We have the freedom to read whatever we want with everyone else in the world. Defined online communities thrive, with people from all over the world connecting through the computer about shared interests like health, sports, and music. Of course, at the center of this community feeling are sharing information and a feeling of common ownership (Fritz 1999; Scanlon and Neuman 2002, 374). However, this feeling of "connection" and community is superficial. Technology creates a barrier between people. This is where plagiarism often begins during the academic use of information. The fact that we do not actually know the authors of the information makes it feel less personal and less egregious when a few sentences are copied and pasted without a citation.

PLAGIARISM PERCEPTIONS

It is impossible to quantify plagiarism in classrooms today. Students are understandably reluctant to accurately self-report, even with formal research studies that guarantee anonymity (Scanlon and Neuman 2002, 378; Ma et al. 2007, 81; Sisti 2007, 228). There have been studies at the university level but far fewer with secondary school students. Students come to high school and college with little to no practical knowledge about plagiarism. They also bring the bad habits and erroneous information about plagiarism learned since elementary school (Davis 1994, 55).

Many students believe that accountability and consequences for copying and pasting from the Internet are unlikely. Technology causes a critical relationship barrier between the author and the digital information consumer. Along with unlimited access, this makes cut and paste an easy, private action. Copy and paste cannot be prevented. While there are well-publicized cases of plagiarism that have been in the news, for many, this is too far removed from the average young adult's life to have any meaning.

At the high school level, students may believe that the consequences for plagiarism will not apply to them if they have never heard of it happening to anyone else. For people who are growing up with unlimited information access, there is an understandable tendency to treat it casually (Tomaiuolo 2007, 19). They know which teachers are unknowledgeable about technology.

This makes copy and paste detection unlikely (Ma et al. 2007, 77; Sisti 2007, 225). To make things more complicated, there is a moral continuum of what they consider to be cheating. Millennials may not value intellectual property the same way as their teachers. For them, the copy and paste of few sentences is a minor infraction compared to purchasing a research paper or directly copying from a library book without a citation (Fritz 1999; Sisti 2007, 225; Evering and Moorman 2012, 38).

As we move forward, plagiarism education for high school and college students will need to emphasize two types of Internet use with different expectations: personal use and academic use. Academic use will need to be accompanied by a higher set of expectations and pedagogy. This will help sort through the various student attitudes that negatively impact ethical digital information use.

PLAGIARISM IN SCHOOLS

Plagiarism is defined by inconsistencies within the educational system. It can be difficult for a student to get a correct answer to a question about paraphrasing and plagiarism by an Internet search. Some teachers care a great deal about plagiarism; others may ignore it. For the average high school and college student, if the teacher is unconcerned with citations and plagiarism, the student will be too (Scanlon 2003, 162). A student can have both types of teachers. Plagiarism often means different things to different teachers. One teacher may consider the copy and paste of a paragraph without a citation to be plagiarism. Another teacher may think plagiarism is the failure to cite one sentence. Some high schools do not have an honor policy with a definition of plagiarism at all. College will be the first time these students are aware of plagiarism. Others may have an honor policy, but after the form is signed, there is no further discussion. There are teachers who handle plagiarism violations within the classroom structure; others will refer to the honor board or give a failing grade. Students who are homeschooled until college present challenges for plagiarism. Without access to the same range of resources, they may not understand plagiarism with digital information at all. High school students whose schools used Turitin.com will have a different perspective about plagiarism in college than those high school students who are using it for the first time.

THE ROLE OF INSTRUCTION FOR PLAGIARISM EDUCATION

Plagiarism Education Instruction

There is no comprehensive, consistent pedagogy for plagiarism in the educational system today. This is astonishing considering the dramatic increase in the accessibility and quantity of information everyone is experiencing. While there will always be students who plagiarize intentionally through laziness or defiance, research shows that much of plagiarism at the high school and university level is unintentional. It is caused by a lack of understanding and skill with citations, paraphrasing, and the ethical management of information (Wilhoit 1994, 161; Roig 1997, 121; Davis 1994, 56; Radunovich, Baugh, and Turner 2009, 30; Evering and Moorman 2012, 37; Childers and Bruton 2016, 13). As educators, we tell students not to plagiarize, but we do not explain how to stop.

Instruction works. It is necessary for students to understand citations, paraphrasing, and the variable authorship and publication cycle of digital sources. This can be in the classroom or through computer modules. There have been many substantive recommendations in the professional literature for proactive instruction to reduce plagiarism. Actively teaching the conventions of paraphrasing, citations, and quotations in writing assignments has been shown to also increase students' overall understanding of plagiarism (Whitaker 1993, 510; Barry 2006, 383; Chao, Wilhelm, and Neureuther 2009, 40; Craig, Federici, and Buehler 2010, 55; Kashian et al. 2015, 251).

Writing and Plagiarism

Plagiarism is a broad, abstract concept. It is not just a problem with the ethical use of information. It is an academic writing problem (Wilhoit 1994, 161). Paraphrasing and summarizing are important areas where students require instruction and feedback. Poor paraphrasing and summarizing are often noted as plagiarism through Turnitin and other plagiarism checkers. Rebecca Moore Howard (1995) has used the term "patchwriting" to describe the process as "copying from a source text and then deleting some words, altering grammatical structures or plugging in one-for-one substitutes" (as cited in Howard 1993, 233).

Learning how to integrate and synthesize secondary-source information is another area of need (Eckstein 2013, 100). Rebecca Moore Howard (1995, 796) and Howard and Davies (2009) have noted that patchwriting, "a blending of the learners and phrases with those of the source," is a sign that "learners employ when they are unfamiliar with the words and ideas about which they are writing." Instead of punishment, this creates an opportunity to work with students on understanding unfamiliar texts and integrating secondary-source information (Howard and Davies 2009). This process can take place in the classroom during the writing process.

When students are inexperienced with the information synthesis of unfamiliar sources, writing revisions, along with practice with paraphrasing and summarizing, is a proven pedagogy. While some students adequately paraphrase basic information, instruction helps students with paraphrasing more complex subject-specific secondary sources (Walker 2008, 391). Revising plagiarized passages provides practice with paraphrasing and understanding different plagiarism scenarios with paraphrasing (Wilhoit 1994, 163). This is a crucial issue that needs further development.

Librarians as Plagiarism Education Teachers

Who should teach students proper citations, paraphrasing, and other conventions to avoid plagiarism? Unless librarians are teaching a defined course, they need to collaborate with classroom teachers. Librarians have professional expertise in the use of sources and can help the situation (Roberts 2007, 46; Gibson and Chester-Fangman 2011, 142) by teaching students about the ethical use of information. Information literacy instruction provides a place to start. Lampert (2004, 351; 2006, 8) suggests that librarians, as research experts, should provide subject-specific plagiarism education (paraphrasing, citations, and other conventions) and secondary-source integration as part of information literacy instruction. While librarians often help students with citations, creating collaborations with faculty for plagiarism education instruction is variable (Gibson and Chester-Fangman 2010, 140). Without a more permanently assigned role for librarians, who have the knowledge and experience in the ethical use of information for plagiarism instruction and student remediation, the delivery of plagiarism education remains inconsistent.

Librarians, teachers, and writing center professionals all have an important stake in plagiarism education, but in 2019, there is no standardized plagiarism education curriculum at any educational level.

Since these research studies have been completed, the quantity of digital information has increased dramatically, amplifying the problem. While many schools have honor codes and institutional policies against plagiarism, it is unclear how much time, if any, is spent proactively teaching students the two key strategies that make the difference in avoiding plagiarism: citation conventions and the proper integration of sources into their writing and research (Lampert 2004, 348).

THE NEW PLAGIARISM: CHALLENGES WITH SOURCES

The new abundance of digital information challenges traditional definitions of plagiarism (Evering and Moorman 2012, 36) and shifts it into a much more involved skill set. Avoiding plagiarism now requires learning authorship, publication cycle, citation, and proofreading for digital resources. Each information type requires instruction.

Books

Books require the most time to locate and use for research. This fact alone has made them less attractive than digital resources. In many schools, the role of print books has shifted to a less dominant research position. Students must physically go to the library to find and then check out a book. Books are the most stable of all research resources with the fewest variables. Print books are retrieved through a library catalog with basic search parameters: author, title, series, or subject. A finite number of results are returned. Books have a long-term, set physical parameter and location on the library shelf. There is no question about authorship or publication. The table of contents and index are consulted to locate relevant information. A finite number of pages to browse create a manageable process. Explaining the role of the book's index is important for the optimal research use of books. Plagiarism with print books is possible. But the average student with Internet access is less likely to plagiarize by retyping sentences or longer passages from a print book.

Digital Sources

Research Databases

A commonality between books and research databases is access through community membership, through either a school library or public library. The quality of information improves because of this community membership. These sources can be accessed from anywhere but require a log-in process at the library's web page. The student needs to understand the purpose of a research database, keyword searching, and the content differences among databases. Research database articles are among the most abstract of any of the digital sources students use for academic purposes. Many students have never seen the original publications where the article originates. Overall, research database articles have more depth than web pages.

While some research databases use natural language searching, these sources generally work best with specific keyword searching. The search results improve with keyword searching, with much more manageable levels than the Internet. Determining relevance for the information found in the article to the information needed requires instruction.

There is a citation tool within the research database for the full citation, but students still need to understand what to do about the parenthetical citation or footnote. Many of these research database articles do not have page numbers when printed, although this is beginning to change. This makes it harder to properly document the source. Many research database articles do not list an author. The publication cycle for these articles can be confusing. A citation generated by the research database can show two or more "homes" for the article. This can erode the student's understanding of the true origin of the source. Students can access this type of source and still not be absolutely sure exactly what they are reading.

Research database articles encourage plagiarism in several ways. As with any digital resource, the ability to cut and paste is present. When a student uses a scholarly research article that is too difficult to understand and synthesize, plagiarism can result. The structure of many research database articles is very similar to a research paper. In fact, many scholarly journal articles are actual research papers completed by professionals in a particular field. The structure of the article can be copied. These articles make it easy for the research (research database article) to dictate the paper instead of the student's ideas dictating the research.

Web Pages

Access to information from web pages is available from absolutely anywhere. "Good enough" information appears in less than a second. The Internet has changed our expectations for information delivery. We now expect information fast, with quality and relevance as secondary concerns. We can look through many web pages to satisfy our curiosity on any number of subjects. It can be difficult to know the difference between facts, original ideas, opinions, and credible information because of the numerous options for information. Web pages have become the de facto information source for all types of personal and academic decision-making. This can create a lack of information discernment, which can impact decisions in every aspect of life.

The potential for plagiarism increases exponentially when students use the Internet randomly for academic secondary sources. Many web pages have very accessible vocabulary, making it more difficult to detect small amounts of copy and paste. The copy and paste of sentences from web pages is the easiest type of cheating that, unlike other types of academic dishonesty, can be completed in complete privacy. The natural language searching of the Internet, where any term is typed into a search box in a web browser, often means less accurate search results. It also increases the number of results returned, often in the millions. Other challenges for using web pages ethically for academic purposes are as follows:

- The author is often not listed.

- The publisher is often hard to find on web pages.

- Web pages do not have page numbers. The only exception is scholarly journal articles found through Google Scholar or similar sites.

- Web pages cannot be easily stored over the time of the research process except through the Favorites option on a web browser.

- Web pages can be moved or removed at any time.

THE NEW SKILL SET REQUIRED BY DIGITAL SOURCES

Digital information requires a new skill set to avoid plagiarism. Students, without instruction, have little ability to avoid plagiarism in academic work. There is a scattering of worksheets, videos, and lesson plans in place on the Internet. This type of instruction is not delivered in an organized fashion in high school or at the university level. Colleges and universities often have web pages, guides, tutorials, and explanations on their websites about paraphrasing, citations, and plagiarism education advice. Students who plagiarize in high school because of a lack of education in this area will likely plagiarize in college. Here is a list of the required skills for students.

Citations

The three major citation-style books can be challenging for some high school and early college students to use. Now, there are so many possible digital sources (images, web pages, social media, personal interviews, e-books, videos, etc.) to use and manage. Sometimes, the needed example for the source is not in the book. Online citation tools have revolutionized this process, but to use these tools effectively, students need to understand sources well enough to be accurate. It is necessary to understand the relationship between the full citation of a source and the parenthetical citation or footnote.

Citation Tools

Research databases now generate a citation. With the often-complicated publication cycle of research database articles, this is a great advantage for students. While the research database citation tool creates a citation, it still must be checked for accuracy. Over the past few years, the most popular online citation tools have shifted beyond the creation of citations to become research platforms. There is a learning curve to know how to use these tools effectively. Authorship and other publication information must be inserted into the proper place in the tool in order to generate a citation correctly. This key information is often not intuitive for digital sources, especially websites.

Digital Source Information Management

The days of checking out library books as the main secondary source for research have disappeared. Students no longer have a stack of books on a desk which have been gathered for a research paper. Digital sources are managed differently through the research process. Printing research database articles and web pages is the best option for highlighting and annotations. This maintains the important information needed for the writing and citation process.

There are schools where printing is discouraged. Several research databases allow students to set up an account where important articles can be stored. Web pages can be stored within the Favorites of the web browser or through Microsoft Word or Microsoft OneNote.

Alternatives to Printing

In many schools, printing is not permitted for economical or environmental reasons. Here are some other options to consider.

Advice for Students

You may have a personal cell phone (or iPad or other device) and school computer to use for your research. Your school computer should be your primary computer for writing and research. You can then treat your cell phone as the digital "viewer" for your sources, instead of printing out the individual pages. Take advantage of any apps your school makes available for Microsoft Office. If you load the Microsoft Office apps on your phone and synch it to your school accounts, you can then view any drafts and research articles from the apps or your e-mail. In other words, you will read the sentences from your phone, then paraphrase, and type in direct quotes using your computer. You may also be able to access these apps to your home computer if you have one. This process will help you use the information more effectively.

Microsoft OneNote is particularly useful. Once you download a research database article to your desktop, you can then attach the article to Microsoft OneNote. Then, use the highlighter and other tools to annotate the article and choose direct quotes and paraphrases. This is also a good place to store live links to web pages you are using in your research or screen captures of information you can use in your research.

Ask your librarian if your research database providers have mobile apps. If so, download these apps to use on your cell phone or other device for accessing your sources.

It is preferable to e-mail the research database article to yourself instead of copy and paste on to a Word document. This will keep the formatting of the article intact. These articles can be maintained in your cell phone in a folder until the end of the project.

For websites, save your computer history until you receive a final grade for the assignment. Save these sites on your bookmark bar, and use a folder for these bookmarks if it is available. If you have used credible, authoritative websites, there is little risk of the web pages being deleted from the website during the research process.

The Microsoft Ink Workspace is a useful tool for web pages. It allows you to take a screenshot of a web page and then underline and highlight the sentences you will use for paraphrases and direct quotes. You can save this file and e-mail it to yourself.

Tools

Check for tools within the research databases which allow you to easily bypass printing. One option is to download articles in PDF format. PDF formats allow you to write on the article and highlight it. Highlight the sentences you plan to paraphrase or use for a direct quote. Save the article, and then e-mail it to yourself.

If there is an option within the research database to open up an account and store articles, you should do so. For example, Gale research databases allow you to highlight and take notes on articles and store them within the database itself.

Advice for Teachers and Librarians

If your school has access to printers but prefers students to not print on a regular basis, this is a good time to ask for special permission to do so for younger students or for classes with inexperienced researchers. Inexperienced researchers will gain an important understanding about digital sources when they can review printed-out pages.

Public and university libraries are usually interested in collaborating with high schools for research projects. These librarians may allow your students to print out research for free or at very low cost if you explain the project and circumstances.

For campuses without printing, librarians will need to make sure that off-campus access to research databases is explained carefully to students. This access should be tested remotely from a cell phone and computer on a quarterly basis for connectivity. The access instructions should be posted in prominent locations on the library's web pages in a password-protected area.

Librarians should actively pursue research databases with the option for mobile apps as a priority. This will increase your student's ability to read and access research articles effectively in digital format across different devices.

Formatting

Quotation marks and the punctuation for citations and footnotes must be correct. The omission or incorrect use can be a source of plagiarism. While problems with formatting areas such as paper headings, charts/diagrams, spacing, and margins are not likely to be a source of plagiarism, a well-formatted paper is easier to read and makes it less likely to be questioned. A Works Cited, Bibliography, or Reference page must also be created properly.

Information Retrieval and Synthesis

Relevant sources must be selected according to the teacher's directions for the research paper. Even when teachers narrow the source types to books, web pages, and research database articles, there can be tens of thousands of options to consider. While reading these sources, students must recognize relevant information. They need to decide among multiple instances of relevant information to use in the research paper.

Paraphrasing

There is inconsistent advice on how to paraphrase on the Internet. Often it is misleading or difficult to apply to a student's unique situation. Solid paraphrasing skills are one of the most important college preparatory skills to teach high school students to ethically manage digital information and avoid plagiarism. Paraphrasing can be accurately taught with the micro-paraphrasing technique in Chapter 2.

Proofreading

School campuses often have an inconsistent academic culture for proof-reading. For many students, proofreading means rereading the paper for basic punctuation and grammar. Digital source use requires moving beyond the hope that a citation "looks right" by including a closer examination of how the sources are used in the paper during proofreading. This helps reduce plagiarism.

- The citation must be correct for the source type. For example, for an e-book, the citation must reflect the e-book file type.

- Accurate authorship must be reflected in the citations. Some have authors listed; others may not.

- The citation information must match. For every different citation or footnote in the text of the paper, there needs to be a matching source on the Works Cited, Bibliography, or References page.

It is also important to proofread the citations created by online citation tools for spelling, capitalization, and completeness.

The Authorship and Publication Cycle for Digital Sources

Most students today have never used print encyclopedias or seen a scholarly journal. There should be instruction to explain the authorship and publication process of digital sources. Without differentiation of various types of sources, words speeding by on a computer lose context and meaning. There is more information about this in Chapter 6.

TURNITIN.COM

It is impossible to discuss plagiarism education without mentioning Turnitin.com. While there are other plagiarism checkers available, Turnitin.com is a consistent leader in this field. Turnitin.com is a web-based subscription service where a student's research paper is checked for plagiarism against a database of manuscripts from other students, a database of books and journals and more than a billion websites. There are differences of opinion surrounding the use of Turnitin.com. These concerns have included the implication that the use of Turnitin implies guilt; it oversimplifies plagiarism and fails to address the reasons why the student plagiarized (Scanlon 2003, 164; Childers and Bruton 2016, 3).

For schools that choose to have Turnitin, it should be viewed as one tool for finding and correcting plagiarism. There will always need to be a review of originality reports to verify the accuracy of plagiarism. It does not include a check of every source imaginable. For example, plagiarism is still possible from unpublished information such as a copied paper from another student whose work is not part of the Turnitin database. The well-documented weaknesses of this system will continue to shift as the program continues to refine itself over time.

Turnitin.com is a very useful tool for finding plagiarism. It is a reactive approach. But because plagiarism is committed by people with different academic experiences and skills, it can never be the "final answer" when it comes to plagiarism. Educators need to determine the reason *why* plagiarism has occurred.

The originality report can be a very useful "self-monitoring mechanism" for students if they are able to make changes before they hand in the research paper to the teacher (Graham-Matheson and Starr 2013, 11; Kashian et al. 2015, 252). For students, this visual display of plagiarism with the chance to correct the errors before a grade is invaluable. These reports provide a good opportunity for writing center professionals, librarians, and teachers to work with students who need to correct errors by providing necessary instruction. It also provides a baseline for the creation of videos, handouts, and other plagiarism information that can be made available to students for the most common plagiarism errors. The mere presence of Turnitin can be a deterrent for students, encouraging greater attention to detail for citations and paraphrasing (Martin 2005, 152; Heckler, Rice, and Bryan 2013, 243; Lofstrom and Kupilla 2013, 238).

The presence of Turnitin can help teachers. Many are understandably overwhelmed by the avalanche of digital sources and what plagiarism "looks like" while using these sources. Even for teachers who are well versed in sources, it allows for initial, objective documentation of plagiarism for teachers to address with students. This saves time and energy (Heckler, Rice, and Bryan 2013, 244).

While there are high schools that use this service, there are challenges. The submission of intellectual property by minors to Turnitin.com's large database is uncomfortable for many schools because it allows the company to make money from these research papers. High schools that do not have a substantial research-based curriculum may find the cost prohibitive. Those schools with a mission of personal integrity expect to be able to trust students without this type of program.

CONCLUSION

Plagiarism is inevitable. Plagiarism checkers like Turnitin.com, while obviously valuable, find plagiarism after the fact. Proactive instruction provides a critical understanding of citations, paraphrasing, and the authorship and publication of digital sources, which naturally reduces plagiarism. Everything changed once digital sources became a primary research source. More working knowledge is now necessary for student researchers to avoid plagiarism, along with a better understanding of digital sources.

Plagiarism cannot be disregarded once we are finished with research papers as students. Technology allows everyone to publish. It is easier than ever to record and post public speeches online. We can expect to create websites; participate in online discussion forums; and write articles, reports, and books throughout our personal and professional lives, which are published on the Internet. Plagiarism can be documented quickly, causing professional and personal embarrassment. The more we do proactively to prevent plagiarism, the less there is to do reactively.

REFERENCES

Barry, Elaine S. 2006. "Can Paraphrasing Practice Help Students Define Plagiarism?" *College Student Journal* 40, no. 2 (June): 377–84. http://search.ebscohost.com/login.aspx?direct=true&db=aph&AN=21375562&site=ehost-live.

Chao, Chia-An, William J. Wilhelm, and Brian D. Neureuther. 2009. "A Study of Electronic Detection and Pedagogical Approaches for Reducing Plagiarism." *Delta Pi Epsilon Journal* 51, no. 1 (Winter): 31–42. https://search.proquest.com/docview/195588928?accountid=41092.

Childers, Dan, and Sam Bruton. 2016. "'Should It Be Considered Plagiarism?' Student Perceptions of Complex Citation Issues." *Journal of Academic Ethics* 14, no. 1 (May): 1–17. doi:http://dx.doi.org/10.1007/s10805-015-9250-6. https://search.proquest.com/docview/1759088668?accountid=41092.

Craig, Paul A., Elizabeth Federici, and Marianne A. Buehler. 2010. "Instructing Students in Academic Integrity." *Journal of College Science Teaching* 40, no. 2 (November): 50–55. https://search.proquest.com/docview/761655869?accountid=41092.

Davis, Susan J. 1994. "Teaching Practices That Encourage or Eliminate Student Plagiarism." *Middle School Journal* 25, no. 3 (January): 55–58. http://www.jstor.org/stable/23024717.

Eckstein, Grant. 2013. "Perspectives on Plagiarism." *Writing on the Edge* 23, no. 2 (Spring): 99–104. http://www.jstor.org/stable/431589.

Evering, Lea Calvert, and Gary Moorman. 2012. "Rethinking Plagiarism in the Digital Age." *Journal of Adolescent & Adult Literacy* 56, no. 1 (September): 35–44. http://www.jstor.org/stable/23367758.

Fritz, Mark. 1999. "COLUMN ONE; Redefining Research, Plagiarism; Going Online to Get Homework Isn't a Novel Thing. To Some Students, It's Not Even Cheating. It's Just Evolved into an Institution; a Big Study Group of Sorts." *Los Angeles Times*, February 25, https://search.proquest.com/docview/421523919?accountid=41092.

Gibson, Nancy Snyder, and Christina Chester-Fangman. 2011. "The Librarian's Role in Combating Plagiarism." *Reference Services Review* 39, no. 1: 132–50. doi:http://dx.doi.org/10.1108/00907321111108169. https://search.proquest.com/docview/849324979?accountid=41092.

Graham-Matheson, Lynne, and Simon Starr. 2013. "Is It Cheating—Or Learning the Craft of Writing? Using Turnitin to Help Students Avoid Plagiarism." *Research in Learning Technology* 21. doi:http://dx.doi.org/10.3402/rlt.v21i0.17218. https://search.proquest.com/docview/2121428750?accountid=41092.

Heckler, Nina C., Margaret Rice, and C. H. Bryan. 2013. "Turnitin Systems: A Deterrent to Plagiarism in College Classrooms." *Journal of Research on Technology in Education* 45, no. 3 (Spring): 229–48. https://search.proquest.com/docview/1448424679?accountid=41092.

Howard, Rebecca Moore. 1993. "A Plagiarism Pentimento." *Journal of Teaching Writing* 11, no. 3 (Summer): 233–46. http://www.citationproject.net/wp-content/uploads/2018/03/Howard-Plagiarism-Pentimento.pdf.

Howard, Rebecca Moore. 1995. "Plagiarisms, Authorships, and the Academic Death Penalty." *College English* 57, no. 7 (November): 788–806. https://search.proquest.com/docview/236929864?accountid=41092.

Howard, Rebecca Moore, and Laura J. Davies. 2009. "Plagiarism in the Internet Age." *Educational Leadership* 66, no. 6 (March): 64–67. http://www.ascd.org/publications/educational-leadership/mar09/vol66/num06/Plagiarism-in-the-Internet-Age.aspx.

Kashian, Nicole, Shannon M. Cruz, Jeong-woo Jang, and Kami J. Silk. 2015. "Evaluation of an Instructional Activity to Reduce Plagiarism in the Communication Classroom." *Journal of Academic Ethics* 13, no. 3 (September): 239–58. https://doi.org/10.1007/s10805-015-9238-2.

Lampert, Lynn D. 2004. "Integrating Discipline-Based Anti-Plagiarism Instruction into the Information Literacy Curriculum." *Reference Services Review* 32, no.4(December):347–55. doi:http://dx.doi.org/10.1108/00907320410569699. https://search.proquest.com/docview/200524962?accountid=41092.

Lampert, Lynn D. 2006. "The Instruction Librarian's Role in Discussing Issues of Academic Integrity." *LOEX Quarterly* 32, no. 4 (January): 8–9. https://core.ac.uk/download/pdf/48440866.pdf.

Lofstrom, Erika, and Paullina Kupilla. 2013. "The Instructional Challenges of Student Plagiarism." *Journal of Academic Ethics* 11, no. 3 (September): 231–42. https://doi.org/10.1007/s10805-013-9181-z.

Ma, Hongyan, Eric Yong Lu, Sandra Turner, and Guofang Wan. 2007. "An Empirical Investigation of Digital Cheating and Plagiarism among Middle School Students." *American Secondary Education* 35, no. 2 (Spring): 69–82. http://www.jstor.org/stable/41406290.

Martin, David F. 2005. "Plagiarism and Technology: A Tool for Coping with Plagiarism." *Journal of Education for Business* 80, no. 3 (January): 149–52. https://search.proquest.com/docview/202820860?accountid=41092.

Radunovich, Heidi, Eboni Baugh, and Elaine Turner. 2009. "An Examination of Students' Knowledge of What Constitutes Plagiarism." *NACTA Journal* 53, no. 4 (Spring): 30–35. http://www.jstor.org/stable/43765409.

Roberts, Tim S. 2007. "Plagiarism and the Internet." *Educational Technology Publications* 47, no. 2 (March/April): 45–47. http://www.jstor.org/stable/44429488.

Roig, Miguel. 1997. "Can Undergraduate Students Determine Whether Text Has Been Plagiarized?" *The Psychological Record* 47, no. 1 (Winter): 113–22. https://search.proquest.com/docview/212759992?accountid=41092.

Scanlon, Patrick M. 2003. "Student Online Plagiarism: How Do We Respond?" *College Teaching* 51, no. 4 (Fall): 161–65. http://www.jstor.org/stable/27559159.

Scanlon, Patrick M., and David R. Neuman. 2002. "Internet Plagiarism among College Students." *Journal of College Student Development* 43, no. 3 (May/June): 374–85. http://citeseerx.ist.psu.edu/viewdoc/download?doi=10.1.1.465.268&rep=rep1&type=pdf.

Sisti, Dominic A. 2007. "How Do High School Students Justify Internet Plagiarism?" *Ethics and Behavior* 17, no. 3 (December): 215–31. https://www.tandfonline.com/doi/full/10.1080/10508420701519163?scroll=top&needAccess=true.

Tomaiuolo, Nicholas. 2007. "Citations and Aberrations." *Searcher* 15, no. 7 (July/August): 17–24. https://search.proquest.com/docview/221036479?accountid=41092.

Walker, Angela L. 2008. "Preventing Unintentional Plagiarism: A Method for Strengthening Paraphrasing Skills." *Journal of Instructional Psychology* 35, no. 4 (December): 387–95. https://search.proquest.com/docview/210332408?accountid=41092.

Whitaker, Elaine E. 1993. "A Pedagogy to Address Plagiarism." *College Composition and Communication* 44, no. 4 (December): 509–14. doi:10.2307/358386.

Wilhoit, Stephen. 1994. "Helping Students Avoid Plagiarism." *College Teaching* 42, no. 4 (Fall): 161–64. http://www.jstor.org/stable/27558679.

2

Paraphrasing and Micro-Paraphrasing

As information continues to proliferate, especially in digital format, it becomes more difficult to determine the difference between general information, known to everyone (common knowledge), and information for which credit must be given. For high school and college students, evidence is presented in a research paper through a direct quote or paraphrase. During the research process, using information by paraphrasing often feels overwhelming, especially with digital resources. This critical part of the research paper writing process is not an intuitive skill. There is an inherent abstract nature to paraphrasing ("put it into your own words"), which can be difficult to discern. Proper paraphrasing helps students avoid accidental plagiarism. Even with citation checkers like Turnitin.com, students need a deliberate educational process to avoid accidental plagiarism.

There are many misperceptions about paraphrasing because no firm educational guidelines are established beyond instructions to "put it into your own words." It can be confusing to decide which original words are permissible to reuse and which words need to be restated. People who are teaching it—or who have to teach it—may find it challenging to do themselves. Often, students attempt to paraphrase too much text and lose the essential meaning of the original sentences. It is often confusing to choose the sentences to paraphrase from the source. Many have experienced variable results when attempting to paraphrase.

MICRO-PARAPHRASING

Micro-paraphrasing, with its clearly defined steps, streamlines the paraphrasing process by emphasizing reading comprehension and the different types of language (unique information, common knowledge, and critical terms) to be analyzed and restated. It offers definite guidelines for the number of sentences that should be paraphrased at one time. The resulting paraphrase is one clear and concise sentence. This makes it easier for teachers to read and grade student work. The paraphrase clearly ends with a parenthetical citation. Results improve when paraphrasing and paraphrasing instruction are considered a reading comprehension issue first and a writing issue second. Instead of the abstract "put it into your own words," micro-paraphrasing creates the paraphrase from the important, unique meaning of the original sentences. A distinct and manageable process for paraphrasing increases students' confidence with this skill and increases the likelihood that they will do it.

There are three distinct reading-based language tasks for students to master within this process.

1. **Identifying common knowledge**. Students need to understand that common knowledge within the original sentences should not be used in the paraphrase.
2. **Identifying the terms in the sentences that cannot be restated**. These critical terms serve as the structure for the new paraphrase.
3. **Identifying the unique information that is important enough to be used as evidence in the research paper.** At the same time, students should also identify what is irrelevant, even if it is not common knowledge.

Paraphrasing with fewer sentences has many advantages for inexperienced researchers. Since micro-paraphrasing uses a maximum of three original sentences at one time, it further ensures the ethical manipulation of the language of others. It is easier to visualize how to change the structure of the original sentences. It also avoids the tendency to read too much when paraphrasing, losing the essential meaning of the sentences. While this approach can also be considered summarizing, this language emphasis creates a prerequisite process for more complex paraphrasing.

Prerequisite Skills for Paraphrasing

Prerequisite skills are necessary for good paraphrasing. While many students have absorbed these information management skills over time, it is still important to review.

One important prerequisite skill for paraphrasing is information discernment. High school and college students need to understand the different characteristics of information when they read sources to decide whether to use a direct quote, paraphrase, or reject information because it is common knowledge or irrelevant. The end goal is always to find information that is appropriate evidence for an argument in a research paper.

Direct quotes should be used for very specific information:

- The use of the primary source as evidence

- Sentences with multiple specific details such as numbers, weights, or titles

- Sentences that are specific enough that they cannot be restated any other way

- Sentences where there is distinct scholarly language

Paraphrases are used for sentences too lengthy for a direct quote with unique information:

- Specialized or general definitions within a subject area

- Notable biographical information that is not commonly known

- General ideas and concepts that can be restated more concisely

Common knowledge is not specific or important enough to be used in the paraphrase. Usually, it should be disregarded. Here are a few examples:

- Well-known subject-area knowledge

- Subject-area knowledge that is part of an instructor lecture

- General information that is easily obtained from an Internet search

The following examples can be used in the classroom during instruction.

Class exercise—Choose paraphrase, direct quote, or common knowledge for each sentence. State a reason for this decision.

1. The Blue Angel Restaurant had several health code violations for salmonella, hepatitis, and rodents.

    (paraphrase)   direct quote   common knowledge

    Reason: Paraphrase. *There is specific information about the types of health code violations but not detailed enough to merit a direct quote.*

2. Since the latest incidents of terrorism, travel overseas has been in sharp decline. People have been advised to cancel nonessential travel to certain countries.

    paraphrase   direct quote   (common knowledge)

    Reason: Common knowledge. *This information is common knowledge and too general to be cited in a research paper.*

3. Walt Whitman's best-known work, *Leaves of Grass,* was self-published.

    (paraphrase)   direct quote   common knowledge

    Reason: *This is unique information that can be paraphrased.*

4. Fighting too often with one enemy means you will teach him your art of war.

    paraphrase   (direct quote)   common knowledge

    Reason: Direct quote. *This sentence is very specific and cannot be paraphrased.*

The relationship between the parenthetical citation and the full source citation is another important prerequisite. Students must have working knowledge of the citation style used at school. Reliable citation generator tools such as NoodleTools can make this process easier. Research databases have built-in citation tools to generate the full citation. Instructors should review the visual relationship between a parenthetical citation for a paraphrase and the full citation for the Works Cited, References, or Bibliography page.

Example 1: This MLA citation begins with the article title since there is no listed author.

"Elvis Presley Biography." Graceland: The Home of Elvis Presley, 2017, www.graceland.com/elvis/biography, Accessed 16 Oct. 2017.

("Elvis Presley Biography") is the MLA parenthetical citation that should be used after the paraphrase.

Example 2

Fitzpatrick, Vincent. *H.L. Mencken.* Continuum Publishing, 1989.

(Fitzpatrick 17) is the MLA parenthetical citation that should be used after the paraphrase. For books, page numbers should be included.

Example 3

Thomas, H.K. (2004) Teaching strategies for improving reading comprehension. *Journal of Reading Education,* 23(4), 245–259.

(Thomas, 2004) is the APA parenthetical citation that should be used after a paraphrase.

There are citation guides for APA, MLA, and Chicago for student use in Appendix E.

Understanding information relevance is also an important prerequisite skill. Encouraging students to read the source carefully has two purposes. First, it provides important background knowledge that will aid in understanding the topic better. This makes it easier to write the paper. Second, students need to read with the purpose of finding relevant information to use as evidence in their research paper. Whether the information is used as a direct quote or a paraphrase, it needs to connect with the research paper as well as possible. This process can be encouraged using a detailed outline.

THE MICRO-PARAPHRASING PROCESS

Micro-paraphrasing is a process with four successive steps. These steps should be defined clearly to students during the instruction. Depending on the students, the micro-paraphrasing steps can be reinforced with additional instruction to build competency.

Step 1: Read the sentences precisely—what does this mean? Without appropriate reading comprehension, paraphrasing is an inaccurate process. An integral part of the micro-paraphrasing instructional process emphasizes precision reading. Students must grasp the essential, unique meaning of the original sentences. The concept of common knowledge should be reviewed with students at this time. As they read the sentences, encourage them to differentiate between what they already know about the topic, what is implied within the original sentences and does not need to be restated, and what is unique enough to provide evidence in a research paper. The common knowledge and irrelevant parts of these sentences are underlined. This paper is about Mother Teresa's lifetime contributions to the Catholic Church and is taken from a research database article about Mother Teresa.

"Mother Teresa." Encyclopedia of World Biography Online, Gale, 1998. World History in Context, https://link.gale.com/apps/doc/ K1631006438/WHIC?u=win5026&sid=WHIC&xid=5208577d. Accessed 18 July 2019.

Example

Agnes [Mother Teresa] spent less than one year in Ireland before leaving to join the Loreto Covent in Darjeeling, India. There, at the foot of Mt. Kanchenjunga, she spent two years as a novice. On May 24, 1931, she took her first vows and the name "Teresa" in memory of Teresa of Avila and Theresa of Liseux ("Mother Teresa").

Explanation: *Mother Teresa chose her name from Teresa of Avila and Theresa of Liseux. The process for becoming a nun is common knowledge. Since we already know the time frame in which she lived, it is unnecessary to include the date of her first vows. The fact that she spent time in Ireland is irrelevant.*

Class exercise—Find the unique information and common knowledge within the sentences:

1. My disaster-resistant roof on my beach house blew off during Hurricane Harvey. *The unique information is "disaster-resistant" and "Hurricane Harvey" since this is a named event.*

2. Harvard's varsity crew team benefits from proximity to the Charles River. *This is completely common knowledge.*

3. Her blog posts written during the earthquake in Mexico include real-time videos of the damage to her house. *The fact that video was recorded in real time is unique.*

4. Car magazines help young boys decide what kind of car they want to drive as adults. *This role for car magazines is common knowledge.*

5. Mother Teresa's brother Lazar is the executor of her estate; he can decide how her name and likeness are used. *This is completely unique information.*

6. Jesuit education has been in existence for over 500 years. *The fact that Jesuit education exists is common knowledge. The number of years is unique information.*

Step 2: Identify critical terms. Critical terms are those words that can't be restated another way. Recognizing which words need to carry over to the paraphrase is an important part of this process. The critical terms are normally names, places, proper nouns, and words that cannot be stated another way. Recognizing these critical terms is challenging. Students have a tendency to overidentify these terms. They need to understand that not all of the critical terms need to be used in the paraphrase, rather only the terms necessary to keep the paraphrase's meaning consistent with the original sentences. Any relevant words that are not critical terms will need to be restated in the paraphrase. In this example, the critical terms are underlined.

Example

Agnes [Mother Teresa] spent less than one year in Ireland before she left to join the Loreto Covent in Darjeeling, India. There, at the foot of Mt. Kanchenjunga, she spent two years as a novice. On May 24, 1931, she took her first vows and the name "Teresa" in memory of Teresa of Avila and Theresa of Liseux.

Explanation: *Not all these critical terms are necessary to write the paraphrase. The name of Mother Teresa's convent is unique, as well as the two saints' names. A concise paraphrase can be written using Agnes, Mother Teresa, Loreto Convent, Teresa of Avila, and Theresa of Liseux.*

Class exercise—Identify the critical terms. Everything else should be restated.

1. A rare dinosaur bone was found by a dog at the shopping mall construction site.

2. A local sports reporter named Nick Jackson "the new Usain Bolt" because of his running speed in the New Balance Nationals Outdoor track meet.

3. The Maryland Hunt Cup is as important as the Preakness Race for the best horses from around the country.

4. Collecting library fines is an important source of revenue for major public libraries.

5. Good teaching is an art, not a science.

Step 3: Determine the new structure. Students should be able to see the "lead" of the original sentences chosen for the paraphrase. This is connected to the reading comprehension process of micro-paraphrasing. Instructors should prompt, "With what idea do these sentences start?" Students should mark the two sentences with related ideas to be paraphrased. These sentences should be in the same paragraph but do not need to be right next to one another. The sentence that is first in the paragraph is dominant for determining a new lead for the two sentences. Using just two sentences for a paraphrase allows the structure to be changed easily, avoiding plagiarism. The new "lead" of the paraphrase should be restructured based on the unique information found in the original sentences. The new paraphrase needs to start differently than the original.

In this example, the critical terms are underlined. The common knowledge and irrelevant information are double underlined. The new lead is circled.

Example

Agnes [Mother Teresa] spent less than one year in Ireland before she left to join the Loreto Covent in Darjeeling, India. There, at the foot of Mt. Kanchenjunga, she spent two years as a novice. On May 24, 1931, she took her first vows and the name "Teresa" in memory of Teresa of Avila and Theresa of Liseux.

Explanation: *These sentences lead with Mother Teresa's experiences before she became a nun. The new lead should be the saints' names.*

Class exercise—Determine the new lead for these sentences.

1. There is a high cost of living on the Hawaiian Islands. There is little manufacturing of consumer goods there. Nevertheless, the population of Hawaii is at the highest level in twenty years.

   Answer: *These sentences lead with the high cost of living. The paraphrase should begin with the high population.*

2. The Bel Fiore Company unexpectedly closed its world tour in London, England. An emergency with a dancer caused them to stop before arriving in Rome, the planned closing city.

   Answer: *These sentence lead with the dance company's early tour closure. The paraphrase should lead with Rome.*

3. There are complaints that tickets for professional wrestling are too expensive. Many well-known wrestlers are multi-millionaires. A recent article noted that the wrestlers support several human rights charities.

Answer: *These sentences lead with the expense of professional wrestling. The paraphrase should lead with human rights charities that are supported by wrestlers.*

4.   The new museum, Nouveau Jour, has fifty important Impressionist paintings. They are also known for their Hyperrealism works. A major donor has just contributed a significant collection of Abstract art, changing the museum's collection drastically.

Answer: *These sentences lead with a listing of the museum's paintings. The paraphrase should lead with the museum's collection, listing the types of paintings differently.*

Step 4: Write the paraphrase and apply the citation. The instructor should review the school's accepted citation style along with the role a citation plays in a paraphrase. The paraphrase should be one sentence only. This provides clarity and the best use of the original information to create an argument. Writing the paraphrase should be a deliberate process where accuracy is checked by students against the original for meaning and for readability. The original sentences are not hidden during this process.

Example

Agnes [Mother Teresa] spent less than one year in Ireland before she left to join the Loreto Covent in Darjeeling, India. There, at the foot of Mt. Kanchenjunga, she spent two years as a novice. On

---

THE MICRO-PARAPHRASING STEPS

Here is a more streamlined list of the micro-paraphrasing steps:

- Read the paragraph for meaning. What is this about?
- Choose two sentences to paraphrase from the paragraph. While the two sentences don't have to be right next to one another, this is preferable.
- Underline the critical terms. These are words that cannot be stated another way and can be used in the new paraphrased sentence. Everything else must be put into your own words.
- As you consider your paraphrase, change the sentence structure so your one-sentence paraphrase begins differently than the original sentences.
- Write the one-sentence paraphrase with the correct parenthetical citation or footnote.

May 24, 1931, she took her first vows and the name "Teresa" in memory of Teresa of Avila and Theresa of Liseux ("Mother Teresa").

Explanation: *It is common knowledge that Mother Teresa lived and worked in India. The fact that she spent less than one year in Ireland is irrelevant. The date of her vows is also irrelevant.*

Acceptable paraphrase:

While at the Loreto Convent, Teresa of Avila and Theresa of Liseux became the inspiration for Mother Teresa's name change from Agnes ("Mother Teresa").

THE MICRO-PARAPHRASING TEACHING PROCESS: PREPARING FOR INSTRUCTION

This instruction can be done by a librarian or classroom teacher with subject-specific research resources. It is appropriate for students from grades eight through twelve and college students. The introductory micro-paraphrasing lesson, especially for grades eight through ten, should be provided away from the source itself, with the original sentences projected onto a screen for students to view. A computer pen is essential for the instructor to interact with the text during this process. For the classwork in this introductory lesson, the original sentences should be relatively straightforward in readability and provided to students on a worksheet. Students should have access to a dictionary and thesaurus.

Providing the introductory classwork on a worksheet gives younger students and those who are new to paraphrasing a chance to interact directly with the words in the original sentences. The parenthetical or full citation for the source should be included on the worksheet with the paraphrasing classwork. The instructor can also write directly on the paper to redirect students in the micro-paraphrasing process. The classwork is normally two paraphrases for students to complete.

Generally, when students are writing research papers, paraphrasing occurs in three different ways:

- Reading the digital source (web page, research database, e-book) on computer screen

- Reading from a print book

- Reading the digital source (web page, research database, e-book) by printing out these pages

For older high school and college students, it is important to provide instruction in the way that they will most likely view the original material. Research database articles or web pages can be cued on the instructor and student computer screens for the example and classwork. Technology can be helpful for this teaching process. Research database articles have built-in highlighters where two or three sentences can be isolated. If student computers allow for it, they can use computer pens to interact with the text directly on the computer screen while they follow the micro-paraphrasing steps. The paraphrase itself should be composed on paper even when the original sentences are shown on the computer screen. This avoids the temptation to copy and paste. At no time should the original sentences be moved to a Word document for manipulation.

Here are other instructor options for presenting the original sentences to be paraphrased in print format to students. This allows students to be more conscious of the source and the citation for the paraphrase. Instructors can isolate the original sentences to be paraphrased or ask students to choose the sentences based on relevance.

- A research database article, web pages, or e-book pages.

- Two pages from a print book. This allows enough text for students to have context in order to choose two sentences to paraphrase based on relevance.

These sentences to be paraphrased should be next to one another and on the same subtopic. The choice of sentences to paraphrase should also be considered in the evaluation of the student's paraphrased sentence.

The types of sentences chosen for the instructor's class example and for classwork can vary in complexity depending on the subject area and the ability level of the students. Instructors should prepare at least two possible answers for the class example and for the classwork if the sentences are isolated in advance. For college preparatory high school students and for college students, the best source for these original sentences is subject-area research database articles. These key digital resources are used throughout high school and college. They also contain the types of language that is necessary to learn micro-paraphrasing:

- Lists of similar facts within the original sentences. The ability to recognize commonality and distill it into concise language is a tool for good paraphrasing.

Original sentences example: The words that need to be distilled are underlined.

> The new university president has an ambitious first year planned. She is focusing on student immigration issues, increasing enrollment, and stabilizing financial aid. Her previous position as the admissions director will help her accomplish these goals.

> **Explanation**: *The paraphrase should combine the three listed items in the second sentence into a more concise term such as recruitment and retention of students.*

- Wordy sentences to determine what's unique and exclude common knowledge, unnecessary details, or irrelevant. It is a significant challenge for students to recognize common knowledge and not include it in the paraphrase.

Original sentences example: Common knowledge and insignificant information are underlined.

> During the mid-1950s, Mother Teresa and <u>her order, the Missionaries of Charity</u>, turned their attention to the victims of leprosy as a <u>high-priority project</u>. The Indian government provided a <u>thirty-four-acre</u> plot of land on which to establish a rehabilitation center for lepers.

> **Explanation**: *The name of the religious order and the size of the plot of land are insignificant and should not be included in the paraphrase. Mother Teresa is a well-known public figure, apart from her religious order. It is implied that establishing a rehabilitation center requires land.*

- Recognizing the inherent "hidden" specificity within language. Part of good paraphrasing is understanding that broad terms and, often, names have more specific, inherent information that is implied. For example, it is well known that Mother Teresa was a nun. That would not need to be stated in a good paraphrase even if it was listed in the original sentences.

Active Instruction: Phase One

This instruction can be timed for the days or weeks before a research paper is assigned. Micro-paraphrasing can also be taught to students as additional instruction at any time during the school year. Librarians who teach information literacy during the research paper writing process can easily incorporate this into regular instruction. If time permits, this instruction should be repeated. Graded homework can help reinforce the micro-paraphrasing concepts.

The first fifteen minutes of class is led by the instructor in active group instruction. This demonstrates how to create a paraphrase by using the four steps with full participation from students. First, the purpose of paraphrasing should be explained to students. The concept of "using the idea" in someone else's writing and putting into your own words is too abstract. Since the purpose of a paraphrase is to serve as evidence for an argument in a research paper, students should focus on understanding the information in the original sentences well enough to use the unique information in their paraphrase in one concise sentence. At this stage, students should also understand the importance of parenthetical citations and bibliographies for paraphrasing.

During this process, the micro-paraphrasing steps should be used in order to build familiarity. Students should understand that when they paraphrase on their own, three original sentences are the maximum number to be used at one time. The goal is the most concise use of the information as possible. Good reading comprehension of the original sentences is at the heart of the micro-paraphrasing technique. Without a clear understanding of the unique meaning of the sentences, the information cannot be used effectively. Students should be encouraged to "say it" to themselves (or out loud) to gain clarity. Good instructor prompts are questions such as "What are these sentences trying to say?" and "What does this mean?" During this reading comprehension discussion, the instructor should be clear on the differences between the common knowledge and unique information in the sentences.

The next step is to determine the critical terms and phrases that must go to the paraphrase. Critical terms are normally proper nouns, dates, names, places, or specialized terms with the understanding that not all of the critical terms need to be used in the paraphrase. These should be clearly underlined for students to see on the screen.

To use the original sentences ethically and avoid paraphrasing plagiarism, the structure must be changed. Fewer sentences make it easier to isolate and identify the lead for the original sentences and decide how to properly change the structure for the paraphrase. In other words, if the original sentences begin with one idea, the paraphrase must begin with a different, unique idea found in the original sentences. The one-sentence paraphrase should then be concisely written based on the unique information found in the sentences with a parenthetical citation.

Active Instruction: Phase Two

The classwork phase is considered the second, highly organic part of the instruction. After students work for about ten minutes, the instructor should walk around to review student paraphrases and make suggestions. Student paraphrases should be reviewed in real time for feedback and redirection. This way they can immediately correct problems with overt copying of words and phrases from the original and copying the sentence structure.

Different classes will need more or less time on the reading comprehension part of the micro-paraphrasing process. When more than two students are having problems with accurate reading comprehension in their classwork, the instructor should stop the class and clarify the meaning of the original sentences. Instructors should expect individual levels of redirection with micro-paraphrasing depending on student ability levels. While two sets of original sentences should be provided to students to practice paraphrasing, the goal is the completion of one good paraphrase. If time permits, individual written feedback can be provided to students on the paraphrasing classwork handout.

Here is a list of common errors to expect from students, which will need redirection during this phase:

- Copying words and phrases from the original which are not considered critical terms.

- Inappropriate use of common knowledge for the new paraphrase.

- Failure to change the structure from the original.

- More than one sentence for the paraphrase.

The emphasis is clearly on using the information concisely. The initial instructional goal is to build familiarity with the micro-paraphrasing process, not complete mastery. Students at all levels require feedback. Adequately grasping the concept is reflected in paraphrases that show a restating of the unique information/idea with no inappropriate copying from the original.

Many students struggle to remember to include the parenthetical citation at the end of the paraphrase. If the paraphrasing practice is completed on paper, then provide the full citation for students. You may need to prompt students for this repeatedly, reminding them that without a parenthetical citation the paraphrase is automatically considered plagiarism. When the original sentences are cued on the computer screen directly from the source, instructors should make students aware of citation tools and parenthetical citation guidelines.

Student Examples

These are examples of good student micro-paraphrasing using two sentences from a paragraph discussing the relationship between Alexander Hamilton and George Washington from the *World History in Context* database from Gale.

- An enduring friendship between Hamilton and Washington helped them both throughout their careers ("Alexander Hamilton").

- Alexander Hamilton's military service led him to form a relationship with George Washington, making way for Hamilton's election as the first secretary of state ("Alexander Hamilton").

- Alexander Hamilton served as an aid to George Washington in the formation of early America ("Alexander Hamilton").

CONCLUSION

Practice and deliberate instruction are essential to reduce plagiarism. Micro-paraphrasing, with four definite steps, gives students a concrete method to be successful. Restating the original sentences through focusing on the unique information is a clearer method than "put it into your own words." This emphasis on reading comprehension and the most concise use of language possible is the counterbalance to the cursory reading encouraged by computer screens and smartphones. When reading is better, writing and research improve.

Micro-paraphrasing instruction can also serve as the basis for a school-wide plagiarism education and prevention program. Deliberate paraphrasing instruction provides a solid basis for instructors and school administrators to make sound decisions about students who have plagiarized in this way. Once a student has been taught this technique, it is impossible to adequately justify accidental paraphrasing plagiarism as an excuse. The steps are straightforward enough to be used as a tool by students and writing center professionals to correct paraphrasing plagiarism when it is committed.

3

Plagiarism Conversations

Students at every educational level have misconceptions about plagiarism. While the instruction described in this book will build a solid skill set to avoid plagiarism, students bring their own misperceptions about plagiarism from their previous academic experiences, which need to be resolved. Discussing plagiarism in an organized, practical way with students is an important part of this process. It bridges a "gray area between building on the ideas of others and stealing them" (Evering and Moorman 2012, 40). Conversations like this "shift from consequences for academic dishonesty to teaching about academic integrity" (Thomas and Sassi 2011, 50). These discussions are designed for students in the eighth grade through the first year of college.

The questions listed in this chapter have multiple purposes. The responses from students can inform the level and types of instruction students need to reduce plagiarism during the research process. It can also determine if students understand the school's academic integrity policies. The questions are standardized, so facilitators can bring students to a unified working knowledge of plagiarism and how to avoid it. Avoiding plagiarism is mastery of a skill set, not a wager to avoid getting caught. The questions and answers in this chapter can be a quick reference to students and classroom teachers who are working on a research project.

STRUCTURING THE DISCUSSION

Use a classroom setting for plagiarism discussions. This allows for comfortable, intimate conversations. Unlike other instruction, these discussions do not need to take place with a research assignment. Online discussions are not recommended. Understandably, many students will not want to put their opinions and perceptions in writing. It's easier to speak freely in a smaller group. When possible, plagiarism discussions should be facilitated by someone who is not in a position of authority over students for grades or academic penalties. This encourages honest exchanges. The facilitator needs to answer questions about the school's academic integrity policy. This individual should also prepare to answer questions about citation conventions and other areas of the research paper writing process. Librarians are particularly suited to leading these discussions since they are professionally familiar with sources and citations. This lets students know that the librarians can help them with plagiarism questions at the reference desk. Ideally, this process takes place over one class period. The questions found in this chapter can be used in a slide presentation, with one question on each slide. Written questions allow time for students to think about the question, especially while someone else is responding. The facilitator can prepare possible answers in the notes section of the slide presentation to help lead the discussion. While there will be students who are naturally opinionated, the facilitator should call on quieter students to get a full range of responses.

Encouraging an open discussion allowing for multiple points of view is critical. It is the only way to lay the groundwork for a unified understanding of plagiarism. The facilitator of this discussion needs to be prepared to hear out student excuses and justifications for their current and past decisions about plagiarism. A productive conversation will extend beyond a review of the honor code, although that certainly should be covered with younger or first-year students. The task is to correct student misperceptions with accurate information while keeping honest exchanges flowing.

EXPLAINING PLAGIARISM

For many, plagiarism is an abstract concept. This will be the first time anyone has formally explained the nuances of plagiarism. Expect resistance from students who have been doing things differently throughout their academic careers. The facilitator's tone needs to be nonthreatening to learn as much as possible from students. Humor is also helpful. Notes should be taken on student responses and the questions they pose to the discussion facilitator. This way, instruction can be planned to fill any knowledge gaps. For example, when I began these discussions with high school students, I learned that very few understood how to paraphrase. I made this a focus of my instruction over a four-month period.

The discussion questions should be a mixture of practical, moral, and situational question types but with an emphasis on practical components. The idea is to create working knowledge of plagiarism. Discussion facilitators should end the discussion with an invitation for students to ask any questions at all about plagiarism. Allow at least ten minutes for this part of the discussion. Encourage students to bring up specific examples when they have been confused about what to do in a given situation about plagiarism. Avoiding plagiarism is a universal challenge in an academic setting. Students will often ask a facilitator about their own personal experiences with plagiarism. It is important to answer honestly because plagiarism is part of everyone's academic experience. When I am asked this question, I honestly tell them about my academic experiences returning to graduate school many years after college graduation. While I was never caught plagiarizing, I was overwhelmed and could very well have plagiarized. Honesty breaks down barriers.

CATEGORIES OF PLAGIARISM QUESTIONS

The following questions are a guide for classroom discussions. The discussion responses are a starting point. Each school community should adapt the questions and responses to its own unique situations. This is also a quick reference for students and teachers.

Practical Plagiarism Questions

Practical plagiarism questions should be primary-type questions for the discussion. These questions can also be presented in a true/false format for a ten-minute warm-up or a full class discussion by facilitators. The goal is for students to be able to apply a solution or procedure in real time for plagiarism issues.

Question: *What is intellectual property?*

Discussion: According to the World Intellectual Property Organization, "intellectual property" refers to "creations of the mind:

inventions; literary and artistic works; and symbols, names and images used in commerce." For example, the instructions for micro-paraphrasing found in this book are a type of intellectual property that is protected by copyright. Intellectual property rights are associated with patents, trademark, and copyright. The owners of the protected material have the right to benefit from their work, so you must get permission before borrowing or reusing this material. Now that everyone can publish on the Internet, respect of intellectual property rights becomes even more important. When authorship is respected, it encourages more people to publish. For students in schools with a morality-based mission, respect for the work of others is also human courtesy.

Question: *What is an idea? What's an example of an original idea? (There is more information on ideas in Chapter 6.)*

Discussion: The concept of an idea can be difficult to grasp. It has not been proven or universally accepted. It does not exist in a set format. An idea can be seen in many ways: a conclusion based on a comparison between two separate things, a statement that is reached based on analysis, or a hypothesis or a concept. Ideas are another type of information, so you need to consider your audience when you're deciding whether it needs a citation.

Example 1: The agenda of the women's organization March On is to "raise collective voices in hope for a better future" for women. *This is the concept the organization uses for its work. It needs a citation because part of the sentence was quoted. It is not common knowledge.*

Example 2: If Hemingway and Fitzgerald were alive today, they would have been considered hopeless alcoholics by medical professionals. *This is a conclusion based on the history of Hemingway and Fitzgerald. It needs a citation because it is a specific conclusion.*

Example 3: The architect's initial plans called for a new slate roof for the arts center because of the board's environmental concerns. *Architectural plans are an idea. The roof has not been installed yet. Environmental concerns are also an idea. Depending on where this information appears, it may need a citation.*

Question: *What is a fact? When does a fact need a citation? When does a fact not need a citation?*

Discussion: Facts are provable knowledge. It is a true statement. When you are deciding about citing a fact, consider whether the fact is common knowledge in this subject area. If it is common knowledge, it does not need a citation. Here are few examples:

Example 1: Presidents in the United States can serve a maximum of two four-year terms. *This is a well-known fact. Even if you used this information for a research assignment in another class, a citation would not be necessary because it is information known by most people living in the United States who have completed high school.*

Example 2: The latest census data noted that the population of Daisy Lake, New Hampshire, is 995. *This is factual common knowledge for the residents of Daisy Lake. It may also be common knowledge for people who live in the nearby towns. Even though it is factual, it is not common knowledge to anyone outside of the Daisy Lake, New Hampshire, area.*

Example 3: Most of Earth's air is composed of nitrogen and oxygen. *This does not need a citation. It is a fact and common knowledge in science. This information can be verified in many places through a basic Internet search.*

Question: *If you get an idea from a web page and use it in a paper or PowerPoint, do you need to be concerned about plagiarism?*

Discussion: No matter where you use someone else's original idea, it needs to be considered for a citation. This includes the use of someone else's ideas in short films, songs, blog posts, images, social media, videos, PowerPoint and other presentations, essays, research papers, posters, models, and any other format that is published or created for a graded academic assignment.

Question: *I'm reading web pages all the time, so I can't keep track of where my ideas come from. How can I possibly cite everything?*

Discussion: This is understandable considering the amount of information the average person receives through web pages. General ideas are well known to everyone. Many of these ideas come from web page browsing, especially from news sources. One example is that veterans of the Iraq War, like many war veterans, sometimes have physical and mental health challenges when they return home. That is a general statement that does not need to be cited. If you write a research paper on health-care problems experienced by the war in Iraq, you need to consult sources that directly out-line these problems. This more specific information about the health conditions will likely need to be cited.

Question: *What's an example of common knowledge?*

Discussion: Common knowledge is information known to everyone within a community, classroom, profession, or other group of people. For example, the name of your school's lacrosse coach is common knowledge within your school community. See Chapter 7 for more information.

Question: *If you change around an assignment from last school year and hand it in this year, is this plagiarism?*

Discussion: Recycling fraud is a very specific type of plagiarism. One component of academic integrity is that each assignment should be original. Secondary sources from previous academic work products should not be reused. This knowledge and work from previous school years now serves as background knowledge of the subject area and should not be used with new work.

Question: *When you are researching, how do you make the decision whether to directly quote or paraphrase what you've read in a secondary source?*

Discussion: Active reading of secondary sources during the research process is an ongoing decision-making process. You need to decide if the information is relevant enough to be used as evidence in a research paper. Wordy sentences that have a relevant idea should be considered for a paraphrase. Often, you can restate two sentences more succinctly than the original. Direct quotes are best used for very specific information and for quotes from the primary source.

Question: *When you are paraphrasing, how much are you supposed to change from the original sentences?*

Discussion: You need to change the original sentences completely. If you change only a few words around, this is plagiarizing. The micro-paraphrasing technique is in Chapter 2. Focus on reading one paragraph from the source. Find two sentences that can be paraphrased. They do not have to be next to one another in the source. Once you have identified the critical terms—those names, places, dates, and other words that can't be restated another way—all the other words and ideas have to be restated in your own words. (The facilitator should review the micro-paraphrasing steps if necessary.)

Question: *Is there ever a time where it is okay to take material from a source, put it into your own words, and not provide a citation?*

Discussion: Putting material from a source into your own words is paraphrasing. There are steps to paraphrasing properly in this book (see Micro-paraphrasing in Chapter 2) to avoid plagiarism. All paraphrases must have a citation except when the information is common knowledge. However, if you copy common knowledge *exactly* from a source, you should cite it.

Question: *Is it okay to change a few words when I use a direct quote in my paper or PowerPoint?*

Discussion: No. Direct quotes must be copied exactly from the source with quotation marks and a citation. This is the case for every way you present your academic work.

Question: *What is a citation?*

Discussion: A citation is a way of recording the sources you use in your research paper or other project. The citation is a list of the author, title of the book or article, publication title, publisher, publication date, and location in the citation-style format used by your school. This helps you be conscious of the source itself, avoiding plagiarism.

Question: *How many direct quotes are appropriate to use on one page of your paper?*

Discussion: Overciting is a red flag for plagiarism in student research papers. If too many direct quotes are used, it appears as if the structure of the paper is being copied from the secondary sources. The priority is always to follow the instructions set by the teacher. A good general recommendation is about two citations for each page of the paper.

Question: *Should your parenthetical citations match the sources listed on your works cited page exactly?*

Discussion: Yes. If a source is cited in the text of your paper, there should be a corresponding citation on the Works Cited or Bibliography page. This is a basic part of proofreading to avoid plagiarism. See Chapter 5 for more information.

Question: *When proofreading my research paper, I can't find one of the sources I used. What should I do?*

Discussion: If the source is important for your paper, then you should make the effort to fix this problem. Do not try to create a citation by memory. Contact the school's librarian for help with this. If the source is not found, you should remove it from your paper.

Question: *I just found a YouTube video snippet that will work perfectly for my PowerPoint. What do I do next?*

Discussion: YouTube videos must be cited like any other source. Refer to your school's citation style manual for more information on this. (Facilitators should be prepared to point students to resources on this topic.)

Question: *Can you use Anonymous or NA as an author for a full citation when there is no name listed with the article?*

Discussion: Authorship is important to understand for web pages. Anonymous or NA should never be used in place of an author's name.

MLA: If there is no author listed, you should begin a citation in MLA format with the article title in quotation marks.

APA: If there is no author listed, you should begin a citation in APA format with the article title without quotation marks.

Chicago: If there is an organization or corporation that created the web page without a named person as the author of the article, use the organization or corporation as the author.

Question: *Does everything on the Internet have an author?*

Discussion: Yes. Authorship must be carefully considered when you use web pages or other content on the Internet for academic work. Even if there is no name listed, there is authorship by the organization or publisher who created it.

Question: *When I make an error on my works cited page with the spacing, is this plagiarism?*

Discussion: There is a difference between intentional plagiarism and more minor errors with formatting like spacing and margins. While spacing errors are not plagiarism, sloppy papers cause teachers to look more in depth at your work, possibly finding other problems.

Question: *When you're writing a paper, what are the signs that you might be plagiarizing?*

Discussion: Here are a few indicators you might be close to plagiarizing.

1. The digital source is side by side on the computer screen with your working document. There is a good chance that you will copy/paste from the digital source to your working document and omit the documentation. Work from printed-out copies of digital sources when possible.
2. Instead of paraphrasing properly from a website, you change just a few words within the original sentences you think may be common knowledge. This type of shortcut can lead to plagiarism.
3. You're behind schedule with the research paper. Feeling overwhelmed or panicked can lead to plagiarism. For example, if you are required to write a twelve-page paper and you have only three pages, it is better to hand in three well-written pages than twelve pages that might contain plagiarism.

Group Work Questions

Group projects are part of academic work across all educational levels. Students need to be prepared for dealing with possible inequities while completing group work.

Question: *What do you do when one person in your group work project doesn't do his or her share?*

Discussion: Anyone who passes off the written work of others as his or her own is plagiarizing. It may also be considered cheating at your school. Facilitators should inform students of this fact but do not expect compliance. Students have difficulty in these types of confrontations with their classmates. At the high school level, many would rather do the work themselves rather than confront a classmate in this way.

Question: *If someone in my group work project plagiarizes, can I be held responsible?*

Discussion: It depends. This question merits a review by the facilitator of each individual responsibility for academic work products. Explain the importance of maintaining all notes and personal work products until the final grade. It's also important to review the final product before handing in the final copy.

Plagiarism Questions for College-Bound High School Seniors and First-Year College Students

This discussion should be held in the spring for high school seniors. For first-year college students, including community college, it can be held during orientation.

Question: *How will college research be different than high school research?*

Discussion: There is a different level of intensity with college research. Many colleges and universities have Turnitin.com or other plagiarism checkers. (The facilitator should explain Turnitin to high school students if the school does not use a plagiarism checker on campus. If community college and first-year students have never used Turnitin.com, explain the full scope of this product as it relates to plagiarism.) College means access to many more research databases and books than high school. The research papers will be longer, with more depth expected. Once the research paper is assigned, teachers normally do not monitor student progress like they do in high school.

Question: *What would you do if you were accused of plagiarism (here) or in college? How would you handle the situation?*

Discussion: There are moral and practical considerations for plagiarism accusations. Facilitators should be prepared for students to express strong opinions about this topic. There will be students who say that they will not admit it willingly, forcing the teacher to "prove it." Others may want to own up to it.

First, you should ask questions. Even though you will be very upset, make sure you really understand the accusations. Either way, it is important to take responsibility for the situation. If you believe you made an unintentional error, explain what you were thinking at the time. Offer to make corrections. If you intentionally plagiarized, take immediate responsibility for your actions at this time. Unless you truly believe that the school has made an egregious error, taking responsibility makes it easier to negotiate on your own behalf. If you're asked to withdraw from school, ask to receive a failing grade for the class instead. Instead of failing the class, ask to redo the paper or receive a zero for this assignment. Be sure to always save your notes, sources, and all other materials you used to write the paper.

Question: *Rank the academic moral offenses from least to most serious (facilitator discussion only).*

Discussion: This question allows you to understand the perceptions of students regarding different types of cheating on campus, including plagiarism. Purchasing a research paper on the Internet is extreme because it means that no original work was completed. It is also a premeditated act. The discussion should also cover the impact that cheating (and plagiarism) has on each individual and the class itself. The cumulative nature of education—where knowledge builds on itself—is subverted by cheating and plagiarism. It is false progress. Copying homework in high schools can be part of a school's culture. This should be addressed based on the school's individual circumstances.

- Copying homework from a classmate
- Cheating on a test
- Purchasing a research paper on the Internet
- Copying and pasting a paragraph from a web page without a citation
- Copying a sentence and then changing a few words without a citation

Teacher Questions about Plagiarism

Student perceptions about what teachers know about plagiarism can inform campus plagiarism policies. This information can also be the basis for discussions and recommendations about how teachers can reduce plagiarism in the classroom.

Question: *What do you think your teachers here know about plagiarism?*

Discussion: This is meant to gauge perceptions about the state of plagiarism on your campus. Do students work differently for teachers who they think may be able to find plagiarism easier than others? The answer is often "yes." Fear of getting caught is a primary reason for high school and college students to try to avoid plagiarism.

Question: *What do you think your chances are of getting caught plagiarizing here (high school)? What about in college?*

Discussion: This question is meant to open a discussion about various academic departments and teachers. The goal of plagiarism education is for students to develop a consistent skill set, not to vary their level of care according to whomever is grading their paper.

Question: *Do you think your teacher can tell if you copy one sentence from a web page?*

Discussion: Once students have a competent skill set to avoid plagiarism in their academic work, they should be less concerned about the perceived knowledge base of instructors.

Question: *Do you think that if a teacher doesn't catch plagiarism the first time, it's a sign that you can continue to do it, especially if you have other work to do for classes where you might be struggling?*

Discussion: Often, students are very busy. They will allow one class to "slide" while paying more attention to other classes that need their attention. The goal is to have the plagiarism education principles applied across all classes consistently.

Academic Integrity Questions

These questions should be adapted to the policies and expectations of the academic community.

Question: *What are the penalties for plagiarism in this class? At this school?*

Discussion: Sometimes, penalties for plagiarism can vary depending on the class and teacher. The facilitator should note whether there is consistent understanding of the penalties for the class and for the school.

Question: *This school has a statement of academic integrity. Do you remember what it says?*

Discussion: The facilitator should be prepared to discuss the school's academic integrity policy in detail. This type of review, especially to define terms such as "unauthorized help," is important.

Question: *Are there instances where you think "accidental plagiarism" should be overlooked?*

Discussion: This question is meant to determine the extent to which students believe that excuses or reasons for plagiarizing will be a mitigating factor. It also allows you to gauge perceptions about the current plagiarism policy in effect.

Question: *What's the difference between accidental plagiarism and intentional plagiarism when penalties or consequences are applied?*

Discussion: Many students believe that if they can show that the plagiarism is minor or accidental, this mitigates any possible consequences. In the context of the school and subject area, the facilitator should discuss the difference between a minor formatting error such as forgetting a quotation mark and the copy/paste of sentences without attribution or omitting a citation from the Bibliography.

Question: *Do you think there are students on campus who are treated differently than others when it comes to accusations of cheating or plagiarism? (This is about any implied status for minorities, foreign students, or sports stars.)*

Discussion: This question may spark a debate. If there is consensus within the class that there is inequity in how the school's honor code is applied, this should be brought to the attention of the school administrator.

Moral Plagiarism Questions

There is a significant moral component for plagiarism. For private and religious schools with a morally based mission, these questions are especially important. Students also need to know what to do in different situations if they are ever accused of plagiarism.

Question: *You hand in a paper and then a short time later realize you plagiarized. What should you do?*

Discussion: This is a decision between asking to fix the paper, drawing attention to your mistake, and saying nothing and hope for the best. Encourage students to contact the teacher, explain the situation, and fix any plagiarism errors before the grading process begins.

Question: *What's the difference between cheating and plagiarism? Which is worse?*

Discussion: The facilitator should be prepared for a discussion of morals. Plagiarism is a type of cheating. This question expands the student's conceptual understanding of plagiarism in a continuum with other forms of cheating like copying homework or taking in unauthorized notes for a test.

Question: *How much do you think your friends are plagiarizing?*

Discussion: There is no need for students to name anyone specifically who is plagiarizing. The facilitator should allow for this discussion to be open ended to understand the extent of the problem more accurately. This question is designed to gauge student perceptions about plagiarism in the class and in the campus community.

Question: *A teacher notes that you and a classmate have used one of the same quotes from the same source in your paper. How will you handle this situation?*

Discussion: During high school, there are fewer possible topics and fewer research databases to choose from for research. If this is a coincidence, especially if you both have the same topic, either you or your classmate should offer to change your source. It is important to maintain all copies of secondary sources until the research paper is returned with a grade. If you intentionally shared the same quote, take responsibility for this. One person should offer to change his or her paper. It is more difficult for this to occur with web pages and books.

Question: *Your friend just told you he plagiarized. You're in the same class. What should you do?*

Discussion: The entire class benefits when teachers and school administrators know about plagiarism. Plagiarism compromises the learning process for everyone. It negatively impacts everyone who does honest work by incorrectly inflating grades. At the high school level, the threat of being socially ostracized for "tattling" often outweighs any concern about inequities to grades. Students can report plagiarism through an anonymous note to the teacher.

Question: *Your roommate showed you where he plagiarized his research paper. You're in the same class. What should you do?*

Discussion: This is difficult because a roommate is someone with whom you share your life every day. It's different than a classmate who you may or may not know well. You can tell your roommate to never do it again if it was intentional or offer advice for next time if it was unintentional. Realistically, it is almost impossible to directly turn in someone you live with for academic misconduct without compromising your own social and academic life on campus. Your campus community may have options to make anonymous reports to faculty or the school administration in this type of situation.

Question: *How much help should parents, tutors, or other "helpers" assist with a research paper before it crosses an ethical line (Radunovich, Turner, and Baugh 2009, 31)?*

Discussion: Proofreading is ultimately the student's responsibility. See Chapter 5 on proofreading. All writers need outside proofreaders and editors because there is a limit to what we are able to objectively recognize in our own work. No one should help rewrite a paper in a significant way. When advice from a "helper" extends to changes in the overall structure of the paper, acknowledgment should be given to this individual or the advice the individual asks for should apply only to minor changes.

CONCLUSION

Discussing such a nuanced concept like plagiarism, especially with inexperienced researchers, reduces fear and anxiety. On most campuses, it is an essential opportunity to "translate" the honor code into usable segments for students to apply in their academic work. It gives depth and breadth to the abstract nature of plagiarism. This process of having a facilitator unpack the more abstract concepts within plagiarism like idea, fact, and common knowledge increases practical understanding. While there are obviously certain nonnegotiable guidelines that should not be crossed by students, these discussions help prepare students for the different ways that teachers and schools will handle plagiarism throughout their academic career. Most important, these discussions set up a comfort level for students to be able to ask questions later about their own work.

REFERENCES

Evering, Lea Calvert, and Gary Moorman. 2012. "Rethinking Plagiarism in the Digital Age." *Journal of Adolescent and Adult Literacy* 56, no. 1 (September): 35–44. http://jstor.org/stable/23367758.

Radunovich, Heidi, Elaine Turner, and Eboni Baugh. 2009. "An Examination of Students' Knowledge of What Constitutes Plagiarism." *NACTA Journal* 53, no. 4 (December): 30–35. http://www.jstor.org/stable/43765409.

Thomas, Ebony Elizabeth, and Kelly Sassi. 2011. "An Ethical Dilemma: Talking about Plagiarism and Academic Integrity in the Digital Age." *National Council of Teachers of English* 100, no. 6 (July): 47–53. http://www.jstor.org/stable/23047881.

4

Citations

Incorrect citations and the omission of citations cause a great deal of plagiarism. Learning citations does not have a formal place in school curriculum at any level. To use information ethically, students need to understand the source and the citation. Digital sources are abstract—literally, they appear as a large group of words on a computer screen without physical boundaries. Citations generated by citation tools and research databases are often the only literal representation of the source itself when students have never seen a scholarly journal or encyclopedia in print. This time of unprecedented digital information access means that citation competence is an urgent skill.

CITATION BASICS

The citation style is determined by your school or the subject area you are studying. The three most commonly used citation styles are the

Publication Manual of the American Psychological Association (APA), *MLA Handbook for Writers of Research Papers* (MLA), and the *Chicago Manual of Style* (Chicago). Two different types of citations are required for each use of an outside source. Parenthetical (in-text) citations document the secondary sources used in a research paper or project within the text of the paper for MLA, APA, and Chicago Author-Date citation styles. Chicago Notes and Bibliography uses footnotes or endnotes instead of parenthetical citations. All three styles require full citations on the Works Cited (MLA), Bibliography (Chicago Author-Date and Notes and Bibliography), and References page (APA).

The Citation Is the Source

Citations represent the source. A full citation should immediately call to mind the individual parts of a source: author, title (article or chapter), publication title(s), publication date, and location. While citations are most commonly identified with research papers, they are necessary any time a source is used for a PowerPoint or any other type of project that will be graded or shown to other people. On the most basic level, citations provide a way for a teacher to verify the source.

APA, MLA, and Chicago citation styles all publish official books. It can be challenging for students and other inexperienced researchers to use these books easily. Digital resources can be published in different ways, often making it difficult to follow the examples in the citation books.

There are so many different types of digital resources available with the potential to enhance the academic work of students, especially videos and other multimedia products. There are no set publication standards for these types of sources. This means that the information needed for the citation can be missing or found in different places. Teaching the citations for books, web pages, and research database articles emphasizes awareness of the authorship and publication process, building respect and understanding for these sources. This eases the way for the advanced analysis skills required to cite other digital products.

The citation is a discrete, complete visual representation of the source. It is possible to teach students the visual indicators of different citations, so they can identify the source and the various components. Citation instruction helps students better understand the source, regardless of whether they use a citation tool or not. Once students begin to see the visual patterns in different types of source citations, it becomes easier to create citations and use citation tools accurately. Proofreading is also easier.

TYPES OF RESOURCES: FINDING THE CITATION INFORMATION

To understand citations, it is essential to first understand the source itself. This is not intuitive. Review each source with students according to the information required for the citation. If possible, librarians should lead this instruction with students as part of information literacy instruction.

The purpose of the examples in this section is to encourage detailed understanding of sources through "reading" the individual parts of the citation. Depending on the citation tool used, there will always be slight variations in citations, especially for digital sources. The accuracy for these examples is based on the best available information.

Print Books

Print books are stable, with no question about the authorship and publication process. As a result, the citation process is straightforward. There is no question about credibility. The subject matter is covered with depth and detail. The author and title are on the front cover. Show students the publication page of a typical book where the information about the publisher and publication dates are located. The publishers of print books have "company" sounding names such as Scribner, Penguin Books, or Oxford University Press. When a book has multiple publication dates, use the most recent date.

The examples in this section can be used for a class explanation about citations, to create a citation guide, or for classwork or homework to build visual recognition skills in students.

MLA

(1) Morrison, Toni. (2) *A Mercy.* (3) Vintage Books, 2008.

    (1)   Author name.
    (2)   Title of book, italicized.
    (3)   Publisher, Publication year.

In-text citation example: (Morrison 28). *The page number will vary depending on the location of the quote or paraphrase.*

How to tell that this is a print book citation:

- The author's name begins the citation.

- The title is italicized.

- There is a publisher name and publication year.

APA

(1) Morrison, T. (2) (2008). (3) *A mercy.* (4) New York, NY: Vintage Books.

    (1)   Author name.
    (2)   Publication year.
    (3)   Title of book, italicized.
    (4)   City, State: Publisher.

In-text citation example: (Morrison, 2008, p. 28). *The page number will vary depending on the location of the quote or paraphrase.*

How to tell that this is a print book citation:

- The author's name begins the citation.

- The title is italicized.

- There is a publisher location, name, and publication year.

Chicago Notes and Bibliography

Note:

1.   Toni Morrison, *A Mercy* (New York, NY: Vintage Books, 2008), 28.

Note that the page number will vary depending on the location of the quote or paraphrase.

Bibliography:

(1) Morrison, Toni. (2) *A Mercy.* (3) New York: Vintage Books, 2008.

    (1)   Author name.
    (2)   Title of book, italicized.
    (3)   Location of publication: Publisher, publication date.

How to tell that this is a print book citation:

- The author's name begins the citation.

- The title is italicized.

- There is a publisher location, name, and publication year.

Chicago Author-Date

(1) Morrison, Toni. (2) 2008. (3) *A Mercy.* (4) New York: Vintage Books.

    (1)   Author.
    (2)   Year of publication.
    (3)   Title of book, italicized.
    (4)   Location of publication: Publisher.

In-text citation example: (Morrison 2008, 67). *The page number will vary depending on the location of the quote or paraphrase.*

How to tell that this is a print book citation:

*   The author's name begins the citation.

*   The title is italicized.

*   There is a publisher location, name, and publication year.

Advice for Teachers and Librarians about Print Books

The use of print books as a secondary source in research should be considered an important part of the college preparatory process. While plagiarism is not eliminated entirely, it is naturally reduced when students use books as sources because they cannot cut and paste information. For yearly research paper assignments, librarians and teachers can collaborate to develop a separate, secondary-source book collection on a set number of student research topics. These books can be made available to students for use in the library only, with the option to copy the cover, publication page, and chapters used for the paper. That way, students have access to the citation information. Plagiarism can be easily checked if students are limited to the books in this collection.

This review of the parts of a book for the citation should begin in the eighth grade with a research assignment. It may need to be reviewed again through the tenth grade depending on the research experience of students. Because of the dominance of digital information, you may find that many students are completely unfamiliar with the print publication process.

Digital Sources

Digital resources introduce different authorship and publication variables, which make creating citations more complicated than books. The boundaries of the information are less apparent. This makes it easy to treat web pages, research database articles, and other digital sources with less value.

Web Pages

The term "web page" is somewhat misleading when discussing sources. The actual source is the *web page article* that is found on a web page within a larger website. At the time of this writing in 2019, there are no publication standards for websites. This means that web pages, along with the possible variations in web page articles, are one of the most important sources to review with students for citation accuracy. While there are certainly some exceptions, the average web page uses language and vocabulary to be accessible to the widest group of people. This makes it easy to plagiarize.

Two types of analyses are required for the appropriate, ethical use of web pages. The first is a "tour" of the parts of a web page. Here are the essential elements.

- Authorship: Is there an individual's name attached to the web page article? This is usually found near the article title. Or does authorship revert to the organization who sponsored the site?

- Article title: The article on the web page is the actual source. The article title is right above the article text.

- Publisher: The publisher is the organization that is responsible for the website content. This can be found in a few different places—next to the copyright sign, above the website title, or in the top left of the home page.

- Publication date: This can be found in a variety of places—near the article title, at the end of the article, or the publication date may revert to the copyright date at the bottom of the web page.

- Website or "container" title: This is the overall title of the "container" where this web page is located. This is above the article.

The second type of analysis for a web page article is content evaluation for credibility, authorship, relevance, bias, timeliness, and currency. It is more difficult to plagiarize from high-quality web pages. There is more information about teaching students how to find credible web pages in Appendix A2. Ideally, librarians should teach this during information literacy instruction. For some web pages, significant analysis is required to determine the authorship and publication information for the citation, even if a citation tool is used.

Advice for Teachers and Librarians about Web Page Citation Instruction. There are two goals for web page citation instruction: (1) create an accurate citation for a credible web page article from a citation guide or by using an online citation tool; (2) recognize a citation by the source type and be able to proofread any errors.

This review for students should take place with a typical web page for the subject area projected on a screen. Appendix A has "Anatomy of a Web Page" lesson plans for each citation style, which explain how to teach students the parts of a web page while they create a citation. There are two types of web page article variations to review: articles with an author and articles without an author.

Here are examples of web page citations with the important visual indicators.

MLA: Web Page Articles

Web page article without an author

(1) "New Kingdom." (2) *Egypt's Golden Empire,* (3) PBS, (4) 2018, (5) www.pbs. org/empires/egypt/newkingdom/index.html. (6) Accessed 23 Jan. 2019.

    (1)   Article title in quotation marks.
    (2)   Web page title, italicized.
    (3)   Publisher of the site.
    (4)   Publication year.
    (5)   URL for this web page article.
    (6)   The day month year the article was last accessed.

    In-text citation example: ("New Kingdom")

How to tell that this is a web page article without an author:

• There is no name at the beginning of the citation to indicate an author.

• There is a URL.

• Accessed date is used only for digital resources.

Web page article with an author

(1) Baker, Peter. (2) "For Trump, the Reality Show Has Never Ended." (3) *Politics,* (4) *The New York Times,* (5) 10 Oct. 2017, (6) www.newyorktimes.com. (7) Accessed 11 Oct. 2017.

    (1)   Author name.
    (2)   Article title, in quotation marks.
    (3)   Web page title, in italics. The print and online versions of the *New York Times* are a mirror of one another. Politics is the section of the newspaper where this article is located in print and online.
    (4)   *The New York Times* is the publisher and the publication title.
    (5)   Publication date.
    (6)   The URL for the article. This URL is abbreviated to www .newyorktimes.com because of its length. The article title is searchable at the *New York Times* website.
    (7)   The day month year the article was last accessed.

    In-text citation example: (Baker)

How to tell that this is a web page article with an author:

• There is an author's name at the beginning of the citation.

• There is a URL.

• Accessed date is used only for digital sources.

APA: Web Page Articles

Web page article without an author

(1) Egypt's golden empire. (2) (2018). (3) Retrieved May 26, 2018, from PBS website: (4) http://www.pbs.org/empires/egypt/newkingdom/index.html

(1)   Title of article.
(2)   Publication year.
(3)   Retrieved from month day, year, from website.
(4)   The URL for the article on the PBS website.

In-text citation example: ("Egypt's Golden Empire," 2018)

How to tell that this is a web page article without an author:

• The citation begins with an article title, not an author's name.

• It notes that the article was retrieved from the PBS website.

• There is a URL.

Web page article with an author

(1) Baker, P. (2) (2017, October 10). (3) For Trump, the reality show has never ended. (4) *The New York Times*. (5) Retrieved from https://www.nytimes.com/2017/10/10/us/politics/trump-corker-feud-tweet-liddle-bob.html

(1)   Author's name.
(2)   Date of publication. Since this is a newspaper article, the date is in year, month day format.
(3)   Article title.
(4)   *The New York Times* is the publisher and the publication title.
(5)   Retrieved from URL.

In-text citation example: (Baker, 2017)

How to tell that this is a web page article with an author:

• There is an author's name at the beginning of the citation.

• There is a retrieved date and website.

• A URL is at the end of the citation.

Chicago Notes and Bibliography: Web Page Articles

Web page article without a person as the author

Note:

1. PBS, "New Kingdom," Egypt's Golden Empire, last modified 2018, accessed January 23, 2019, http://www.pbs.org/empires/egypt/newkingdom/index.html.

Bibliography:

(1) PBS. (2) "New Kingdom." (3) Egypt's Golden Empire. (4) Last modified 2018. (5) Accessed January 23, 2019. (6) http://www.pbs.org/empires/egypt/newkingdom/index.html.

(1) The organization, PBS, is responsible for the article.
(2) The article title in quotation marks.
(3) The title of the web page name.
(4) Last modified year is the copyright date since there is no other publication year.
(5) The accessed date is the last date you viewed the article.
(6) The URL for this article on PBS website.

How to tell that this is a web page article without a named author (person):

• There is the name of a corporation, not a person at the beginning of the citation.

• The article title is in quotation marks.

• The citation has a URL.

Web page article with an author

Note:

1. Peter Baker, "For Trump, the Reality Show Has Never Ended," *New York Times*, April 2, 2018, Politics, accessed April 5, 2018, https://www.nytimes.com/2017/10/10/us/politics/trump-corker-feud-tweet-liddle-bob.html

Bibliography:

(1) Baker, Peter. (2) "For Trump, the Reality Show Has Never Ended." (3) *New York Times*, (4) April 2, 2018, (5) Politics. (6) Accessed April 5, 2018. (7) https://www.nytimes.com/2017/10/10/us/politics/trump-corker-feud-tweet-liddle-bob.html

(1) Author's name.
(2) The article title in quotation marks.
(3) *The New York Times* is the publisher and the publication title.
(4) Publication date.
(5) Website title. The print and online versions of the *New York Times* are a mirror of one another. "Politics" is the section of the newspaper where this article is located in print and online.
(6) The accessed date is the last date you viewed the article.
(7) The URL for this article on the *New York Times* website.

How to tell that this is a web page article with an author:

- There is an author at the beginning of the citation.
- The article title is in quotation marks.
- There is a URL.

Chicago Author-Date: Web Page Articles

Web page article without a person named as author

(1) PBS. (2) 2018. (3) "New Kingdom." (4) Egypt's Golden Empire. (5) Accessed January 23, 2019. (6) http://www.pbs.org/empires/egypt/newkingdom/index.html.

    (1)   The organization, PBS, is responsible for the article.
    (2)   Publication date.
    (3)   The article title in quotation marks.
    (4)   Web page title.
    (5)   The last date the article was viewed.
    (6)   The URL for the article on the PBS website.

In-text citation example: (PBS 2018)

How to tell that this is a web page article citation without an author:

- There is not an author's name at the beginning of the citation.
- There is a URL.

Web page article with an author

(1) Baker, Peter. (2) 2018. (3) "For Trump, the Reality Show Has Never Ended." (4) *New York Times,* (5) April 2, 2018, (6) Politics. (7) Accessed April 5, 2018. (8) http://www.newyorktimes.com.

    (1)   The author's name.
    (2)   Publication date.
    (3)   The article title in quotation marks.
    (4)   The publisher *and* the name of the publication.
    (5)   The date of publication.
    (6)   The web page title. The print and online versions of the *New York Times* are a mirror of one another. "Politics" is the section of the newspaper where this article is located in print and online.
    (7)   The accessed date is the last date the article was viewed.
    (8)   The URL for the article on the *New York Times* website.

In-text citation example: (Baker 2018)

How to tell that this is a web page article citation with an author:

- There is the name of an author at the beginning of the citation.
- There is a URL.
- The article title is in quotation marks.

Advice for Students: Web Page Articles. If you are not entirely sure if you will use a web page article as a source, print out the web pages anyway. At any time, web pages can be moved, or the links can be broken. This way, you can maintain the parts of the source and create the citation. Maintain the search history in your web browser until the project is complete, especially if you don't have access to a printer.

Research Database Articles

Research database articles are one of the most authoritative and credible type of digital resources. They are also abstract. Research database articles originate from a wide range of publications. We do not see the entire publication during a research database search. The articles are in a results list from what could be hundreds of different publications according to the frequency that the search keywords appear in the article. It can be difficult to fully grasp the boundaries of a source you have never seen outside of a computer screen. Many students have never used a print reference book or encyclopedias. Many don't read print magazines or newspapers. They have never seen a scholarly journal. Library reference collections, the source of many research database articles, have transitioned to digital versions too.

Students only need to determine the relevance of the article to the research topic after a keyword search. These resources are available through the library's website, providing wide access to many authors, research, and topic areas from a variety of publications. The citations for research database articles can be more complex because these articles have been published in more than one place. There is also a time delay between when the article is written and when it finally appears in a research database. The writing in research databases is usually more sophisticated than web pages and makes these sources more difficult to plagiarize without detection. The length is appropriate for most research projects, generally from 3 to 10 pages long.

Most research databases produce the full citation for the article through a citation tool within the database. This citation tool is important to use since many of these articles go through a complicated publication cycle, originating in books, encyclopedias, and journals before becoming available in the database. Instruction is necessary for the parenthetical citation or footnote for each type of article. Like web page citations, the goal is to have students recognize the type of source by the citation and be able to proofread any errors. The visual recognition of what type of source the research database article originated from helps students choose information more accurately for the information need. The basic publication information is found at the top of the research database article. The fact that research databases produce a citation makes it important to offer instruction on the parts of the citation.

Scholarly Journal Research Database Articles. One of the most important types of articles found in a research database is a scholarly journal article. Scholarly journals are written for a community of professionals, often as part of a professional association. Many of these articles are research based. *The Journal of the American Medical Association* and the *National Council of Teachers of English* are two examples of scholarly journals. Members normally receive the journal in the mail on a monthly or quarterly basis. Sometimes, the journal is also published online, available to everyone. The evidence found in research databases is clearer and more relevant for research.

Here is how the publication process often proceeds for scholarly journal articles:

- Author writes an article about a professional topic.

- Author sends in article to scholarly journal.

- Editor reviews the article. It is rejected outright or conditionally "accepted" and sent out to peer reviewers.

- The article is sent back to the author for necessary changes. It can also be rejected at this stage if any problems are found.

- After changes are made, the article is reviewed again by the editor and scheduled for publication.

- The article is published in the journal. The journal is made available to subscribers by mail and/or open access on the journal's website.

- The entire issue is made digitally available through a research database for searching.

These sources always have an author. Scholarly journal articles have page numbers in the citation because they are often printed in journal/magazine format. The page numbers should be visible at the bottom of the article. There is a significant time between when the article was originally published and when it appears in a research database article.

Here are citation examples of scholarly research database articles. All these articles will have authors.

MLA: Scholarly Journal Research Database Article

(1) Larsen, Torill. (2) "Creating a Supportive Environment among Youth Football Players." (3) *Health Education,* (4) vol. 72, no. 6, (5) 2015, (6) pp. 570–586. (7) *ProQuest,* (8) https://search.proquest.com/docview/1 715874529?accountid=41092.

    (1)   Author name.
    (2)   Article title in quotation marks.
    (3)   Title of the scholarly journal, italicized.
    (4)   Volume (vol.) number, issue (no.) number.
    (5)   Publication year.
    (6)   The page range of the article from the scholarly journal.
    (7)   Title of research database, italicized.
    (8)   The URL for the article in *ProQuest,* the research database.

In-text citation example: (Larsen 571). *The page number will vary (between 570 and 586) depending on the location of the quote or paraphrase.*

How to tell that this is a scholarly journal citation:

• There is an author at the beginning of the citation.

• The article title is in quotation marks.

• *Health Education,* a scholarly journal title, is italicized.

• Vol. 72, no. 6 is the volume and issue number. This is always part of scholarly journal research citations.

• Scholarly journal citations always include a page range from the original publication—570–586.

• *ProQuest* is a research database.

APA: Scholarly Journal Research Database Article

(1) Larsen, T. (2) (2015). (3) Creating a supportive environment among youth football players. (4) *Health Education,* (5) 72(6), (6) 570–586. (7) Retrieved from ProQuest Research Library database.

    (1)   Author name.
    (2)   Publication year.
    (3)   Article title.
    (4)   Journal title, italicized.
    (5)   Volume number (issue number).
    (6)   The page range for the article from the scholarly journal.
    (7)   The database name where the article was found.

In-text citation example: (Larsen, 2015, p. 576). *The page number will vary (between 570 and 586) depending on the location of the quote or paraphrase.*

How to tell that this is a scholarly journal citation:

- There is an author name at the beginning of the citation.

- *Health Education,* a scholarly journal title, is italicized.

- vol. 72, no. 6 is the volume and issue numbers. This is always part of scholarly journal citations.

- Scholarly journal citations always include a page range from the original publication—570–586.

- *ProQuest* is a research database.

Chicago Author-Date Scholarly Journal Research Database Article

(1) Larsen, Torill. (2) 2015. (3) "Creating a Supportive Environment among Youth Football Players." (4) *Health Education* (5) 72 (6): (6) 570–586. (7) https://search.proquest.com/docview/1715874529?accountid= 41092. (8) doi: http://dx.doi.org/10.1108/HE-04-2014-0054

    (1)   Author name.
    (2)   Publication year.
    (3)   Article title in quotation marks.
    (4)   Scholarly journal title, italicized.
    (5)   Volume number (issue number).
    (6)   The page range for the article from the scholarly journal.
    (7)   The URL for the article in ProQuest, the research database.
    (8)   The doi is a link that will remain consistent throughout the existence of the article.

In-text citation example: (Larsen 2015, 577). *The page number will vary (between 570 and 586) depending on the location of the quote or paraphrase.*

How to tell that this is a scholarly journal citation:

- There is an author at the beginning of the citation.

- The article title is in quotation marks.

- *Health Education,* a scholarly journal title, is italicized.

- 72 (6) is the volume and issue number. This is always part of scholarly journal citations.

- Scholarly journal citations always include a page range from the original publication—570–586. *ProQuest* is a research database.

Chicago Notes-Bibliography Scholarly Journal Citation

Note:

1. Torrill Larsen, "Creating a Supportive Environment among Youth Football Players," *Health Education* 72, no. 6 (2015): 574, doi:http://dx.doi.org/10.1108/HE-04-2014-0054.

The page number in the Note will vary (between 570 and 586, in this instance) depending on the location of the quote or paraphrase. The doi, a permanent link to the article, is included when available.

Bibliography:

(1) Larsen, Torill. (2) "Creating a Supportive Environment among Youth Football Players." (3) *Health Education* (4) 72, no. 6 (2015): (5) 570–586. (6) doi:http://dx.doi.org/10.1108/HE-04-2014-0054. (7) https://search.proquest.com/docview/1715874529?accountid=41092.

    (1)   Author.
    (2)   Article title in quotation marks.
    (3)   Scholarly journal title, italicized.
    (4)   Volume number, issue number (Publication year).
    (5)   The page range from the scholarly journal.
    (6)   Doi. This is a link which will be consistently assigned to this article over the long term.
    (7)   The URL for the article in *ProQuest*, the research database.

How to tell that this is a scholarly journal citation:

• There is an author at the beginning of the citation.

• The article title is in quotation marks.

• *Health Education*, a scholarly journal title, is italicized.

• 72, no. 6 is the volume and issue number. This is always part of scholarly journal research database citations.

• Scholarly journal citations always include a page range from the original publication—570–586.

• *ProQuest* is a research database.

Reference Source Research Database Articles. Another important type of research database article is from reference sources. These articles are scanned from encyclopedias and specialized reference sources into a research database. Specialized encyclopedias and reference books are first published in print format. These books often cover one general topic, with separate entries on various aspects of this topic.

Research databases compile these entries and make them available for keyword searching. These articles are normally relatively short, usually between one and three pages when printed out. There may be multiple volumes of these books, which will be reflected in the full citation. Some of the articles will have a named author; many will not. When you download the article, check if page numbers are included on each page. If so, the page number should be included in the parenthetical citation or footnote. Often, the page range noted in the full citation is for the page range location of the article in the book or encyclopedia, not the article from the research database.

MLA Research Database Reference Source Article Citation—No Author

(1) "Drake." (2) *Contemporary Black Biography,* (3) vol. 86, (4) Gale, (5) 2011. (6) *Biography in Context,* (7) https://link.galegroup.com/apps/doc/K1606005056/BIC?u=baltcntycpl&sid=BIC&xid=c5b45282. (8) Accessed 4 Aug. 2018.

(1) Article title in quotation marks.
(2) The title of the book where the article originated, italicized.
(3) The volume number where this article was located within the original set of reference books.
(4) Publisher name.
(5) Publication year for *Contemporary Black Biography.*
(6) The name of the database where the article first originated, italicized.
(7) The URL for the article in *Biography in Context,* the research database.
(8) The accessed date is the last date that the article was viewed.

In-text citation example: ("Drake"). *There are no page numbers in the full citation.*

How to tell that this is a research database article from a reference source without an author:

• "Drake" begins the citation. If there was an author, it would be listed in Last Name, First Name format. The article is a biography about the singer Drake.

• *Contemporary Black Biography* is a reference book where the article originated. It is italicized.

• *Biography in Context* is a research database. It is italicized.

MLA Research Database Reference Source Citation—Author

(1) Shirer, Frank R. (2) "Pearl Harbor." (3) *Dictionary of American History,* (4) edited by Stanley I. Kutler, (5) 3rd ed., (6) vol. 6, (7) Charles Scribner's

Sons, (8) 2003, (9) pp. 271–273. (10) *U.S. History in Context*, (11) http://
link.galegroup.com/apps/doc/CX3401803190/UHIC?u=win5026&s
id=UHIC&xid=8dc4dbf0. (12) Accessed 12 June 2018.

(1) Author name.
(2) Article title in quotation marks.
(3) Title of book where the article originated, italicized.
(4) Stanley I. Kutler is the editor of the book, *Dictionary of American History*, where the article originated.
(5) 3rd edition means that the book has been published three times, with revisions each time.
(6) This is volume 6 in a larger set of reference books.
(7) The publisher of the book where the article originated.
(8) The publication year for *Dictionary of American History*.
(9) The page range for the article in the book.
(10) The name of the research database where this article was found.
(11) The URL for the article in *U.S. History in Context*, the research database.
(12) The accessed date is the last date the article was viewed.

In-text citation example: (Shirer). *No page number is used with the parenthetical citation unless page numbers print out on the article. The page range listed in this citation is from the original source of the article*, Dictionary of American History.

How to tell that this is a research database article from a reference source with an author:

• *U.S. History in Context* is a research database.

• The author's name, Shirer, Frank R., begins the citation.

• *Dictionary of American History* is the title of the reference book where this article originated. It is italicized.

• edited by Stanley I. Kutler; books have editors.

• There is a URL that indicates Gale, a publisher of research databases.

• Charles Scribner's Sons is a book publisher. This indicates the original source of the article was a book.

APA Research Database Reference Source Article Citation—No Author

(1) Drake. (2) (2011). (3) In *Contemporary Black Biography* (4) (Vol. 86). (5) Detroit, MI: Gale. (6) Retrieved from https://link.galegroup.com/apps/doc/K1606005056/BIC?u=baltcntycpl&sid=BIC&xid=c5b45282

(1) Article title in quotation marks.
(2) Year of publication for *Contemporary Black Biography*.

(3)   The title of the book where the article originated.
(4)   The volume of the encyclopedia within the *Contemporary Black Biography* encyclopedia set where the article originated.
(5)   Location of publication: Publisher.
(6)   The URL from a Gale research database.

In-text citation example: ("Drake," 2011). There are no page numbers listed in the full citation.

How to tell that this is a research database article from a reference source without an author:

- Drake begins the citation. If there was an author, it would be listed as Last Name, First Initial format. The article is a biography about the singer Drake.

- *Contemporary Black Biography* is the reference book where the article originated. It is italicized.

- Biography in Context is a research database. It is italicized.

APA Research Database Reference Source Article Citation—Author

(1) Shirer, F. R. (2) (2003). (3) Pearl Harbor. (4) In S. I. Kutler (Ed.), (5) *Dictionary of American History* (6) (3rd ed., Vol. 6, pp. 271–273). (7) New York: Charles Scribner's Sons. (8) Retrieved from http://link.galegroup.com/apps/doc/CX3401803190/UHIC?u=win5026&sid=UHIC&xid=8dc4dbf0.

(1)   Author name.
(2)   Publication year for *Dictionary of American History.*
(3)   Article title. Pearl Harbor is capitalized in its entirety because it is a proper noun.
(4)   Stanley I. Kutler is the editor of the book, *Dictionary of American History,* where the article originated.
(5)   The book where the article originated, italicized.
(6)   3rd edition means that the book has been published three times, with revisions each time. This is a multivolume set of books—this article was found in volume 6. The page range from the book is indicated by pp. 271–273.
(7)   This is the city of publication and the publisher.
(8)   Retrieved from URL for this article.

In-text citation example: (Shirer, 2003). *No page number is used with the parenthetical citation unless the page numbers print out on the article. The page range listed in this citation is from the original source of the article,* Dictionary of American History.

How to tell that this is a research database article from a reference source with an author:

* *U.S. History in Context* is a research database.

* There is an author at the beginning of the citation.

* *Dictionary of American History* is the title of the reference book where this article originated. It is italicized.

* "In S. I. Kutler (Ed.)" indicates a book editor.

* Charles Scribner's Sons is a book publisher. This indicates that the original source of the article is a book.

* There is a URL that includes Gale, a publisher of research databases.

Chicago Author-Date Research Database Reference Source Article Citation—No Author

(1) "Drake." (2) 2011. (3) In *Contemporary Black Biography.* (4) Vol. 86. (5) Detroit, MI: Gale. (6) *Biography in Context* (7) (accessed June 11, 2019). (8) https://link.galegroup.com/apps/doc/K1606005056/BIC?u=baltcntycpl&sid=BIC&xid=c5b45282.

(1) Article title in quotation marks.
(2) Year of publication for *Contemporary Black Biography.*
(3) Title of the reference book where the article originated.
(4) The volume of the encyclopedia within the *Contemporary Black Biography* encyclopedia set where the article originated.
(5) Location of publication: Publisher.
(6) The name of database where the article was found.
(7) The accessed date is the last date the article was viewed.
(8) The URL for this article in *Biography in Context,* a research database.

In-text citation example: ("Drake 2011). *No page numbers are listed in the full citation.*

How to tell that this is a reference source research database article without an author:

* "Drake" begins this citation. If there was an author, it would be in Last Name, First Name format.

* *Contemporary Black Biogr*aphy is the reference book where the article originated. It is italicized.

* Biography in Context is a research database. It is italicized.

Chicago Author-Date Research Database Reference Source
Article Citation—Author

(1) Shirer, Frank R. (2) 2003. (3) "Pearl Harbor." (4) In *Dictionary of American History,* (5) 3rd ed., (6) edited by Stanley I. Kutler, (7) 271–273. (8) Vol. 6. (9) New York: Charles Scribner's Sons. (10) *U.S. History in Context* (11) (accessed June 12, 2018). (12) http://link.galegroup.com/apps/doc/CX3401803190/UHIC?u=win5026&sid=UHIC&xid=8dc4dbf0.

(1)   Author name.
(2)   Publication date of *Dictionary of American History.*
(3)   Article title in quotation marks.
(4)   Title of the book where the article originated, italicized.
(5)   3rd edition means that the book, *Dictionary of American History,* has been published three times, with revisions each time.
(6)   Stanley I. Kutler is the editor of the book where this article originated.
(7)   The page range for the article from the book.
(8)   *Dictionary of American History* is a multivolume set of encyclopedias. This article is found in volume 6.
(9)   Location of publication: Publisher.
(10) The name of the research database where the article was found.
(11) The accessed date is the last date the article was viewed.
(12) The URL for the article in *U.S. History in Context,* the research database.

In-text citation example: (Shirer 2003). *No page number is used with the parenthetical citation unless the page numbers print out on the article. The page range listed in this citation is from the original source of the article,* Dictionary of American History.

How to tell that this is a research database article from a reference source with an author:

• *U.S. History in Context* is a research database.

• There is an author at the beginning of the citation.

• edited by Stanley I. Kutler; books have editors.

• *Dictionary of American History* is the title of the reference book. This is italicized.

• Charles Scribner's Sons is a book publisher. This indicates that the original source of the article is a book.

• There is a URL which includes Gale, a publisher of research databases.

Chicago Notes and Bibliography Research Database Reference Source Article Citation—No Author

Note:

1. "Drake," in *Contemporary Black Biography* (Detroit, MI: Gale, 2011), 86, https://link.galegroup.com/apps/doc/K1606005056/BIC?u=baltcnt ycpl&sid=BIC&xid=c5b4528

Bibliography:

(1) "Drake." (2) In *Contemporary Black Biography.* (3) Vol. 86. (4) Detroit, MI: Gale, 2011. (5) *Biography in Context* (6) (accessed June 12, 2019). (7) https://link.galegroup.com/apps/doc/K1606005056/BIC?u=baltc ntycpl&sid=BIC&xid=c5b45282.

   (1)   Article title in quotation marks.
   (2)   Title of book where the article originated, italicized.
   (3)   The volume of the encyclopedia within the *Contemporary Black Biog*raphy encyclopedia set where the article originated.
   (4)   Location of publication: Publisher, publication date.
   (5)   Name of research database where the article was accessed.
   (6)   The date when the information was last viewed.
   (7)   The URL for the article from *Biography in Context,* the research database.

How to tell that this is a reference source research database article without an author:

•   "Drake" begins this citation. If there was an author, it would be in Last Name, First Name format.

•   *Contemporary Black Biog*raphy is the reference book where the article originated. It is italicized.

•   *Biography in Context* is a research database.

Chicago Notes and Bibliography Research Database Reference Source Article Citation—Author

Note:

1. Frank R. Shirer, "Pearl Harbor," in *Dictionary of American History,* ed. Stanley I. Kutler I. Kutler (New York, NY: Charles Scribner's Sons, 2003), 6, http://link.galegroup.com/apps/doc/CX3401803190/UHIC?u=win5026&sid=UHIC&xid=8dc4dbf0.

Bibliography:

(1) Shirer, Frank R. (2) "Pearl Harbor." (3) In *Dictionary of American History,* (4) 3rd ed., (5) edited by Stanley I. Kutler, (6) 271–273. (7) Vol. 6. (8) New York, NY: Charles Scribner's Sons, 2003. (9) *U.S. History in Context* (10) (accessed June 12, 2019). (11) http://link.galegroup.com/apps/doc/CX3401803190/UHIC?u=win5026&sid=UHIC&xid=8dc4dbf0.

(1)   Author name.

(2)   Article title in quotation marks.

(3)   Title of the reference book where the article originated, italicized.

(4)   3rd edition means that the book has been published three times, with revisions each time.

(5)   Stanley I. Kutler is the editor of the reference book, *Dictionary of American History,* where the article originated.

(6)   The page range for the article from the book.

(7)   *Dictionary of American History* is a multivolume set of encyclopedias. This article is found in volume 6.

(8)   Location of publication: Publisher, publication date.

(9)   *U.S. History in Context* is a research database.

(10)   The accessed date is the last date the article was viewed.

(11)   The URL for the article from *U.S. History in Context,* a research database.

How to tell that this is a research database article from a reference source with an author:

•   *U.S. History in Context* is a research database. This is italicized.

•   There is an author at the beginning of the citation.

•   *Dictionary of American History* is the title of the reference book. This is italicized.

•   Charles Scribner's Sons is a book publisher that published the book, *Dictionary of American History,* in 2003.

•   There is a URL that includes Gale, a publisher of research databases.

Advice for Teachers about Research Database Articles. The ethical, competent use of research database articles for high school students is a critical college preparatory skill. You will be able to easily manage your students' use of research database citations because it is created accurately through the interface of the research database. The proper use of parenthetical citations for research database articles will require instruction.

Plagiarism grows when students do not fully understand sources they are using for research. Research database articles originate from publications that your students have never seen or used before in print format.

Advice for Librarians about Research Database Articles. A review of research database articles and the citation should be done before the first major research assignment for inexperienced researchers. After this, review the full citation and parenthetical citation for each source type as part of information literacy instruction. If you have copies of magazines, scholarly journals, or reference books in print format, you should show these to students during information literacy instruction.

BREAKING DOWN CITATIONS

Building Visual Familiarity of Citations: Advice for Teachers and Librarians

No student should be expected to memorize any citation style. However, an ongoing visual review of citations helps reduce plagiarism and improve student proofreading. Multiple-choice warm-up questions can be developed for a general review or to target specific problem areas. These can be delivered by a librarian before or after information literacy instruction or by an instructor anytime during the research process. These warm-up sessions can also include true/false questions and questions about a screenshot of a web page or research database article publication information.

Here is a list of elements that can be visually learned and retained by students by the tenth grade:

- Date format for the school's citation style: Dates can vary within different types of publications. Review these variations—year; month/year; day/month/year. Show these dates in isolation for the correct format and within different citation types.

- Quotation marks versus italics for different titles: books, web page articles, websites, magazines, scholarly journals, book chapter titles.

- Basic parenthetical citation format for books, web pages, and research database articles.

- For more experienced researchers, you can review visual recognition of full citations with one element missing.

This review instruction is easily delivered in five or ten minutes at the beginning or end of information literacy instruction or anytime by an instructor. Warm-up questions can be projected onto a screen. You will find examples beginning in Appendix G.

Citation Guides

A citation guide is a one-page, two-sided print handout with citations tailored to an assignment. It isolates the correct citation format for the assignment, allowing students to mentally disregard other incorrect options. While the official citation-style guide books are authoritative, these can be difficult for students to find the exact example they need. Since digital resources can be successfully published with key citation elements missing, a citation guide provides a clear road map. While it can be digitally posted on a teacher's learning management system and the library's web page, the paper format is a stable way to provide citation examples that have been tailored to the assignment. For example, if a teacher requires government information websites for sources, the citation guide can reflect this. Students can attach the citation guide to their research project folder for easy access.

Work can be reviewed away from an Internet connection with a citation guide. It is a personalized, stable way to proofread, teach, and create citations. While many students use online citation tools, the handout citation guide is another way to present this information. Plagiarism excuses are reduced when the citation process is presented to students by more than one method. It normally includes the following:

• The basic format of the citation for each type of resource.

• An example of a citation that is comparable to the source students will use for the assignment.

• Any additional information needed by students.

Citation guides in paper handout format help students manage the level of detail required to check their work. It is easier to make side-by-side comparisons between a paper citation guide and citations on a printed rough draft. There is a guide for each citation style in Appendix E of this book.

Advice for Students about Citation Guides

The citation guides in this book can help you during the citation process. If you receive a citation guide, use it to make sure your citations are accurate. Even if you use an online citation tool, it is useful to check your citations against another objective source for accuracy. If you need more assistance, check with your librarian.

Advice for Teachers about Citation Guides

Citation guides are important for teachers too. This is a good time to work with a librarian who can help you with this. Librarians are professional experts on resources and citations. For example, if you will be assigning a PowerPoint presentation each quarter where your students will use images from the Internet, a librarian can create a citation guide for this. A general citation guide can provide you with a model for using citations within your teaching content. The citation guide is also a teaching tool. While you or a librarian is explaining the citation process, students can use the citation guide to follow along. This can also be an answer key to correct student citations throughout the school year. It is a concrete plagiarism deterrent for students.

Even if your students use an online citation tool, this guide can be used by your students to compare their work to this model. If a collaboration with a librarian is not possible, there are also general citation guides in this book that you can adapt for your needs. When the sources you ask students to use in the assignment instructions coordinate with the citation guide, you will gain consistent results.

Advice for Teachers: Teaching Citations

The competent use of citations is essential in this unprecedented time of digital information access. Citations are at the center of avoiding plagiarism. You do not have to be an expert on citations to make them part of your teaching. It is a learning process.

You can build familiarity and visual recognition of citations in your students over the course of a school year. Competency increases quickly when citations are expected often and with consistency. Your grading expectations for citations should be matched with the instruction you have provided. Even one class period of citation instruction is a good investment.

Regardless of your subject area, do not assume that another teacher or subject area has provided adequate instruction for citations. Expectations for citations can vary within a school. A common mistaken belief is that English department is solely responsible for teaching citations and basic research skills. Even if this is the case in your school, citation competency cannot be gained through just one subject area.

Even if full research papers are not part of your teaching, citations should have a role in your class if you will be using information from the Internet or any other outside, secondary source for assignments. Your students may be using secondary sources for presentations or other projects where citations for images or direct quotes are appropriate. At the very least, you may be using outside sources for handouts and postings on your school's learning management system.

Requiring citations from your students does not need to be complicated. Unless you believe that a student has intentionally misled you with a source, an incorrect citation with the basic information does not mean that a student is guilty of academic misconduct. You can ask for corrections. There is more information about this in Chapter 5.

There are options for integrating citations if you are not currently doing so. Your first choice should be to have your school librarian help with this process. If a librarian is not available, there is a lesson plan in this book to explain citations for each source type. You will find adaptable citation guides beginning in Appendix E. The goal is consistency with citations throughout the school year. If you leave students to their own devices with citations, there is a high likelihood of errors and plagiarism.

Your school may subscribe to an online citation tool. If so, it means that it has been screened for accuracy and appropriateness. If you would prefer this option, require your students to use this same tool. You should also open your own account. This gives you the opportunity to create your own citations for your class content and check student work when needed. The librarian can also fully introduce the school's online citation tool to students and make sure each student has an active account. A citation tool is not a substitute for instruction. Students still need instruction for different source types, especially for digital resources where they have never seen the print version.

It is reasonable for students to be able to correct any errors during the rough-draft stage of the research process after instruction. Incorrect citations are not necessarily plagiarism unless it appears to be purposely misleading. Problems with punctuation or other minor issues should be corrected. However, omitting a citation should be viewed as plagiarism. For middle and high schools without a full-time librarian, it is imperative that teachers review citations with college-bound students. There are guides and lesson plans in this book.

Librarians Teaching Citations

Librarians are in the best professional position to teach citations as experts on sources, especially digital sources. This lets students see librarians as a source of objective assistance for plagiarism.

Here are some ways to impact your students' competence with citations:

- If your library budget allows, purchase an online citation tool for your school. You may want to ask for suggestions from teachers and your school administration before purchase. Along with active outreach to students, teachers, and parents, prepare online and print handouts with instructions on account setup and best practice examples.

- When you are teaching information literacy, use the first five minutes for a citation multiple-choice warm-up. You can use the warm-ups in Appendix B as models.

- Prepare a basic citation guide for distribution at the library.

- When providing information literacy instruction for a research assignment, offer to make a citation guide for the teacher and students.

- When teaching searching skills with research databases and web pages, explain the authorship and publication information of the source you choose from the results list. This builds familiarity with the parameters of a source.

Online Citation Tools

Online citation tools are an excellent way to create and manage citations. While these tools organize citations throughout the life of a research project, they do not provide understanding of the source itself. Use of online citation tools by students has made it more important than ever to incorporate citation instruction. A citation tool should be introduced to students only after instruction for the parts of each resource type.

Online Citation Tools: Advice for Librarians

Look for opportunities to demonstrate the citation tool to your school community. There may be time during a school assembly, orientations, or class time. Provide instructions for the use of the citation tool in handout format and posted on the library's website.

Online Citation Tools: Advice for Teachers

Citation tools should be introduced after you or your librarian has reviewed the parts of each resource. This is an important prerequisite. Accuracy with citation tools improves once students know the parts of each source. For best results, ask your students to use the same citation tool for the entire school year. This makes it easier for you to see the visual patterns in your students' work.

Online Citation Tools: Advice for Students

A good online citation tool is an excellent way to create and organize citations. Your library probably subscribes to at least one online citation tool for you to use. This is better than choosing a citation tool randomly from the Internet. Citation tools are normally listed on your library's web page.

It is essential to follow your teacher's instructions about citations. If a specific citation tool is recommended, you should use it. If your teacher provides a citation guide and you decide to use a citation tool, check your citations from the citation tool against the teacher's citation guide to make sure they agree. Do not use online citation tools for research database articles. Use the citation tool on the article page. Some research databases will allow you to export the citation to your citation tool. The publication process for research database articles can be complex; the research database article citation tool will capture this accurately.

A citation tool works only as well as the information you type into it. If you don't have enough information to complete the boxes of the citation tool, check the source again. Be aware that not all citation tools are created equal. Even when you use a citation tool, you must be conscious of the publication and authorship of a source to use it accurately. You are still responsible for the accuracy of your citations. Consider checking your citations against the resources found in this book.

RESOURCES
Websites

APA Style: www.apastyle.org. The Quick Answers: References section of this web page is especially helpful.

Chicago-Style Citation Quick Guide: http://www.chicagomanualofstyle.org/tools_citationguide.html.

The MLA Style Center: https://style.mla.org. This is a useful quick guide to creating citations.

The Owl at Purdue: https://owl.english.purdue.edu/owl/. This website provides excellent models for all three major citation styles.

Books

The Chicago Manual of Style. 2017. 17th ed. Chicago, IL: University of Chicago Press.

MLA Handbook. 2016. 8th ed. New York, NY: Modern Language Association of America.

Publication Manual of the American Psychological Association. 2009. 6th ed. Washington, DC: American Psychological Association.

Turabian, Kate L. 2017. *A Manual for Writers of Research Papers, Theses, and Dissertations.* 9th ed. Chicago, IL: The University of Chicago Press.

5

Reducing Plagiarism in the Classroom

Librarians and teachers can do a great deal to reduce plagiarism in the classroom, both individually and through collaborations. Combining information literacy with plagiarism education through teacher and librarian collaborations is a particularly effective way to build awareness for ethical research and use of information. This chapter takes a practical approach for recognizing plagiarism in student work and reducing it through integrating plagiarism education. For librarians, this chapter will explain how librarians, as information experts, can bring visibility to plagiarism education in schools.

TEACHER AND LIBRARIAN COLLABORATIONS

Plagiarism can be reduced through teacher and librarian collaborations. This is a natural extension of information literacy instruction or for separate classes for plagiarism education.

Advice for Teachers about Collaborations for Plagiarism Education

You will find that most of the plagiarism committed by your students is unintentional. This is not a problem you need to solve alone. Collaborating with your school's librarian for plagiarism education can make a big difference without requiring an overhaul of your current classroom priorities. Here are some of the professional services that your school's librarian can offer you and your students, which will help reduce plagiarism:

- It is important to expect your students to cite their work when it is appropriate to do so. You should never assume that your students know how to cite sources properly. Whether or not your students use citation tools, a librarian can thoroughly review your school's citation style with your students. This can be done at the beginning of the school year or anytime a research project is assigned.

- Librarians can create citation guides tailored for an assignment, which you can also utilize to correct student papers. You can also request a general citation guide covering examples for each type of resource, as well as the elements of formatting a research paper.

- Online citation tools don't solve the problem of plagiarism entirely. Students need to be familiar with the parts of digital sources in order to use citation tools accurately. As professional experts on sources, librarians can easily review the digital resources your students will use for the research assignment during information literacy instruction, allowing both you and your students to become familiar with the publication cycle. The librarian can also assist your students in opening up accounts and using your school's chosen citation tool effectively.

- Before a major research assignment begins, discuss an extended definition of plagiarism with your students, as outlined in Appendix H. A librarian can lead this discussion with you by providing visual examples of the parts of plagiarism that relate to sources.

When you are present in the classroom during a librarian's information literacy and plagiarism education instruction, it serves two important purposes. First, it allows you to review these concepts, especially with citations and digital sources, making it easier to help students through the research process. Second, your presence confirms the importance of this instruction with your students. They know you will be more aware of the possibility of plagiarism in their academic work products. You also have the opportunity to review key concepts later with your students. This type of direct instruction means you will see better work products.

If you have a good working relationship with your school librarian, consider a deep collaboration for a research paper. Deep collaborations with a librarian normally extend beyond one instructional session. The librarian can emphasize information literacy and plagiarism education throughout the process while you focus on teaching the research paper content. During these deep collaborations, scheduling regular research time for your students at the library allows students to ask questions in real time, clarifying misconceptions about plagiarism and research. You and the librarian can organically add brief instruction if necessary, depending on student issues at the moment. These "teachable" moments for students individually or as a group are invaluable.

When you know you will be away from school for a planned absence, consider asking your school librarian to work with your classes on the instruction in this book. It is a good opportunity to reinforce awareness of plagiarism without taking regular class time.

Advice for Librarians about Collaborations for Plagiarism Education

Regular, consistent communication with teachers is everything. Establish an approximate time frame for your plagiarism education classes. For example, a review of your school's citation style with a citation guide may take twenty minutes. Other plagiarism instruction may take an entire class period. This added information gives teachers help for planning, especially on days when there may be shortened schedules.

Working within the school calendar is a way to schedule instruction with subject-area teachers. You can ask to deliver instruction during the same time every school year. For example, many research papers are written in the spring. This is a good time for annual information literacy and plagiarism education instruction classes. Citation review is appropriate for the first week of school. At the high school level, this can allow you to deliver differentiated, consistent instruction each school year as students advance. Plagiarism discussions and paraphrasing classes are appropriate to schedule at the end of a semester or the beginning of a new one before new course content begins.

Plagiarism is reduced when students understand sources. This is also an important component of information literacy instruction. Show students examples of online publications that are in print and on television such as the *New York Times*, Fox News, and *Newsweek*. Demonstrate the physical differences in depth for a book chapter, web page, and research database article on the same topic.

STRATEGIES FOR REDUCING PLAGIARISM IN THE CLASSROOM

Advice for Teachers

Students can plagiarize in countless ways because of the Internet. Back in 1998, Jamie McKenzie (1998) prolifically declared, "Students now wield an electronic shovel that makes it possible to find and save huge chunks of information with little reading, effort or originality." For schools without Turnitin.com or another formal plagiarism checker program, it's much easier to find blatant, intentional plagiarism than unintentional, especially small amounts of information that have been copied and pasted. Unintentional plagiarism is so prevalent because until now, your students have never been taught how to avoid it. That's the bad news. The good news is that expecting your students to use information ethically is not an impossible task. Whatever you can do in your classroom makes a difference. You don't need to wait for a school- or district-wide mandate to begin this instruction. It is very manageable.

There is a balance between ignoring plagiarism and allowing it to overshadow your work as a teacher. Given the sheer volume of digital information your students have at their fingertips, ignoring the ethical use of sources will not work, especially for college prep students. The overall goal is to raise your student's awareness of ways to avoid plagiarism, not to throw down a plagiarism "gauntlet" where catching students consumes your time and energy. This is achievable through clear, consistent, reasonable expectations and secondary-source (particularly digital) education for your students.

It's easy to start with the basics. There are many things you can do. A detailed definition of plagiarism, along with any other academic expectations, should be prominently noted on your syllabus and learning management system with details and examples (Wilhoit 1994, 162; Craig, Federici, and Buehler 2010, 55). Even though you may not be required to do so, show the correct citation documentation in your teaching materials for information you borrow from a secondary source or other teachers (Price 2002, 101; Thomas and Sassi 2011, 48). This visual awareness helps your students learn the citation style over time. It also indicates your own respect for the intellectual property of others. Be careful of allowing students digital or extended print access to the research papers of their classmates for peer review. This can offer opportunities for plagiarism.

It is impossible to reduce plagiarism without citation instruction for your students. The correct use of citations is an important foundation for the ethical use of information during the research process. You do not have to be an expert on citations to expect your students to use them properly. You can learn along with them over the course of the school year. The goal is to create a group of citation resources to consult when questions arise. Citation guides in this book can be used as examples for students and as a grading tool for you. A citation guide is an important element for success, even if your students use an online citation tool because it explains the parts of the source. It provides students a way to proofread citations created by citation tools. Your librarian can assist you in creating citation guides tailored to an individual assignment.

Since many students use online citation tools already, require them to use the same citation tool for consistency. You should have your own account with this citation tool. This will make it easier for you to grade papers and answer questions. If your school library subscribes to a citation tool, this should be your first choice. Your school librarian can help students open up accounts and review the best use of the citation tool.

Purchase a copy of the official citation-style book for your classroom. This can be an easy reference for you and your students when questions arise. You will need to tell your students to use the index of these books in order to find the necessary information. These books are updated every several years, making this a good investment. You can also ask to borrow a copy from your school library for the school year.

If your school uses Turnitin.com, allow your students to correct plagiarism problems before handing in the final copy. Encourage your school administration to assign someone (outside of your class) to work with students individually on problems from Turnitin's originality reports. This process of correcting plagiarism is a powerful part of the pedagogy. Many examples and citation guides in this book provide resources for your teaching in this area.

There are many good resources about "plagiarism-proof" assignments for teachers at all grade levels, which are not covered in this book. It is especially important in smaller school communities to change your research paper topics each school year for middle school and high school students to discourage the reuse of papers by siblings and close friends who may be a year or so apart in age. Collect a one-paragraph writing sample from students on a topic in your subject area at the beginning of the course. This will give you a relative indicator of abilities with vocabulary and sentence structure.

You can establish consistent parameters for research assignments in order to reduce plagiarism. Reduce over-citing or under-citing by asking students to cite only a maximum of two or three times for each page of the research paper. One block quote for every five pages of research paper is appropriate. Require students to send you a digital and print copy of any research assignment. Even if you only grade the print copy, the digital copy will give you links for web pages and research database citations to check as necessary.

The Use of Secondary Sources to Reduce Plagiarism

Another way to reduce plagiarism for inexperienced researchers is to regulate the allowable types of secondary sources for the research assignment. One goal of student research is the use of unique secondary sources. To discourage unnecessary citations, exclude the following sources from use in your students' research papers except for background knowledge:

• Information that can be found in your textbook.

• Class lectures and class notes.

• Any knowledge that can be considered below grade level for the research assignment.

• Basic biographical information about well-known people does not need to be cited.

Books, research database articles, and web pages properly prepare college-bound high school students for college research. The ethical use of these resources, with instruction, is straightforward. Social media content (even from credible, well-known people), blog posts, or any other "media"-type source that lack clear publication standards make it harder to create a citation, and it will be harder for you to check. YouTube, on the other hand, has become a good source for interviews and primary-source information and should be permitted as source when appropriate for high school students. Abstracts from research database articles should not be allowed as a source for high school and first-year college students. These are normally broad, general statements about the topic, making it easier to plagiarize.

Web pages are the easiest way for students to plagiarize. Most web pages have very accessible language, making them easy to copy. It is more difficult to plagiarize with books and research database articles because the information is more specialized and specific with a more academic vocabulary. Books, in particular, require more effort to plagiarize. When you ask students to use websites as resources, it is important to require that only the most credible, authoritative sites are used. Your school librarian can explain this website evaluation process to your students as part of information literacy instruction. While not at the same level as research database articles and books, the most credible websites have better depth, better vocabulary, and more unique information. This credibility means a more defined editorial process that makes the various parts of the web page—author, article title, publisher, publication date more apparent, making citations more accurate.

Plagiarism can be further reduced by requiring sources for the research project, which have page numbers—books and scholarly journal research database articles. These sources, because they have page numbers, create a more linear citation and footnote process. It is also easier to check these types of sources when you have a question. Students will know that this type of citation needs to be accurate. The citations from research databases will have a very uniform look. There are examples in Chapter 4 and Appendix E. It is not necessary to check the intricacies of these citations if the overall look is consistent.

Your students will benefit from a well-defined research process. Show students examples of research papers that have been completed correctly (Colella-Sandercock and Alahmadi 2015, 79). This provides a good reference point to meet the assignment expectations. Research papers should be a process with monitored benchmarks by a proposal, outline, and rough draft. If the final paper has any major differences that have not been discussed with you, there may be plagiarism (Craig, Federici, and Buehler 2010, 54; Colella-Sandercock and Alahmadi 2015, 79). Require multiple drafts, and ask students to turn in these rough drafts with the final paper. This discourages students from buying or borrowing papers (Wilhoit 1994, 163).

A big research paper can create stress in students. They need practice with writing and the use of sources. Subject-area research database articles are a great source to use for class assignments throughout the school year (Pearson 2011, 58).

You will be surprised about the misconceptions your students have about plagiarism. During the research process, you may want to dedicate a short period of time each week during class to take student questions about plagiarism (Colella-Sandercock and Alahmadi 2015, 80). Chapter 3 in this book provides a working definition of plagiarism and questions that can serve as the basis for a discussion in your classroom. Consider asking your school's librarian to lead this discussion on a day when you will be away from the classroom.

Once you and/or the librarian have explained everything about your plagiarism expectations and students have had time to practice these skills, students need to be accountable for plagiarism. In middle school and high school, consequences for blatant plagiarism are especially important. You may decide to handle plagiarism violations yourself through failure of the assignment or notifying parents. As a teacher, you need to determine your comfort level with how your school administration handles plagiarism while determining consistent policies for your classroom.

One of the main premises of this book is that students need to experience an educational process in order to avoid plagiarism, especially with digital resources. That said, unintentional plagiarism is still plagiarism. You should decide which errors merit point reductions and which errors constitute plagiarism in student work products. Allow students to correct citation errors during the rough-draft stage.

Plagiarism Problems and Solutions

Here are some plagiarism issues you may face with possible solutions.

Plagiarism issue: You have explained that evidence from a secondary source—one or two sentences—should be inserted into the text of the paper with quotation marks to support a claim with a parenthetical citation or footnote. The student has copied and pasted a paragraph from Wikipedia without attribution.

Solution: This is blatant plagiarism. You have various options: notify your school administration, student fails the assignment, contact parents and honor board hearing, if applicable.

Plagiarism issue: Your student's Bibliography has a citation where you can't easily determine the source type.

Solution: This falls into the category of a misleading or false citation. Ask the student to produce the source in a short period of time. If the student was present for instruction but cannot clarify the source, this should be considered intentional plagiarism. If the student needs help locating the source, the librarian should be consulted.

Plagiarism issue: A citation has the correct information but there is an error in italics, punctuation, or spacing.

Solution: Allow the student to correct these errors at the rough-draft stage. If it is in the final paper, reduce points.

Plagiarism issue: A student, who claims to have great personal interest in the subject area, hands in a paper with no citations. He claims to have retained all of the information in the paper from years of self-study without any way to trace the sources.

Solution: A basic premise of research is that new secondary sources should be consulted to write the paper. The student should rewrite the paper with appropriate citations. There is no compromise with this.

Plagiarism issue: While reviewing a student paper, you find a sentence within a paragraph that you believe has been copied from a secondary source. When confronted, the student says it is common knowledge.

Solution: This merits a discussion with the student. If the sentence is common knowledge, ask the student to eliminate it from the paper. If not, tell the student to cite it.

CITATIONS AND PLAGIARISM

Advice for Teachers: When to Expect Citations from Students

Here are some indicators for when information should be cited in your student's academic work.

- All paraphrases, direct quotes, and block quotes.

- The use of advanced words or phrases.

- The use of unique words or phrases.

- All digital images in PowerPoint or other presentations should be cited.

- Any information that is not common knowledge and/or beyond the scope of your classroom discussion. Examples: Barack Obama used a desk belonging to Robert Kennedy in his Senate office. Henry Knox managed the logistics for Washington's crossing of the Delaware River.

- The more specific the information, the more likely it is that it needs a citation. Examples: all units of measurement; elapsed time; costs; dates of critical events that are not common knowledge; years of events when not common knowledge; specific numbers of items or people.

- Information outside of the subject area that is not common knowledge. For example, information about the British monarchs may need to be cited in a paper about British literature.

Recognizing Plagiarism through Citation Errors

This is a list of problems with citations that may indicate plagiarism.

- There is more than one source by the same author cited in the paper and on the Works Cited/References/Bibliography page without the appropriate differentiation in the text of the paper through parenthetical citations or footnotes. For example, a student uses one website for two or three different articles by the same author. The student uses the author's last name (Trueman) throughout the paper without differentiating the article.

- A long page range for quotes or paraphrases in the parenthetical citation or footnote. Example: (Reagan 241–252). A citation with page numbers should note one page number or, at the most, a range of two pages.

- There is a source on the Works Cited/References/Bibliography page which does not have any parenthetical citations or footnotes in the text of the paper.

- There is a source quoted in the text of the paper that is not on the Works Cited/References/Bibliography page.

- Citations are confusing and incomplete. There are citations that are seriously incorrect, indicating a lack of understanding of the overall process.

Here are some possible indications of plagiarism in the structure of research papers and essays:

- There is too much quoted material. This means that the *structure* of the paper was copied from the source.

- Excessive use of one source in the text of the paper to the exclusion of others listed on the Works Cited page. For example, one source is used five times, while the rest of the sources are used once.

- A student has plagiarized through the omission of a source and then claims to not understand a basic part of the process such as the use of footnotes. You know they were present when the instruction was provided.

- The sources and quotes in the student's paper don't line up with the overall topic (Ryhn 1998, 22).

- There are no citations at all. The student writes from "what he knows."

- As you read the paper, there are consecutive citations from one source. Example: Paragraph one in the paper cites (Smith 14), and the next paragraph has a citation for (Smith 15).

- A sentence within a paragraph that is different in tone, structure, or vocabulary than the sentences surrounding it.

- A sentence that is completely out of context with the other sentences around it.

- A paragraph that is different in tone, structure, or vocabulary than the other paragraphs.

- A paragraph that is completely out of context with the other paragraphs around it.

- A sentence that is ambiguous. This indicates a lack of understanding of the source. The student has used a source in a paraphrase with vocabulary he or she does not understand (Whitaker 1993, 512). While this may not be plagiarism, it bears further investigation.

- A disjointed paragraph or group of sentences, indicating a piecing together of different sentences from sources.

- Parenthetical citations that are in the same position for each paragraph in the paper. For example, the first three paragraphs have a parenthetical citation after the last sentence. Ideally, the parenthetical citations should be in a variety of places throughout the text.

- The use of British and other foreign spellings by American students used without a citation: centre, fibre.

- The use of advanced vocabulary. Examples: singularly focused; acid fueled attempt; disunity; communist expansionist commitment; ubiquitous.

- Two students in your class have the same sentences, paper structure, or other major similarities. This bears further investigation.

- Skipping footnotes in the paper. Students may skip footnotes and claim "ignorance" about the proper footnoting procedure, pointing to the Bibliography as a list of sources. If the student can't discuss the ideas presented in the paper or the subject matter, the chances are good that the paper is plagiarized (Ryhn 1998, 22).

Citation tools have made the grading process somewhat easier for teachers. Citations from research database articles will have a complete, uniform appearance. There are examples in Chapter 4. You do not have to correct the intricacies of these citations. You do not have to be overly concerned with punctuation problems in citations although these should be corrected during the rough-draft stage.

For middle school and high school students who are most likely to copy and paste from Google, Google should be the first place teachers should check when you suspect that sentences have been plagiarized (Ma et al. 2007, 80). Place the sentence or word cluster in quotation marks when you search for the original source through Google.

PROOFREADING TO AVOID PLAGIARISM

Advice for Teachers

Proofreading directly impacts the quality of student writing and incidences of unintentional plagiarism. Typically, proofreading means the process of correcting spelling, punctuation, grammar, and sentence structure. Since digital sources now dominate research, proofreading needs to expand to include a thorough review of how these sources are used in the paper. Students should be expected to review the proper placement of quotes and paraphrases along with the citations and footnotes. This is an area where student skills will be very scattered. Proofreading is a very abstract concept for students to grasp without definite parameters. This section covers proofreading issues that directly or indirectly impact plagiarism.

Here are the most common scenarios:

- Students don't know how to proofread at all.

- Citation tools are trusted as long as the citation looks correct.

- A teacher, tutor, or someone else will do it for them, so the student never learns.

- Expectations for proofreading are unclear and usually do not include a mandatory review of citation documentation in the text of the paper.
- "Research paper fatigue" sets in. Students are tired at the end of the research process, so proofreading suffers.
- Everyone in the class is proofreading differently with inconsistent results.

Content-area teachers get understandably frustrated with student proofreading skills. The reality is that students need a structure for the process. They will be the result of their past education in this area. They simply may not know how to do it. Many students are accustomed to completing work at the last minute, compromising the quality of their writing. This "last-minute" mentality is often part of the school's culture, making it difficult to have students revise work properly. With a set scope for proofreading, teachers can improve student writing and reduce plagiarism through consistent expectations. It is possible to change the school culture over time within your subject area. Your students will rise to the standards that you set. It's a good investment of time for students to understand that proofreading requires time and attention to detail. It helps them get more familiar with the ethical, appropriate use of different sources and the school's citation style. The more practice you provide your students, the better they will be at this important skill.

When you have planned absences from the classroom, your school librarian can easily review proofreading citations with your class. This type of review is also very appropriate for homework and school days with shortened class periods.

Advice for Librarians

Proofreading is an area of concern among most teachers. This should be taught as a class separate from information literacy instruction. You can help students through this process by the Can You Spot the Problems? exercise in Appendix D. When you take the initiative and offer this class to teachers who do research papers, it creates another important avenue for instruction to students. Even if the class does not have an active research paper, students benefit from a review of the principles of proofreading as it relates to the use of sources. Another class idea is to create a mock Works Cited, Bibliography, or References page with multiple errors and have students correct it.

Advice for Students

Proofreading is essential. Along with grammar, spelling, punctuation, and readability, review your citations and the use of quoted and paraphrased information within the text of your paper. Fatigue at the end of the process is no excuse for not completing this critical activity.

The appearance of your paper matters. Typos and other unnecessary errors cause you to lose points. These unnecessary errors are visually distracting to the teacher. You can never be certain about a teacher's interpretation of an error in your paper, so it's important to always do your best work. When you take care of proofreading details consistently, your writing gets better. As you get better at writing, it becomes an easier and smoother process. Teachers will always have different expectations. When you move past these expectations to complete thorough, detailed proofreading, your writing will excel.

PROOFREADING GUIDELINES

Here are the important guidelines for proofreading to avoid plagiarism. Please refer to Chapter 6 for more information.

A Note about Citation Tools and Proofreading

You still need to review your citations after using an online citation tool. If the resulting citation has parts that are repeated or for whatever reason doesn't look right, go back and make sure you have put the correct information about the source in the designated box in the citation tool. The option to enter only a URL and relying on the citation tool to read the web page parts is particularly risky. If you use this option, check the citation against a citation guide for accuracy. Use the same citation tool for your sources (with the exception of research database articles) for consistency.

Title Formats

Check the title formats for books, web pages, research database articles, e-books, chapters, and essay titles mentioned in the text of the paper. For MLA and Chicago, book and periodical titles are italicized. Titles of articles, poems, essays, and other smaller works are in quotation marks. For APA, book and periodical titles are italicized. Titles of articles do not have italics or quotation marks. For more information, see Chapter 6.

References/Bibliography/Works Cited Page

• This is the last page of your paper.
• Citations should be alphabetized with a hanging indent.

- Verify your spacing according to the citation style your school uses.

- Correct any font or capitalization errors from the copy/paste from a citation tool.

Parenthetical Citations and Footnotes

- A general guideline is that each page of your paper should have a maximum of two or three citations. This includes direct quotes and paraphrases.

- If you have more than three citations on a page of your paper, review these citations carefully. You may be able to eliminate the weakest one. Check your teacher's instructions for this.

- Compare your sources to your parenthetical citations and footnotes. There should be a parenthetical citation or footnote for each source you have cited in your paper. It is a good idea to check off your use of a source in the text of your paper from your Works Cited, Bibliography, or References page.

- Check that the format for the parenthetical citation or footnote is correct.

- Check the superscript numbers of your footnotes and the placement at the bottom of the page in ascending order.

Direct Quotes and Paraphrases

Many plagiarism accusations begin with problems with direct quotes and paraphrases. Direct quotes are used for very specific information that cannot be restated any other way. All information from primary sources should be a direct quote. Paraphrases are used for more lengthy sentences from a secondary source when you can use the idea, but rewrite the sentences more concisely in your own words.

Direct Quotes

Locate all of the direct quotes in your rough draft. Beginning with the first page of your paper, compare the quotes in your paper to the sentences you have highlighted in each source. This review also gives you a chance to reconsider the quotes you have chosen for your paper. You may decide to eliminate a quote or add a new one. If you make any changes, adjust your Works Cited, References, or Bibliography page. Check to make sure that the quoted material is copied exactly. Your quote should be one or two sentences only. There should be quotation marks at the beginning and end of the quote.

Direct Quote Parenthetical Citations and Footnotes

Check the parenthetical citation or footnote for each direct quote in your paper to make sure it is correct. The quotation marks must be properly placed within the text of your paper. Chapter 6 offers examples about how to do this properly.

Paraphrases

Beginning with the first page of your paper, compare the paraphrases in your paper to the sentences you have highlighted in each source.

- Review the micro-paraphrasing steps to ensure you have not plagiarized. See Chapter 2 to review the steps.

- Do not use quotation marks for paraphrases in the text of your paper.

- Each paraphrase needs a parenthetical citation or footnote.

Paraphrase Parenthetical Citations and Footnotes

The parenthetical citation should be at the end of the paraphrase (sentence) you created. It is not at the end of the paragraph unless the last sentence of the paragraph is a paraphrase. The same general rules about placing a direct quote properly within the text of the paper apply to paraphrases. See Chapter 6 for more information.

Here are some additional guidelines for direct quotes and paraphrases.

- Web page articles never have page numbers except in certain circumstances such as an article in PDF format.

- Books will always have page numbers. Scholarly journal articles have page numbers. For other types of research database articles, check if page numbers are from the original publication printout with the article.

- Each type of source has a different parenthetical citation and footnote format. Whether it is for a direct quote or paraphrase, confirm that each parenthetical citation and footnote is correct for each source. There is more information about this in Chapter 4.

Block Quotes

Block quotes should be used sparingly: one block quote for every five pages in the research paper as a general guide.

Review the Teacher's Grading Rubric and Assignment Expectations

Did you meet all of the necessary requirements for the assignment? Teachers are very specific about expectations. Review your teacher's grading rubric and assignment instructions. Make sure you have used the types of sources your teacher has required. Check off the items you have completed. If you have anything missing, make a plan to complete it as soon as possible.

Reviewing a Rubric

This is a typical grading rubric in an English class for an essay that requires the use of primary and secondary sources in MLA format. The areas that connect to proofreading are underlined with an explanation (courtesy of Brendan Bailey).

Grade	Description
A (100) / A– (92)	The paper is exemplary. It not only meets, but far exceeds minimum requirements for the assignment. (1) It is nearly entirely free of errors in grammar. It has a (2) clear thesis, strong topic sentences, meaningful use of primary source and secondary source quotations, and an effective conclusion. (3) All MLA formatting is correct. (4) It includes a Works Cited formatted correctly. It shows a careful attention to detail and mature vocabulary choice. The writing is sophisticated. It is one of the best in the class.

(1) **It is nearly entirely free of errors in grammar**. Errors in spelling and grammar can be an indicator that a teacher should look more closely at your paper. The grammar check program in Microsoft Word will not be enough to find all grammar errors. Read each sentence out loud, beginning at the end of your paper with the last sentence and working your way through until you reach the first sentence. Make any necessary corrections. You will also want to ask a trusted, competent individual to read your paper for these types of errors during the proofreading process.

(2) **Meaningful use of primary-source and secondary-source quotations.** Information used in the paper from primary sources should always be connected directly to the evidence you use from secondary sources. In other words, secondary sources are evidence to use to make your points about quotes from primary sources.

(3) **All MLA formatting is correct**. MLA formatting means that the spacing, font, margins, and all other elements are correct. Appearance matters when you are writing a paper.

(4) **It includes a Works Cited formatted correctly**. Even if you use an online citation tool, you have to check your citations and how the citations are arranged on the Works Cited page.

   (a) It is the last page of the paper with your last name and page number in the top-right heading.

   (b) The citations are double spaced, with double spacing between each citation.

   (c) Make sure all titles, quotation marks, and italics are stated properly.

   (d) Check the citations for a Times New Roman 12-point font. Sometimes, fonts may not transfer correctly when you copy and paste from a citation tool.

   (e) The citations are alphabetized correctly.

   (f) Each citation has a hanging indentation.

More Proofreading Guidelines: Advice for Students

While proofreading should take place continuously as you are writing the paper, it is critical especially at the rough-draft stage and at the very end before the final paper is due. Plan to finish your final rough draft a day or two in advance. Proofread it; then set it aside. A break from the paper will help you proofread more clearly when you go back to it. It will be easier to find any errors. This is a good time to ask a trusted, competent, objective person to read your paper for suggestions. If you are short on time, at least allow a few hours between your final proofreading and handing in the final copy.

Here are some other ideas to make the proofreading of your sources easier:

• **The research database citation tool is primary.** All research databases have a built-in citation tool, usually next to the article. This is always the preferred citation. Research database articles often go through a complicated publication process, making this citation more accurate than an outside online citation tool. You still need to review this citation for accuracy and correct any obvious errors such as problems with the capitalization of a title or an author's name that is not listed in the correct format.

- **Track direct quotes and paraphrases.** Carefully keep track of your direct quotes and paraphrases within each source. Choose two different colors to highlight the text so you can immediately see the difference between the two different types of information. Highlight direct quotes in one color, and mark the sentence with a "Q" as a direct quote in the margin. When you use sentences as a paraphrase, use a different color highlighter. Mark the sentences as a paraphrase with a "P" in the margin. This makes it easier to track these two different types of evidence while writing your paper.

- **Draft citation list.** Create a draft Works Cited/References/Bibliography page as soon as you begin researching. As you use a source, create the citation and place it on the draft. It is easy to eliminate sources you have not used at the end.

INTEGRATING PLAGIARISM EDUCATION

Advice for Teachers

Here are some suggestions for ways for you to integrate plagiarism education into your research project without a librarian collaboration. You may need to allow a few more days for the process to incorporate plagiarism education lessons, but this is a good investment of time.

First, decide on the parameters for the secondary sources you will have students use in the research project. For example, you may want them to use only research database articles and books. Decide on the minimum number of sources as well as the number of quotes, paraphrases, and direct quotes required. A good rule is to require one or two quotes or paraphrases for each page of research paper. This allows for practice in synthesizing secondary-source information while allowing your students' own ideas to be the majority of the writing. One block quote for every five pages of research paper is reasonable. Including a block quote is important because most students need practice with this. Determine your primary source, if applicable.

Once you have reviewed the exercises in this book, create a schedule for homework and classwork to reinforce the concepts. It is a good idea to open up time once a week (or more, depending on your stance on this) for students to be able to ask plagiarism questions. At this point, you should also decide your stance on unintentional and intentional plagiarism for your students. Unintentional plagiarism should be handled with point reductions—many of these errors can be corrected at the rough-draft stage. Intentional plagiarism can be handled in different ways, depending on the policies of your school.

Next, gather citation resources for yourself and your students. This can include, but is not limited to, variations of citation guides from this book, copies of your school's citation-style book, websites with citation examples, and a good online citation tool. You're ready to introduce the research project to students. Before you talk about the specifics of the research project, discuss the definition of plagiarism found in Appendix H. This definition should be prominently displayed on the assignment handout and through your learning management system. You should decide, based on your initial conversation about plagiarism with your students, if more extensive conversations about plagiarism should be scheduled. If you need more time to discuss plagiarism, see Chapter 3.

It is important to review digital sources and citations with students. Show students the location of the research databases you would like for them to use either within your library's website or through a public library. Review the interface of the home page of the research database along with the built-in citation tool. There is an important distinction between the keyword searching required for research databases and natural language searching for web pages. Keyword searching is focused on a concise use of language. Basic keywords focus on concise language such as places, names, titles, political movements, species, and other concepts that may be described by a proper noun or very specific language.

Example keywords

- Ruth Bader Ginsburg cancer. There are many articles written about Ruth Bader Ginsburg. This will narrow it down to articles that mention her cancer diagnosis.

- *Gulliver's Travels* satire. Including the keyword satire will search only for articles that discuss the use of satire in this book.

- Focal brain stimulation. This is a very specific term in the study of the brain.

- Global warming. This is an example of a very broad, general term. It would be better to search for a particular type of global warming.

If you are allowing students to use web pages as sources, review the web page evaluation criteria found in Appendix A2 with a credible, subject-area web page as an example. Then complete the "Anatomy of a Web Page" lesson. Both of these lessons will give your students an understanding of credible content and the publication parts of web pages.

Consider completing the warm-up reviews for the citation style for five to ten minutes during the first week of the research process. Paraphrasing without plagiarism is a skill that requires practice. It is essential to build in time for this instruction. If you are short on class time, ask students to paraphrase for homework; then you can provide feedback.

Advice for Librarians: Leading the Way with Plagiarism Education

Depending on your training and professional priorities, you may believe that the use of print books as secondary sources is an essential part of the research process. In order to maintain professional viability, we need to relax this stance. The future of classroom instruction by librarians should be focused on the management and instruction for digital sources, ahead of managing any print collections. Now that digital information is so immediately accessible from anywhere at any time, fewer students will see the library as a *place* where research must be conducted. As professional information providers, librarians have a good opportunity to respond to this reality.

High school librarians have a professional obligation to prepare college-bound students with the skill set to avoid plagiarism with digital sources, especially if there is a low number of research-based assignments assigned over the course of a school year. College librarians, who have the same obligation, have to assume that incoming students have not received any formalized instruction during high school about plagiarism. The avalanche of digital information available to students means that ignoring plagiarism education is no longer an option.

There's a harsh reality for librarians across educational levels. Teachers are the ones who control how the time is used within the classroom. At professional meetings everywhere, librarians are continually discussing the challenges in creating collaborations with teachers. As important as plagiarism education is, it is unnecessary to be on a never-ending campaign to get classroom time for this. Yes, our students need it, and librarians have the professional expertise to provide it. Everyone in education is aware of the problems caused by digital information but may not look to librarians first to solve it. We have to lay the groundwork first.

At the middle school and high school levels, the first thing for librarians to do is to gather citation resources for plagiarism education. Most college and university libraries have this information online for students already. You can make these resources available to students and teachers in print handout format and on your library's web page.

Here are some ideas:

- Have three to five copies of your school's citation style (or styles) at the library near the reference desk. This is for any student checkouts and for your use for any questions at the reference desk.

- If the library has subscribed to a citation tool, create instructions for how to set up an account and any best practices for using the tool. Post this to the library's web page, and have handouts available at the library. Look for opportunities to present the citation tool to students in groups. This gives you an opportunity to demonstrate the best practices while steering them away from less reliable options.

- Citation guides are important, even if your school has a citation tool or you know your students are using one frequently. You should hand out a copy of a citation guide for each information literacy class you teach, as well as pointing students to the same information on your web page. You need a few different types in handout form and posted on the library's web page. Citation guides can be personalized to your school community or a particular research assignment. Here are a few examples:

  - A citation guide with web pages, research database articles, and books. Each part of the citation should be marked with the part of the source. There are examples of citation guides in Appendix G of this book.
  - A citation guide with "nonstandard" sources. The meaning of "nonstandard" has different meanings in different schools. A basic nonstandard guide should include images, YouTube videos, PDF articles from the Internet, Google Books, chapters and smaller works from textbooks, and anthologies and e-books. While these sources are common, many teachers are unfamiliar with the citations for these sources.
  - A guide that shows how to set a quote or paraphrase in the text of a paper.
  - Depending on the experience of your students, a detailed guide for formatting a paper in your school's citation style.
  - Delineate the steps for micro-paraphrasing with a few examples of good and bad paraphrasing.

Don't hesitate to jump into plagiarism education instruction. You can offer micro-paraphrasing classes all year long. Students benefit greatly with repeated practice and feedback for this skill. If this is a new type of instruction for you, ask for at least forty-eight hours' notice before a class to prepare. You will learn by the experience. After each class, reflect on the class and plan to improve. As experts with a professional stake in the use of sources, librarians have to be proactive in establishing relationships with students, teachers, writing centers, and school administrators for a role in plagiarism education (Gibson and Chester-Fangman 2011, 41). When you are in the classroom for information literacy instruction, tell students that you will review research papers and other projects for possible plagiarism. Librarians, who are not involved in the grading process, are in the perfect position to offer objective, "no fault" advice to students for how to correct errors in research papers.

Putting plagiarism education on the map at your school could mean assisting students who need to make corrections to plagiarized work, "sponsoring" Turnitin or another plagiarism checker through the library, offering assistance at the reference desk, or providing class instruction. The idea is to set up a consistent communication schedule with your school community about plagiarism education instruction. You know which communication channels work best to reach students and teachers at your school. At the beginning of the school year, ask to be invited to academic department meetings for subject areas that assign student research. At that time, you can offer to assist with plagiarism education through paraphrasing classes or any of the lessons found in this book or by consulting with students who have plagiarized for remediation. Let your school administration know about your instructional offerings in this area, and ask to be part of any academic integrity committees.

Throughout the school year, look for open opportunities to provide this instruction, either as an extension of information literacy instruction you normally do or as a separate class. Substituting for teachers with planned absences can be a good opportunity to provide this instruction. If the average teacher in your school teaches five classes each day, you can easily see over one hundred students. This may be 10 percent of your school population. If you have lessons prepared in advance, it may be possible to substitute for teachers who miss school because of illness.

Use the instruction in this book with the research resources you have available through the library. If you do not have a full selection of research databases, consider using databases through your local public library. Here are some other ways to address the concept in your school.

- Freshman orientation is a good time to begin a discussion of plagiarism with students. Using the plagiarism discussion questions in Chapter 3 can be a starting point. You can also use library orientation for transfer students to understand plagiarism.

- Overall, teachers will likely be less familiar with digital resources than you. Create a workshop on plagiarism education for teachers for professional development days or before school starts in August, which includes a review of research databases and online citation tools.

Out of all of the instruction in this book, a separate class where you can provide instruction and feedback for students for micro-paraphrasing is the most important. Mastery of paraphrasing helps avoid accusations of plagiarism across all educational levels. Paraphrasing classes can be held at any time throughout the school year, making it easy for teachers to schedule for a day that works for them. There are so many misperceptions and incorrect information about how to paraphrase without plagiarizing by students and teachers that it is impossible to overstate the importance of teaching this skill.

If you have limited time or opportunities for new instruction, there are ways in which information literacy instruction and plagiarism education can directly intersect:

- When you are teaching research database searching skills, review the authorship and publication cycle for research database articles. When students understand each source, it is easier to remember that each source needs to be properly documented.

- Librarians often teach relevance skills to students during information literacy instruction for digital sources. This relevance discussion normally entails a review of the depth, authorship, and credibility of the information. The next logical instructional step is the proper placement of the sentences in the text of the paper with documentation.

- The lack of publication standards for web pages make it essential to teach the parts of a web page that belong in the citation. This can be easily included in a lesson about searching and web page evaluation skills (see Appendix A2). Again, this makes it easier to understand the source and document it properly.

- Take any opportunity to create a citation with students when you're reviewing sources.

If you work alone, without support staff in the library, discuss the importance of this instruction for students with your school administration and ask for help when you are away from the library teaching. One option is to ask the subject area teacher of the class you are teaching to supervise the library while you are in the classroom with students. We can't assume that students are able to interpret honor codes on their own and successfully manage digital information without unintentional plagiarism.

If you have the space, keep copies of print encyclopedias and other reference books. This can help build context for the research database articles that originate from these books. The same can be said for having a selection of newspapers and magazines for your students so you can demonstrate the print publication cycle. These are found in databases like *ProQuest*.

Librarians: Helping Students Who Have Plagiarized

Learning how to avoid plagiarism is a process. For teachers, librarians can be true partners in plagiarism as "detectives" for possible plagiarism and for remediation after the fact. For librarians, helping students remediate after plagiarism is a good way to work directly with students and raise your profile on campus. Plagiarism can be a very emotional topic for students, parents, and teachers. The library or writing center can be an objective place, outside of the classroom, to rectify the situation (Colella-Sandercock and Alahmadi 2015, 80). Here is a remediation process to follow with students. It is easier to assume this role when you have a track record of providing plagiarism instruction to your school community.

- Ask the teacher or school administrator to send you the plagiarized paper in advance of meeting with the student. Speak to the teacher to learn what has already been discussed with the student about this situation.

- Make a list of all of the errors that constitute plagiarism in advance of meeting with the student.

- Review the corrections needed with the student. You should explain the concept that is the source of the plagiarism with examples.

- Provide a citation guide or other materials with examples necessary to correct errors. The student should correct the paper and return it to you.

- Ask students to sign a list of errors with the necessary corrections to acknowledge the situation. Send a copy of this to the teacher, parents, and school administration if necessary. The school administration can decide whether this list should be maintained in the student's file.

REFERENCES

Colella-Sandercock, Julia, and Hanin Alahmadi. 2015. "Plagiarism Education: Strategies for Instructors." *International Journal of Learning, Teaching and Research* 13, no. 1 (August): 76–84. Accessed January 3, 2019. https://www.ijlter.org/index.php/ijlter/article/viewFile/395/190.

Craig, Paul A., Elizabeth Federici, and Marianne A. Buehler. 2010. "Instructing Students in Academic Integrity." *Journal of College Science Teaching* 40, no. 2 (November): 50–55. https://search.proquest.com/docview/761655869?accountid=41092.

Gibson, Nancy Snyder, and Christina Chester-Fangman. 2011. "The Librarian's Role in Combating Plagiarism." *Reference Services Review* 39, no. 1: 132–50. doi:10.1108/00907321111108169.

Ma, Hongya, Eric Yong Lu, Sandra Turner, and Guofang Wan. 2007. "An Empiri-
    cal Investigation of Digital Cheating and Plagiarism among Middle School
    Students." *American Secondary Education* 35, no. 2 (Spring): 69–82. http://
    www.jstor.org/stable/41406290.

McKenzie, Jamie. 1998. "The New Plagiarism: Seven Antidotes to Prevent High-
    way Robbery in an Electronic Age." *The Educational Technology Journal* 7,
    no. 8 (May). Accessed March 24, 2018. http://fno.org/may98/cov98may
    .html.

Pearson, Nancy Guillot. 2011. "Classrooms That Discourage Plagiarism and Wel-
    come Technology." *English Journal* 100, no. 6 (July): 54–59. https://search
    .proquest.com/docview/875295434?accountid=41092.

Price, Margaret. 2002. "Beyond 'Gotcha!': Situating Plagiarism in Policy and Peda-
    gogy." 2002. *College Composition and Communication* 54, no. 1 (Septem-
    ber): 88–115. http://www.jstor.org/stable/1512103.

Ryhn, Julie J.C.H. 1998. "Student Plagiarism in an Online World." *ASEE Prism* 8,
    no. 4 (December): 20–24. http://www.jstor.org/stable/43530181.

Thomas, Ebony Elizabeth, and Kelly Sassi. 2011. "An Ethical Dilemma: Talking
    about Plagiarism and Academic Integrity in the Digital Age." *National
    Council of Teachers of English* 100, no. 6: 47–53. http://www.jstor.org/
    stable/23047881.

Whitaker, Elaine W. 1993. "A Pedagogy to Address Plagiarism." *College Composi-
    tion and Communication* 44, no. 4 (December): 509–14. http://www.jstor
    .org/stable/358386.

Wilhoit, Stephen. 1994. "Helping Students Avoid Plagiarism." *College Teaching*
    42, no. 4 (Fall): 161–64. http://www.jstor.org/stable/27558679.

6

Student Resources

A NEW WAY TO LOOK AT PLAGIARISM

This chapter is a reference for high school and college students during the research process. You will find all types of information to help you better understand print and digital sources, which makes it easier to use sources ethically.

The Internet

The Internet has changed research forever. For academic work, everything you see, read, hear, and watch on the Internet needs to be cited except the most basic ideas or facts within a subject area. You need to cite the words, images, videos, and anything else created by another person.

There are few exceptions to this rule. Many of these sources on the Internet are published in different ways. This means that along with determining the credibility and relevance of sources to your topic, individual authorship *must* be considered with every source you consider using even if an author's name is not listed.

Publishing is now easier than ever before because of the Internet. You will most likely publish your work in some way on the Internet during your academic career. You may have done so already. To overcome the barriers of technology, the Internet needs to work with a sense of humanity and community. Everyone deserves attribution and validation for original words and ideas. It is the right thing to do.

The Internet has created an amazing abundance of information for everyone. Now that we're all living online, it has become easier to recognize the names and work of others. So many people have remote personal and professional relationships and collaborations. We've heard of more people; we "know" more people and their work, making it easier to detect plagiarism, especially with information that is important enough to be quoted.

Catching Plagiarism

Many schools have formal plagiarism checker programs with mandatory use. Even for schools without these programs, instructors who assign writing during a course notice how you express yourself. There will always be subtle differences between your writing and the writing of others. Instructors can easily check your suspected sentences through Google.

Anyone who teaches in a course in high school and college has a professional aptitude in the subject area. College professors are published experts in their subject areas, who read the professional research continuously. As your education progresses, the likelihood increases dramatically that if you plagiarize, the instructor will find it. The consequences for plagiarism are serious. Plagiarism can result in failure of an assignment, failure of a course, or your removal from school. Plagiarism, or even sloppiness that might be considered plagiarism, causes instructors and others in a position to help you academically and professionally to not trust you. It compromises your credibility.

As someone who has been to school and who has different personal interests, you probably know a lot about various topics without looking up the information. This is considered general, common knowledge. The chances of you exactly duplicating a sentence you have read somewhere over the course of your education is remote if the source is not directly in front of you. A general rule is that the more specific the information, the more likely it is to need a citation. However, if you and a friend are in the same class with the same topic and have assisted one another with sources or proofreading assistance, you do need to be careful to not copy one another's words and ideas.

It's important to have confidence in your own thoughts and ideas when you're writing. Your ideas and analysis are meant to be the main focus of a research paper. The information you add from secondary sources is just evidence you use to help prove your points. If you have any doubts about your work, ask your teacher, your librarian, or your school's writing center for help.

Release your old perceptions about plagiarism. Avoiding plagiarism is just about following a skill set. Even if you're attending a school that has Turnitin.com, it is important to minimize your unintentional plagiarism and be able to correct yourself when you do it. This chapter provides you with advice and practical guidelines about plagiarism.

How Do You Know You Are Running the Risk of Plagiarism?

1. A Word document and a research database article or web page article are open on your computer screen side by side. This can lead to too much copy and pasting.

2. It's the night before the paper is due, and you have just started writing and researching. Without time to organize and develop your ideas, you may borrow too much from secondary sources.

3. You have placed your quotes and/or paraphrases in the text of the rough draft of your paper with empty brackets at the end of the sentence. You plan to come back later to fill in the citation documentation. Backtracking like this can make it difficult to remember which source you used and your original intention for the information.

4. You do not have an outline of your paper before the writing, and the research process begins. This can cause you to choose random information from sources to build your paper instead of following an outline to choose sources to match the arguments you are making in your paper.

5. You have cut and pasted two original sentences from a source onto a Word document to paraphrase. To identify the critical terms and change the structure, micro-paraphrasing needs to take place on a separate paper and then be typed onto your draft.

TYPES OF INFORMATION
Common Knowledge

Along with writing well, an important task when writing a research paper is deciding which information needs a citation. Common knowledge is "what everyone knows." This "common knowledge" does not need a citation. The first type of common knowledge is your personal common knowledge. You have retained information from your experiences such as places you have visited, hobbies, and viewing media and through the people you know. The Internet has given everyone the opportunity to know more about politics, news, entertainment, sports, and many other topics. Your ability to talk about these topics with a general understanding is your personal common knowledge.

The second type of common knowledge is academic. Academic common knowledge can be something you remember from your reading or class discussions during previous academic years. It's the knowledge you retain from being in school like basic math, the laws of science, and important parts of American history. When you're reading secondary sources, determining common knowledge is an art, not a science. It takes time and experience to learn this skill. You are making an educated judgment call each time you decide whether information needs a citation.

For academic work, it's easiest to think about common knowledge in terms of the subject area. For example, you are taking an introductory biology class. It's the spring, and you've been assigned a research paper. Here's what you have so far:

- A textbook covering various parts of biology

- Class notes from teacher lectures

- Concepts you've been taught in class which coordinate with the textbook and teacher lectures

- Tests, quizzes, essays, and other graded assignments on the biology topics

You have a basic level of knowledge about biology based on everything listed earlier. What you've learned in this class can be considered common knowledge about biology. It means that you now know enough about the various aspects of biology to choose a specific topic to write your paper that is outside of what you have learned in class. Usually, this subject-area common knowledge is not unique or specific enough to be good evidence to use as quotes and paraphrases in a research paper. But if you do use it, it doesn't have to be cited. Your teacher (the audience), who is grading the paper, knows this already.

When deciding whether information for a research paper needs a citation, here are a few questions to ask yourself. If the answers are "yes," then what you are reading is common knowledge.

- Does everyone know this? Even if you can't remember the exact details, can you look it up quickly by an Internet search? For example, you may have learned that bees are critical for the pollination of flowers. The fact that honeybees are a major pollinator can be quickly verified with an Internet search. This is common knowledge. It doesn't need a citation.

- Have I read this information somewhere before—in my textbook or on the Internet? If yes, then this information is background knowledge or common knowledge.

- Have I learned or heard this information before either through current class lectures or a previous school year? If yes, then this information is background knowledge or common knowledge.

When you are using information outside of the subject area in your paper, this should be cited. If you decide that a sentence is common knowledge, you can't copy it exactly from a source without a citation. You also can't change around one or two words and not cite it. This is plagiarism. If you decide to use the common knowledge sentence, *completely* restate the idea in a new sentence. Then you don't need a citation.

The typical advice is, "When in doubt, cite it." This is only partially true. Too many unnecessary citations can raise red flags. It's also more challenging to manage a lot of citations accurately and ethically. The information you cite should be very specific and outside of what you've already been taught to be effective evidence for the arguments in your paper.

Relevant and Irrelevant Information

If you have ever received information literacy instruction while you have been in school, you have probably heard the term "relevant information." Relevant information is the sentences from the secondary source which can be evidence for the arguments you are making in your paper. This is the information you will use for quotes and paraphrases. These sentences are normally not common knowledge. (Remember, common knowledge is usually not specific or unique enough to be used as a quote or paraphrase.) You will need a citation for relevant information.

Irrelevant information falls under the category of "who cares?" It may be on the overall topic but is not specific or important enough to be used for a quote or paraphrase. For example, Rosa Parks's husband, Raymond, was a barber. This is not common knowledge for most people. But it does not relate to her role as a civil rights advocate and should not be used in a paper at all.

Ideas, Facts, and Opinions

Ideas, facts, and opinions are different types of information. It's important to know the difference to decide whether the information needs a citation. An idea is something that has not been factually accepted or realized in a set format. There is sometimes an overlap between ideas and opinions. Opinions are ideas, analyses, or interpretations that can be created by one person or shared by a group. For example, the analysis of a literary work is the opinion of the author who wrote the article. This is an expression of the author's ideas about the meaning of the literary work. Groups can share opinions. The Sierra Club has the opinion that the environment should be protected from pollution through regulations.

Facts, on the other hand, are statements that cannot be disputed.

Examples of Ideas and Opinions

- A script for an episode of a television program. This is an idea for a television program episode.

- Movie and book reviews. These are the opinions and ideas of the author of the review about the movie and book.

- Plans to renovate a house. This is the idea for how the house should be built.

- Comparisons between two characters in a literary analysis article. This comparison, using a literary work, is the author's opinions (ideas). Another author might view the two characters differently.

- An interpretation of the symbolism in a literary work or historical event. This type of analysis from the author is the author's opinion about the literary work or historical event. Another author will have different ideas about the same things.

- Sometimes, ideas come from an analysis of data from research. The data is factual, but the conclusions—what it all could mean—are an idea. You will often read a paragraph at the end of a scholarly research article which discusses problems with the study or ideas for future research.

- Any information that can be considered "compare and contrast" of two or more different things. This includes similarities and differences between related concepts.

- Any type of criticism. This criticism can be from a person or a group.

- Personal, social, or cultural values and basic religious beliefs. These are the ideas by which people live.

- Written analysis of research data. The data is factual; the conclusions drawn from the data (what it could mean) are ideas.

- . Articles that quote experts on a topic then draw a conclusion. A common type of scholarly journal article is a literature review. These conclusions (ideas) are opinions of one author of the work of others.

- Recommendations about what is necessary to solve a problem or change a situation. These are ideas that are not fully realized.

- Television news programs now feature opinions from experts. The news is factual information. The interpretation or discussion of these events is opinion.

What's a Fact?

A fact is something that has been proven to be true. It is measurable, verifiable, and observable consistently over time. Facts are accepted by everyone.

- A physical description of any object that currently exists.

- Basic factual premises that are widely accepted. Examples: Water is the combination of hydrogen and oxygen atoms. Two plus two equals four.

- Data gained from experiments, research, surveys, or polls.

- Concepts such as gravity, electricity, and weather that are understood as true by everyone.

Here are a few examples of factual statements:

- The stock market hit the lowest point this week since the crash of 2008.
  The stock market is a measurable experience over time. This sentence will need quotation marks and a citation because it is a dated event.

- The leaves from many different types of trees change color in the fall and then fall to the ground.
  This is an observable physical process. This fact does not need a citation.

- All twenty-five Latin students at Loyola Blakefield received highest honors on the National Latin Exam for 2018.
  This sentence notes several small unique facts: twenty-five students, Latin, highest honors and National Latin Exam. Exam grades are factual. This is news within a community and perhaps regionally. If this sentence is published, it will need quotation marks and a citation.

- The invention of television did not eliminate radio.
  It is factually accurate that television and radio both exist today. This is factual common knowledge. It does not need a citation.

- The National Weather Service is the federal government's official source for weather information.

   The National Weather Service is a well-known expert in weather issues in the United States. It does not need a citation.

- High-definition television has a higher resolution than standard-definition television.

   This is a scientific certainty. It does not need a citation.

RECOGNIZING DIGITAL SOURCE PARTS

Digital sources are often from journals, reference books, or other publications you have never seen in print. You need to be able to recognize these publications, so you understand what type of source you are using.

Titles of Reference Books and Specialized Encyclopedias

Your library may have print reference books available for research. This can range from a multivolume set of general encyclopedias to specialized encyclopedias that are normally one volume covering a general subject area. More likely, you will be using entries from reference books, which are found in research databases as articles. These sources will provide you with a credible but more general overview of a topic. These types of articles are informative but not research based like many scholarly journal articles. Here are some examples of reference book titles you may see in a citation from a research database:

Dictionary of American History

European Writers: The Romantic Century, Vol. 7

Dictionary of the Middle Ages

Worldmark Encyclopedia of the States

Europe Since 1914: Encyclopedia of the Age of War and Reconstruction

Titles of Magazines and Newspapers

Most school librarians do not keep back issues of magazines and newspapers. You will use research databases to find magazine and newspaper articles for research. Here is a list of some common magazine and newspaper titles. These are credible sources but normally not scholarly.

The Washington Post

Discover

Foreign Affairs

The Wall Street Journal

The New York Times

The Los Angeles Times

U.S.A. Today

Smithsonian Magazine

Forbes

Scientific American

The New Yorker

Research Database Articles: Scholarly Journal Titles

It is important to know the type of source you are using from a research database. Your sources need to match the topic of your paper. Sometimes, you need general information; other times, you will need deeper research. Many scholarly journals feature articles based on research completed by professionals in different fields. This research could be survey results, experiments, evaluations, studies, or any number of research scenarios. After reviewing an article and using the research database citation tool, you should be able to recognize a scholarly journal title. If you have a scholarly journal article, you know that you have a highly credible source. The scholarly journal title will be italicized within the citation. Here is a list of scholarly journal titles as examples. These titles have an "academic" sound to them. There are many more. Note that these titles often have "Journal," "Review," and similar types of words in the title. It is common for scholarly journals to cover one professional area.

The Journal of Higher Education

College and University Teaching

Modern Language Notes

Critical Survey

The English Journal

Websites: Article Titles and Web Page Titles

There are two important titles for web pages. Since each website is published differently, you need to consider the different titles before you create the citation or use a citation tool.

1. **Web Page Article Title**

   The paragraphs of text you read to find a quote or paraphrase is the web page article. The web page article title is right above these paragraphs. The web page article title is specific and describes what you'll read in the paragraphs.

2. **Website Title**

   The website title is a more general description of the information on the web pages in the website. The website title, often along with the publisher, is listed above the article title on the web page. It is the "container" where the web page article is found within the website. The font for the web page title is larger than that for the web page article title.

Volume and Issue Number

Volume (vol.) and issue numbers (no.) always appear in the citation of scholarly journal research database articles. They provide important information about the publication. Volume is the number of years the publication has been in existence. The issue number is the number of issues published during a particular year. Here's how to recognize the volume number and issue number.

MLA

   vol. 28, no. 1

APA: The first number is the volume number; the second number is the issue number.

   28 (1)

Chicago

   28, no. 1

Book Publishers

Book publishers are part of print books, e-books, and research database articles. Book chapters and excerpts can sometimes be found on websites and through Google Books. Research databases often have articles that are reprinted from books and specialized encyclopedias—these book titles will be part of the full citation. For print books and e-books, the publisher is found on the publication page, usually one of the first few pages of the book. Book publishers are not italicized in any citations.

Indiana University Press

John Wiley and Sons

Vintage Books

MacMillan

Penguin Books

WHAT TYPES OF INFORMATION NEED A CITATION?

Problems with citations, especially through omission, are a leading cause of preventable plagiarism. Once you know the citation style your school or class is using, get a copy of the official manual to use as a reference. You can also bookmark the official citation-style website on your web browser. Even if you believe your instructor is unconcerned with citations, it is important to do them correctly.

Regardless of which type of project you are working on, all information needs to be considered for a citation whether it is in print or digital. Here is a partial list of information types that should be cited.

Abstracts from research database articlesArchitectural drawings

Archival material

Artifacts

Artworks

Audio recordings

Blog posts

Books, including textbooks, audio books, book chapters, e-books, back cover, and inside book jacket written material

Class lectures

Class notes

Conference proceedings

Court cases

Data from surveys, lab experiments, or any other similar research

Diaries

Dictionaries

Dissertations

E-books

E-mail

Films, all types

Government documents of any type

Handouts—informational handouts and teacher handouts

Images, born digital

Images (from books)

Instant messages

Instructional manuals

Interviews: personal interviews that are conducted by you. This also includes newspaper, television, and other interviews you can access from any source.

Journals—online and print

Letters

Magazines—online and print

Manuscripts

Maps

Meeting notes

Movies

Newspapers—online and print

Oral histories

Organization records

Pamphlets

Patents

PDF documents found on the Internet

Photographs, born print

Podcasts

PowerPoint or any other similar presentation viewed in person or on the Internet

Radio broadcasts

Research database articles

Reviews of performances, books, or art

Scientific reports, including clinical trial reports and lab reports

Social media: Twitter, Facebook, and all other similar sites

Song lyrics

Speeches

Statements—published

Statistics

Surveys

Television programs

Text messages

Textbooks

Videos, including YouTube and all video types found on the InternetWebsites, all types

Wikipedia

Working papers

AUTHORS AND EDITORS

When you use a citation tool, you need to recognize if the source has a named person as author from the citation. The APA citation style recognizes groups and organizations as authors when there is no name attached to the source. This is important for how your citation should be handled in the Works Cited, References, and Bibliography page and with in-text references.

Recognizing Authors in a Citation

Here is an example of a source with an author. It is at the beginning of the citation.

MLA

Ganguli, Tania. "Through Early Challenges at LeBron James' I Promise School, Seeds of Success Are Sown." *ProQuest*, 21 Nov. 2018, https://search.proquest.com/docview/2136597400?accountid=41092.

Chicago (Notes and Bibliography)

Ganguli, Tania. "Through Early Challenges at LeBron James' I Promise School, Seeds of Success Are Sown." *Los Angeles Times*, November 21, 2018. ProQuest.

Chicago (Author-Date)

Ganguli, Tania. 2018. "Through Early Challenges at LeBron James' I Promise School, Seeds of Success Are Sown." *Los Angeles Times*, November 21, 2018. ProQuest.

APA

Ganguli, T. (2018, November 21). Through early challenges at LeBron James' I Promise School, seeds of success are sown. *Los Angeles Times*. Retrieved from ProQuest database.

In this example, the source does not have an author. The parenthetical citations and footnotes will lead with the article title.

MLA

"Pearl Harbor." *Gale Student Resources in Context*, Gale, 2017. *Student Resources in Context*, http://link.galegroup.com/apps/doc/XYQXGW118124201/SUIC?u=win5026&sid=SUIC&xid=b457f42e. Accessed 12 Dec. 2018.

Chicago (Notes and Bibliography)

"Pearl Harbor." In *Gale Student Resources in Context*. Detroit, MI: Gale, 2017. *Student Resources In Context* (accessed December 12, 2018). http://link.galegroup.com/apps/doc/XYQXGW118124201/SUIC?u=win5026&sid=SUIC&xid=b457f42e.

Chicago (Author-Date)

"Pearl Harbor." 2017. In *Gale Student Resources in Context*. Detroit, MI: Gale. *Student Resources In Context*. http://link.galegroup.com/apps/doc/XYQXGW118124201/SUIC?u=win5026&sid=SUIC&xid=b457f42e.

APA

Pearl Harbor. (2017). In *Gale Student Resources in Context*. Detroit, MI: Gale. Retrieved from http://link.galegroup.com/apps/doc/XYQXGW118124201/SUIC?u=win5026&sid=SUIC&xid=b457f42e.

Author Name Formats

The author's name should be stated in the citation as it appears on the source itself. If there is more than one author, use the order of names as it appears on the source for your citation. The basic format is Last Name, First Name. Middle names and middle initials are used for authors only if it is included in the source itself. When an author has a middle name, it is placed after the first name for MLA and Chicago. A middle initial is an abbreviation for a middle name. A middle initial is handled the same way as a middle name, placed after the first name. Example: Kelly, William T. APA uses initials for both first names and middle names.

Authors with middle names
Example: Margaret Tredick McFarland

MLA: McFarland, Margaret Tredick

Chicago Author-Date: McFarland, Margaret Tredick

Chicago Notes and Bibliography footnote: Margaret Tredick McFarland

Chicago Notes and Bibliography bibliography: McFarland, Margaret Tredick

APA: McFarland, M.T.

A book or article written by two authors
Example: Margaret Padrezas and Beverly Jones

MLA: Padrezas, Margaret, and Beverly Jones

Chicago Author-Date: Padrezas, Margaret, and Beverly Jones

Chicago Notes and Bibliography: Padrezas, Margaret, and Beverly Jones

APA: Padrezas, M & Jones, B.

Editors

Editors have a prominent role in the publication and citation process. Editors decide the contents of a book when there are chapters written by different authors. The name of the editor of a book can be found on the front cover or on the publication page. Editors are an important part of research database article citations when the article originated from an edited book. These examples show how the editor's name appears in the full citation.

MLA

You will see "edited by" and then the editor's name in the full citation. The editor's name is stated with the first name first.

Examples

edited by D. L. Kirkpatrick
edited by Diane Telgen and Kevin Hile

APA

The abbreviation for editor(s) is capitalized after the names in parentheses in the full citation. Use an "&" between the names of two editors. When an editor has a middle name, use this as a second initial.

Examples

H. Bloom (Ed.)
K. S. Sisung & G. A. Raffaelle (Eds.)

Chicago

Examples

Edited by Richard Tulane—full citation
ed. Richard Tulane—footnote

TITLE FORMATS

Italics versus Quotation Marks for Titles

Accuracy with italics and quotation marks is important to avoid confusion about the type of source you are using.

MLA

MLA Titles: Italics

Books and e-books: *Dracula*
Magazines: *The New Yorker*
Newspapers: *The Washington Post*
Research database names: *JSTOR*

Poems that are book length: *Beowulf*
Scholarly journals: *The Journal of the American Medical Association*
Website titles: *Technology Update*

MLA Titles: Quotation Marks

Article titles for magazines, newspapers, web pages, scholarly journal articles, and other types of research database articles: "The Decline of the Bee Population"

Book chapters: "The Marriage of F. Scott Fitzgerald"
Poems (short poems): "The Raven"
Short story titles: "The Tell-Tale Heart"

Chicago Author-Date and Notes-Bibliography

The guidelines are the same for both types of Chicago citations.

Chicago: Italics

Books and e-books: *Dracula*
Magazines: *The New Yorker*
Scholarly journals: *The Journal of the American Medical Association*
Newspapers: *The Washington Post*

Chicago: No Quotation Marks or Italics

Research databases: JSTOR
Website titles: Classics Today

Chicago: Quotation Marks

Article titles for magazines, newspapers, web pages, scholarly journal articles, and other types of research database articles: "The Decline of the Bee Population"

Book chapters: "The Marriage of F. Scott Fitzgerald"
Poems (short poems): "The Raven"
Short story titles: "The Tell-Tale Heart"

APA

APA Titles: Italics

Books and e-books: *Dracula*
Magazines: *Time*
Newspapers: *The New York Times*
Scholarly journals: *The Journal of the American Medical Association*

APA Titles: No Italics or Quotation Marks

Article titles for magazines, newspapers, web pages, scholarly journal articles, and other types of research database articles: The insulin wars
A work in an anthology: Baseball as the bleachers like it

DATES AND PAGE NUMBERS

Locating Publication Dates for Sources

You need to be able to easily find dates on sources in order to create an accurate citation or use a citation tool. The publication year gives you important information about the source. When you have a choice of sources, current information is always better. Omitting a date or using the wrong date format in a citation can result in a loss of points or cause misunderstandings about your citations. Here are some basic guidelines for finding the publication date on different sources.

Books

Print books and e-books will always have a publication year. This is found on the publication page, one of the first few pages at the front of the book.

Web Pages

Publication dates on web pages vary.

- There is normally a copyright year at the bottom of the web page. If there is no other date listed, this can be used as the publication date for the citation.

- Newspapers and other similar publications on the Internet will have a day, month, and year for the publication date. This is located near the article title.

- For all other web page articles, check for the date near the article title and author name. You should also check at the end of the article.

Research Database Articles

The publication date will be near the top of the article with the author, article title, and publication information. When you use the citation tool within the research database, the publication date will automatically be part of the citation.

Publication Date versus Copyright Date

You will find the most accurate publication dates for web page articles from news sources or other publications that publish content on a regularly scheduled basis. These sources will also have a copyright date for the overall website. For example, a news article published in the *New York Times* and posted on its website today will have a publication date of December 6, 2018. The copyright date will be listed on the bottom of the web page as 2018. The publication date is December 6, 2018. This is a more specific date and should be used for the citation. Many websites have only a copyright date.

Accessed Dates for Digital Sources

For MLA and Chicago, the accessed date is the last date you viewed the digital resource. For Chicago, the accessed date is used only when there is no publication date. You need to include the word "accessed" in the citation. Book citations will never have an accessed date. APA uses a retrieved date, the last day you used the source.

MLA: Accessed Day Month Year
Chicago: accessed Month Day, Year
APA: Retrieved Month Day, Year

Month Abbreviations

For Chicago and APA, spell out the months in the citation and in the text of your paper. MLA prefers month abbreviations in full citations, and spell out the month in the text of your paper.

Date Variations

MLA: Use the Day Month Year format based on what is available from the source. This format should also be used for the accessed date.

2 Aug. 2018

Aug. 2018

2018

Date Variations for Parenthetical Citations

APA: The year of publication is primary in the citation after the author's name. For sources with more specific publication information available, the publication month and day follows the publication year after the comma.

(2018)

(2018, September)

(2018, September 7)

(2018, Fall)

(2018, November/December)

Chicago Author-Date: The only date in the parenthetical citation is the year of publication. There may be a month, day, and year of publication in the full citation for newspaper articles and other more specifically dated publications.

(2018)

PAGE NUMBERS IN SOURCES

With digital sources, it can be confusing to know when to use page numbers with your parenthetical citations and footnotes. This is important in reducing plagiarism. A general guideline is that when page numbers print out with the article pages for digital sources, you need to use a page number in the parenthetical citation.

- Books and e-books will always have page numbers.

- The average web page does *not* have a page number. There are some exceptions for PDF documents, but this will be obvious when you see it.

- Scholarly journal articles from research databases will have page numbers. These page numbers correspond with the original printing in the print version of the journal. The page numbers will print out on the article.

- When you generate the full citation for research database articles that originate from reference sources and encyclopedias, a page range is often listed. You do not have to use a page number for these sources unless the page numbers print out on the article.

NONSTANDARD SOURCES

Many valuable nonstandard sources are located on the Internet. A nonstandard source means any source that is not an image, web page article, or a research database article. Some citation tools such as NoodleTools accommodate all types of sources.

Example: YouTube Videos

MLA

(1) "How the Power of Attention Changes Everything." (2) *YouTube,* (3) uploaded by Jeff Klein, (4) 17 June 2014, (5) www.youtube.com/watch?v=vfvD_jt9R-s. (6) Accessed 5 Dec. 2018.

(1) Title of video in quotation marks.
(2) *YouTube* is the name of the website, italicized.
(3) "uploaded by" is the creator of the video.
(4) Publication/uploaded date.
(5) URL.
(6) Accessed date.

Chicago Author-Date

(1) "How the Power of Attention Changes Everything." (2) 2014. (3) Video file. (4) YouTube. (5) Posted by Jeff Klein, (6) June 17, 2014. (7) Accessed December 13, 2018. (8) http://www.youtube.com/watch?v=vfvD_jt9R-s.

(1) Title of video in quotation marks.
(2) Publication year.
(3) Type of file.
(4) Name of website where the video originated.
(5) Posted by the creator's name.
(6) Date of publication or upload.
(7) Accessed date of the video.
(8) URL of the video.

Chicago Notes and Bibliography

(1) "How the Power of Attention Changes Everything." (2) Video file. (3) You-Tube. (4) Posted by Jeff Klein, (5) June 17, 2014. (6) Accessed December 13, 2018. (7) http://www.youtube.com/watch?v=vfvD_jt9R-s.

(1) Title of video in quotation marks.
(2) Type of file.
(3) Name of website where the video originated.
(4) Posted by the creator's name.
(5) Date of publication or upload.
(6) Accessed date of the video.
(7) URL of the video.

APA

(1) Klein, J. (2) (2014, June 17). (3) *How the Power of Attention Changes Every-thing* (4) [Video file]. (5) Retrieved from http://www.youtube.com/watch?v=vfvD_jt9R-s.

- (1)   Name of video creator.
- (2)   Date of publication/upload.
- (3)   Title of video, italicized.
- (4)   Type of file.
- (5)   Retrieved from URL.

For other nonstandard sources found on the Internet, follow the basic model of web page citations. Analyze the source before you use a citation tool, or build the citation yourself. Jot down this information:

- Is there an author listed?

- What is the title of this "source"?

- Is there a larger title of the web page or "parent" organization?

- Who published it?

- When was it published?

- What is the URL?

QUOTATIONS AND PARAPHRASING

Block Quotes

Block quotes, when you use a longer quote from a primary or secondary source in the text of the paper, should not be overused. The two primary ways for you to cite in your paper are one- or two-line quotations in the text of your paper or paraphrases. Block quotes are secondary to the use of one- or two-line quotation and paraphrases. A good general rule is one block quote for every five pages of a research paper. Too many block quotes can make it appear that you are trying to piece your paper together with some-one else's words in your paper. This can raise a plagiarism accusation.

Block quotes are set apart from the text of your paper. In all citation styles, the block quote begins 1 inch from the left margin and 0.5 inch from the other text. Use a block quote for sentences that are specific and important to your topic and can't be broken up and used as smaller one- or two-line quotes and still make sense. Here are some times when using a block quote is appropriate:

- The opinion of an expert who agrees or disagrees with your thesis. The opposing viewpoint is an especially good reason to use a block quote. Then, you can refute this opinion.

- A specific conclusion from research or an important analysis.

- Present an additional challenge or problem with the subject.

- Important lines of poetry that you will analyze.

- Dialogue between characters in a literary work which you will then analyze.

- Monologue of a literary character which you will then analyze.

Using the author's name in the introductory sentence makes the parenthetical citation easier to create. While there are slight variations for each of the three major citation styles, here are some overall guidelines:

- Use a block quote when you are quoting more than four lines of text and more than three lines from a poem. Type the sentences exactly how they appear in the source.

- No quotation marks should be used for the block quote itself.

- The parenthetical citation should be after the last sentence in the block quote, after the period. If you do not use the author's name in the block quote introductory sentence, make sure that this is included in the parenthetical citation, along with a page number, if it is a book or scholarly journal research database article. Example: (Miles 2017, 75).

- The block quote itself should be single spaced.

MLA

For more information, see pages 76 and 77 in the MLA Handbook, Eighth Edition.

This example is a block quote from a scholarly journal article published in 2017 by William Kelly about children reading web pages. It is from page 56. Since the author's name is mentioned in the introductory sentence, the parenthetical citation has only the page number. You will also have a full citation on your Works Cited page, which begins with Kelly, William. If your block quote is from a web page (without a page number), the author's name in the introductory sentence means that you will not need a parenthetical citation.

Example

Kelly noted the need to address the information avalanche in young children:

Information evaluation of web pages will become an urgent skill as children begin to read web pages as early as fourth grade. Introducing information evaluation into the elementary school curriculum will mean adjusting the training for student teachers in this area. It also offers an opportunity for the library science and teaching professions to collaborate to shape information use in an important way. Personal decision making through reading web pages is so pervasive that this is an urgent curricular priority across educational levels. (56)

APA

For more information, see page 29 of the *Publication Manual of the American Psychological Association*, sixth edition.

This example is a block quote from a scholarly journal article published in 2017 by William Kelly about children reading web pages. It is from page 56. Since the author's name and publication year are mentioned in the introductory sentence, the parenthetical citation has only the page number. You will also have a full citation on your References page, which begins with Kelly, W. If the block quote is from a web page (without a page number), the author's name, along with the publication year in the introductory sentence, means that you will not need a parenthetical citation.

Example

Kelly (2017) noted the need to address the information avalanche in young children:

> Information evaluation of web pages will become an urgent skill as children begin to read web pages as early as fourth grade. Introducing information evaluation into the elementary school curriculum will mean adjusting the training for student teachers in this area. It also offers an opportunity for the library science and teaching professions to collaborate to shape information use in an important way. Personal decision making through reading web pages is so pervasive that this is an urgent curricular priority across educational levels. (p. 56)

Chicago Author-Date

This example is a block quote from a scholarly journal article published in 2017 by William Kelly about children using web pages. It is from page 56. Since the author's name and publication year are mentioned in the introductory sentence, the parenthetical citation has only the page number. You will also have a full citation on your References page, which begins with Kelly, William.

If the block quote is from a web page (without a page number), the author's name, along with the publication year in the introductory sentence, means that you do not need to include the author's name in the parenthetical citation.

Example

Kelly (2017) noted the need to address the information avalanche in young children:

> Information evaluation of web pages will become an urgent skill as children begin to read web pages as early as fourth grade. Introducing information evaluation into the elementary school curriculum will mean adjusting the training for student teachers in this area. It also offers an opportunity for the library science and teaching professions to collaborate to shape information use in an important way. Personal decision making through reading web pages is so pervasive that this is an urgent curricular priority across educational levels. (56)

- Use a block quote when you are quoting more than one hundred words of text. Type the sentences exactly how they appear in the source.

- No quotation marks should be used for the block quote itself.

- The parenthetical citation should be after the last sentence in the block quote, after the period. If the source has a page number (book or research database article), make sure this is included in your parenthetical citation. Example: (Miles 2017, 75).

- The block quote itself should be single spaced.

- A block quote has an introductory sentence. You can use the last name of the author and the publication year in this sentence. If you do this, then your parenthetical citation will include only the page number. Example: (75).

Chicago Notes and Bibliography

This example is a block quote from a scholarly journal article published in 2017 by William Kelly about children reading web pages. It is from page 56.

Example

Kelly noted the need to address the information avalanche in young children:

> Information evaluation of web pages will become an urgent skill as children begin to read web pages as early as fourth grade. Introducing information evaluation into the elementary school curriculum will mean adjusting the training for student teachers in this area. It also

offers an opportunity for the library science and teaching professions to collaborate to shape information use in an important way. Personal decision making through reading web pages is so pervasive that this is an urgent curricular priority across educational levels.1

- Use a block quote when you are quoting more than one hundred words of text. Type the sentences exactly how they appear in the source.

- No quotation marks should be used for the block quote itself.

- Use the author's name and publication year in the introductory sentence. The superscript number for your footnote will be placed after the period of the last sentence of the block quote.

- The block quote itself should be single spaced.

Placing a Quote or Paraphrase in the Text of Your Paper

Less is more for direct quotes. Paraphrases should be only one sentence. Paraphrases do not have quotation marks.

MLA: Direct Quote from a Research Database Article

Example 1

"Coeducational high schools were found to have 15% less bullying over a four-year period as compared to single sex schools" (Durkin 25).
The parenthetical citation is after the closing quotation mark. The period is placed after the parenthetical citation.

Example 2

Durkin said, "Coeducational high schools were found to have 15% less bullying over a four year period as compared to single sex schools" (25).
The author's name is used in the text of the sentence, so only the page number is necessary in the parenthetical citation.

MLA: Paraphrase

Example 1

Bullying decreases by 15% in coed high schools (Durkin 25).
There are no quotation marks. The period for the sentence is after the parenthetical citation.

Example 2

Durkin said that bullying decreases by 15% in coed high schools (25).

There are no quotation marks. The period for the sentence is after the parenthetical citation. The author's name is in the text of the sentence, so only the page number is necessary for the parenthetical citation.

APA: Direct Quote

Example 1

Durkin found that "coeducational high schools were found to have 15% less bullying over a four-year period as compared to single sex schools" (2017).

The author's name is used in the text of the sentence. The publication date 2017 is placed in parentheses after the closing quotation mark. The period is outside of the closing parentheses.

Example 2

Durkin (2017) found that "coeducational high schools were found to have 15% less bullying over a four-year period as compared to single sex schools" (p. 25).

The author's name and the publication year are used in the text of the sentence. There is a separate parenthetical citation for the page number.

APA: Paraphrase

Example 1

Bullying decreases by 15% in coed high schools (Durkin, 2017, p. 25).

The author's name, publication year, and page number are part of the parenthetical citation.

Example 2

Durkin (2017) noted that bullying decreased by 15% in coed high schools (p. 25).

Since the author's name and publication year are in the text of the sentence, there is a parenthetical citation for the page number.

Chicago Author-Date: Direct Quote

Example 1

"Coeducational high schools were found to have 15% less bullying over a four-year period as compared to single sex schools" (Durkin 2017, 25).

The author's last name, publication year, and page number are noted in the parenthetical citation at the end of the sentence.

Example 2

Durkin (2017) found that "coeducational high schools were found to have 15% less bullying over a four-year period as compared to single sex schools" (25).

The author's name and publication date are in the text of the sentence. The page number is in a parenthetical citation at the end of the quote.

Chicago Notes and Bibliography: Direct Quote

Note the use of a superscript note number instead of a parenthetical citation at the end of the sentence.

Example 1

"Coeducational high schools were found to have 15% less bullying over a four-year period as compared to single sex schools."[1]

Example 2

Durkin found that "coeducational high schools were found to have 15% less bullying over a four-year period as compared to single sex schools."[1]

Chicago Author-Date: Paraphrase

Example 1

Bullying decreases by 15% in coed high schools (Durkin 2017, 25).

The author's last name, publication year, and page number are noted in the parenthetical citation at the end of the sentence.

Example 2

Durkin (2017) noted that bullying decreases by 15% in coeducational high schools (25).

The author name and publication date are in the text of the sentence. The page number is in a parenthetical citation at the end of the quote.

Chicago Notes and Bibliography: Paraphrase

Example 1

Bullying decreases by 15% in coed high schools.[1]

Example 2

Durkin noted that bullying decreases by 15% in coeducational high schools.[1]

MICRO-PARAPHRASING

You should use a paraphrase when the sentences contain an important idea but it's too wordy for a direct quote. Your paraphrase should consist of *unique* information that was found in the two sentences, which can be used as evidence in your paper. Your goal is to create a new sentence that begins differently than the original that is a clear, concise restatement in your own words with a citation.

Don't paraphrase common knowledge for use in your paper. For example, if you are writing about the contributions of Rosa Parks to the American Civil Rights Movement, you do not need to use the information that she is considered the first lady of the civil rights movement. You also need to avoid irrelevant information. Rosa Parks's husband was a barber. This is not common knowledge, but it is not relevant for your paper topic. The steps for micro-paraphrasing are in Chapter 2.

Here are a few additional guidelines for a more concise paraphrase.

For sentences that have lists, apply a more general, descriptive term to encompass the items in the list. The critical terms are underlined in this example.

Example

Dr. Simone Duvall is the first woman of color to be appointed to the prestigious position of Director of the Centers for Disease Control and Prevention this week. Over the past ten years, she has had positions with increasing levels of responsibility at Harvard Medical School as a medical researcher, clinical professor and head of the Department of Microbiology.

Explanation: *Look for opportunities to condense lists in a sentence. Technically, "medical researcher," "clinical professor," and "head of the Department of Microbiology" are critical terms that can't be restated any other way. Since our goal is a concise paraphrase, there is a good opportunity to condense these titles into "positions with increasing levels of responsibility." Names and proper nouns are always considered critical terms. "Woman of color" is a unique critical term. We don't* *know specifics from the original sentences about her exact nationality, so "woman of color" is the only term to use. "Dr. Simone Duvall," "Director of the Centers for Disease Control and Prevention," and "Harvard Medical School" are all critical terms that should be used in the paraphrase. It's not necessary to mention the number of years she worked there. To get an important job, it's understood that she has experience.*

Correct paraphrase: After several important medical research positions at Harvard Medical School, Dr. Simone Duvall is the first woman physician of color to be appointed the director of the Centers of Disease Control.

When putting the original sentences into your own words, don't use clunky language as a synonym. For example, don't substitute "young woman" for "girl." "Girl" can be a critical term that is used in the paraphrase.

Examples: The first words in this list are concise and can be used as critical terms from the original sentences in the paraphrase. The second words are clunky and should not be used as synonyms for the paraphrase.

> book—monograph
> doctor—medical professional
> teacher—faculty member
> school—educational institution

When paraphrasing information about well-known people, look for built-in meanings based on the person's name recognition. They are well known enough that we have working knowledge of who they are and what they do. You don't have to include what this individual does in your new paraphrased sentence. The meaning is implied within the person's name. In the first example, Neil deGrasse Tyson is an astrophysicist. It is unnecessary to include Astrophysicist Neil deGrasse Tyson in a paraphrase. Neil deGrasse Tyson can stand alone in the sentence.

Examples

> Neil deGrasse Tyson: astrophysicist
> Nancy Pelosi: Speaker of the House, politics
> Laura Bush: First Lady, librarian
> J.K. Rowling: Harry Potter books, author
> Mother Teresa: work with the poor and sick, Missionaries of Charity

On the average, the two sentences you will paraphrase will probably have about four or five critical terms that can't be restated any other way. Focus on names, dates, places, proper nouns, and other very specific terms when you identify the critical terms. Check a dictionary or thesaurus for assistance if you have trouble deciding if a word should be considered a critical term.

Examples of other critical terms

Laws and acts: Taft-Hartley Act
School names: University of Maryland
Wars and names of battles: North African Campaign
Technical terms: Public Value Mapping framework, anti-inflammatory, bandwidth
All titles: *One Flew over the Cuckoo's Nest, CSI Miami*
Names of professions: teacher, librarian, doctor
Religions: Catholic, Baptist
Weather conditions: drought, erosion, rain, snow

Dates in sentences you're considering for a paraphrase are technically critical terms—dates can't be restated any other way. But consider if you really need the date in the new paraphrased sentence. The goal is always a clear, concise, new sentence. Often, the other writing in your paper points to a time already, making it unnecessary to repeat the date in your paraphrase.

THE MECHANICS OF PLAGIARISM

Copy and Paste

Copy and paste from a source is a primary cause of plagiarism. Do not copy and paste sentences directly from a digital source directly to a Word document. When you copy and paste sentences (or an entire paragraph) onto a Word document and change around a few words, this is plagiarism, even if you cite it.

In high school and the first few years of college, you will make fewer errors if you use just a few sentences at a time in a direct quote or paraphrase. For a direct quote, retype these sentences, add the parenthetical citation or footnote, and put the full citation on your draft Works Cited/References/Bibliography page right away. Since it is only one or two sentences, it will take just a few minutes. Retyping helps you to understand the material better. It also gives you an opportunity to reconsider the quote, helping you to decide if it is the right evidence to support your points. This can help improve your writing. Micro-paraphrasing can't be completed correctly if you copy and paste the sentences from the source onto a Word document. It's important to create the paraphrase first, type it on your document, and apply the citation.

Here are two more reasons you should *not* copy and paste digital material directly onto your draft research paper or other project for a direct quote or paraphrase. All of these can lead to plagiarism accusations.

1. You may forget to add the parenthetical citation or footnote after you copy and paste. A temporary "place holder" in the document for the

citation may cause confusion for you later. You don't want to put the wrong source into the "place holder" for the information.

2. You always need to know the boundaries where your writing and information borrowed by others begins and ends. If you copy and paste sentences and forget to include quotation marks, this is difficult to determine.

One of the most important ways to avoid plagiarism during the research process is to print out copies of your digital sources. If you do not have access to printing, many research databases allow for highlighting of articles with the option to save the article. You can also maintain articles by screenshots and saving through Word or another similar program.

These Errors Are Not Considered Plagiarism (But You'll Probably Lose Points)

•   Punctuation errors with citations.

•   Spelling problems with the author's name or title of the source.

•   Problems with spacing or margins.

•   The Works Cited, References, or Bibliography is not alphabetized.

Plagiarism Problems and Solutions

Here are several examples of plagiarism with a solution.

Plagiarism Problem

You purchased a research paper and used a paragraph from it to increase your required word count. The rest of the paper is your own writing.

Solution

This is intentional plagiarism. There is no way to justify this. If you are accused of plagiarism with this, admit it immediately and accept the consequences gracefully.

Plagiarism Problem

You forget a parenthetical citation (MLA, APA, Chicago Author-Date) or footnote (Chicago Notes and Bibliography) for a paraphrase or direct quote in your paper.

Solution

This is considered plagiarism. Once you have placed a quote or paraphrase in your rough draft, add the citation immediately. You can then highlight the sentences on the rough draft, visually marking it to remind yourself to review it again during the proofreading process.

Plagiarism Problem

You copy and paste too many sentences for a direct quote with a citation within the text of your paper, or you have more than one block quote for every five pages of your research paper.

Solution

This makes it appear as if you're trying to fill up space in your paper with quotes instead of your own ideas and analysis. A direct quote should be one or two lines within the text of your paper. If your quote is more than four sentences, use a block quote. See the earlier material in this chapter for instructions on how to use block quotes. A good rule of thumb is one block quote for every five pages of research paper.

Plagiarism Problem

You have a citation but forget to put quotation marks around a direct quote.

Solution

Even though this error is most likely due to poor proofreading, it is considered plagiarism. It creates confusion about the source of the information. For web pages and research database articles, highlight and annotate direct quotes in a consistent color. Keep direct quotes highlighted in your rough draft until you proofread one final time.

Plagiarism Problem

There are too many citations in the text of your paper.

Solution

This creates the impression that you used your sources to create the structure of your paper. Your analysis should be the majority of your paper. Review your teacher's instructions. A good guideline is to use a maximum of two to three citations for each page of your paper.

Plagiarism Problem

You did not attach your Works Cited, References, or Bibliography page to the end of your paper.

Solution

This is plagiarism that can be prevented during the proofreading process. As soon as you realize this mistake, offer to provide the page as soon as possible to your teacher.

Plagiarism Problem

The entire paper is written based on your own knowledge without any secondary sources.

Solution

If this is the case, it means that your paper is too general. Research papers require the use of evidence from secondary sources to support your thesis. The teacher can't objectively determine whether you copied the information or if you actually have this type of knowledge from memory. Offer to rewrite the paper, using secondary sources according to your teacher's instructions.

Plagiarism Problem

You use one source with page numbers consecutively to cite information in your paper.

Solution

This is plagiarism because it appears as if you are using the structure of a source to write your paper. Your use of sources should vary throughout your paper.

Plagiarism Problem

You use a parenthetical citation in the text of your paper without a corresponding source on your References, Works Cited, or Bibliography page.

Solution

This is a proofreading issue that can be considered plagiarism. In the rough-draft stage of your paper, check off each parenthetical citation or footnote with a corresponding source on your References, Works Cited, or Bibliography page.

Plagiarism Problem

You change around a few words from a sentence on a web page you think is common knowledge. You use this sentence in your paper without a citation.

Solution

This is plagiarism. If you copy the sentence exactly, you need a citation, whether it is common knowledge or not. If you are sure this is common knowledge, completely restate the sentence in your own words, not just change a few words around. Refer to the micro-paraphrasing technique in Chapter 2.

Plagiarism Problem

There are too many original words in your paraphrase. You included a citation or footnote.

Solution

This is plagiarism, even if you cited your paraphrase. If a paraphrase is difficult to do, consider using a direct quote instead. Review Chapter 2 on the micro-paraphrasing technique.

Plagiarism Problem

One source is cited many more times in the text of your paper than the other sources you have listed on your Works Cited, References, or Bibliography page.

Solution

This appears as if you have used the structure of this one source to write the paper. Vary the sources you use throughout your paper. Instead of overusing a source, eliminate a source if it is not useful. Ask for assistance at your school's writing center, from your librarian, or from your teacher.

Plagiarism Problem

You haven't had time to write the research paper so you decide to use a few paragraphs from a research paper you completed last school year. You use proper citations for the use of this material.

Solution

You can never reuse anything you have written before. It doesn't matter if you reuse one sentence, one paragraph, or an entire paper. It is plagiarism. This is called recycling fraud, a specific type of plagiarism. An important part of academic integrity is that each assignment is completed from scratch with completely new material. It is a better idea to hand in fewer pages of work that is completed properly than commit plagiarism.

Plagiarism Problem

You have used a (web page, research database article, book) source for citations in your paper. But you've misplaced the source—the printed-out pages are lost. You use your memory to recreate the citation.

Solution

Do not recreate the citation from your memory about the source. Misleading citations are a common cause of plagiarism accusations. When citations are completed correctly, there is an overall consistent appearance. This is an important reason to complete your proofreading process a few days before the paper is due. Maintain your web browser history throughout the research process for web page sources. A librarian can help you locate lost sources.

Other Practical Ways to Avoid Plagiarism

• Use information from sources that you understand. If you use a source that is too advanced, it is more difficult to use the information without plagiarizing.

• Do not copy and paste. This is explained further in this chapter.

• When you type in a direct quote or paraphrase for your paper during the rough-draft stage, do the parenthetical citation and full citation on your Works Cited/References page in the correct format at this stage. If you change your mind about using a source, it is easier to remove this information, along with the citations, than it is to recreate it from scratch later. For Chicago Notes and Bibliography, keep a running list of footnotes.

• If your school has a formal plagiarism checker such as Turnitin.com, you will use this in the way your teacher advises. For students in schools without these programs, do not rely solely on free plagiarism checkers on the Internet to determine if you have plagiarized. You do not know the reliability of these free tools.

• Librarians are experts on sources and plagiarism. If you have any questions, please ask a librarian or someone from your school's writing center. That person will not report your questions about plagiarism to your teacher.

HONOR POLICIES AND HONOR AGREEMENTS

Here's a typical definition of plagiarism from a middle and high school:

Plagiarism—(1) The intentional or unintentional taking of the (2) ideas or writings of another and presenting them as one's own (3) without attribution is not permitted. This includes the use of research papers, term papers, or critiques (4) previously handed in to this or any other institution, (5) materials accessed from the Internet or other electronic sources (e. g. phone, e-mail, etc.) encyclopedias, dictionaries or any other source. Additionally, (6) presenting an author's exact wording without marking it as a quotation is considered plagiarism, even if the source is cited.

(courtesy of Loyola Blakefield)

Let's unpack what this really means:

(1) The "intentional or unintentional taking of the ideas or writings of another" means that it doesn't matter if you plagiarized accidently because you didn't know or if you did it on purpose. If you use the ideas or writing of another person without a citation, it's still considered

plagiarism, no matter what the circumstances. You can say it was an accident or that you didn't know but it's still considered plagiarism.

(2) Deciding if you've used someone else's ideas is sometimes difficult. See Chapter 2 for more information about the use of ideas.

(3) Attribution—the use of a citation.

(4) "Previously handed in" means that you can't ever hand in work from a previous grade or another class. This is a type of plagiarism called recycling fraud. It doesn't matter that it's your work. Educators are part of a relatively small professional community who communicate with one another often about assignments.

(5) "materials accessed from the Internet or other electronic sources (e. g. phone, e-mail, etc.) encyclopedias, dictionaries or any other source": *Everything* needs to be considered for a citation. It doesn't matter how you access the information—phone, computer, or another device. The Internet and the possible types of sources are increasing exponentially every day. A partial list of sources is in this chapter.

(6) "presenting an author's exact wording without marking it as a quotation is considered plagiarism, even if the source is cited."—If you use a direct quote from a source and forget quotation marks, it is considered plagiarism, even with a citation. This misrepresents the information as a paraphrase. Your use of quotation marks is important to check when you proofread.

YOU HAVE BEEN ACCUSED OF PLAGIARISM: WHAT SHOULD YOU DO?

First of all, if you did plagiarize, do not lie about it. Plagiarism which is found by Turnitin.com is an objective report which will be difficult to argue against. Even if your teacher found it without a plagiarism checker, assume that the teacher has the incident fully documented.

Here is a process to consider:

• Gather all of the sources you used in the paper. If there is a misunderstanding, you will need to be organized to make your case.

• If you have received instruction about citations or other aspects of plagiarism, this may work against you. The assumption is that once you have been taught these principles that you will use them correctly in your academic work.

- Depending on the severity of the violation, negotiate. You can offer to do a new assignment or have a failing grade for the course instead of expulsion. Your goal is to stay enrolled in school.

RESOURCES

APA Sample Paper Resources: https://www.apastyle.org/learn/faqs/view-sample-papers. You can compare your paper to the examples here.

Chicago Manual of Style—Author Date Sample Citations: https://www.chicago manualofstyle.org/tools_citationguide/citation-guide-2.html. A useful quick guide for Chicago Author-Date Citations.

Chicago Manual of Style—Notes and Bibliography Sample Citations: https://www.chicagomanualofstyle.org/tools_citationguide/citation-guide-1.html. A useful quick guide for Chicago Notes and Bibliography citations.

MLA Handbook, Eighth Edition. Modern Language Association of America, 2016.

The MLA Style Center: https://style.mla.org. This website includes a quick guide and templates for creating MLA citations.

7

Common Knowledge

Common knowledge is a very complex concept. Identifying the differences between common knowledge and information that must be cited is one of the pillars of proactive plagiarism education. This chapter shows librarians and teachers how to show students the differences in information so it can be used appropriately and ethically.

COMMON KNOWLEDGE AND PLAGIARISM

The Internet has changed everything about what we consider to be common knowledge. With so much information at our fingertips for basic information, citations for everything are now unnecessary. Information that is readily available in similar versions on different websites is normally not original. The chances that we've heard or learned it before are great, even if we can't remember the exact details. There is great value in original ideas, evaluations, and conclusions from knowledgeable, talented people. The work completed by these authors is worthy of our consideration through citations.

The Internet is so vast that it is difficult to see the picture clearly. The continuous viewing of social media and web pages gives the average student the impression of knowing much more than he or she actually does. Web pages and social media give us a "good-enough" understanding of many more different subjects than the average person can read about in a book over the course of a lifetime. Digital natives have access to an enormous amount of information but lack the experience to know how to use it ethically and appropriately.

Digital information for both personal and academic common knowledge is coming from the same source—a computer screen. Just because students may be reading a lot of information on computers and personal devices, teachers should not assume that they can properly understand and use this information. For people who are reading social media posts and various web pages throughout a day, along with websites for academic purposes, it can be hard to keep things straight. This is not easy. It can also be a gamble for your students who have a different frame of reference than you.

Moving forward, students will need to understand that two different information types are on the Internet: personal and academic. Information considered for academic use has to be considered with a different set of standards than information for personal use.

Recognizing Common Knowledge

Common knowledge is an important information type to recognize for research. It is generally viewed as information that is known to everyone within a group of people. During the academic research process, students need to decide which information needs a citation. Apart from the process of writing, this decision-making about citations is a primary concern, especially for inexperienced researchers.

As a general rule, common knowledge does not need a citation. This includes factual information that is readily available in different places on the Internet. What is considered common knowledge also depends on the context of how the information is used. Information that is well known in one subject area may not be known in another subject area. There are general common knowledge and field-specific common knowledge. "General common knowledge is information such as historical dates and facts which can be easily verified in general reference sources such as an encyclopedia. Field specific common knowledge is information known to a specific community such as an institution, a city, an ethnic group, or an academic discipline" (Shi 2011, 308).

Reading Sources with Attention to Detail

A major factor in plagiarism is the failure to recognize unique, specific information written by an author and cite it properly. Information has degrees of specificity that when recognized help students decide on the correct use of citations in their academic work. The more general the information, the more likely that it is common knowledge.

Students must learn to differentiate between common knowledge and the proprietary words and ideas of others through experience and instruction. They need practice in the analysis of sentences. Digital information has released the boundaries between sources. Now, all knowledge is truly connected. We are all consciously and unconsciously influenced by what we have heard, what we have learned in school, and what we have read (both in books and on a computer screen). For example, my writing of this book was heavily influenced by the plagiarism researchers who raised the ideas in this book before me. We learn as we go along, based on what we hear, read, and see.

Where do we tell student researchers to draw the line? It will always be a judgment call. A more meaningful reading of secondary sources is more important than ever to be able to differentiate between different types of information in order to respect authors and use the information ethically.

Determining common knowledge from information that must be cited is not intuitive. Some factors that determine student aptitude in this area are as follows:

1. Previous research paper writing experience. Evaluating secondary-source information requires experience reading different types of information and using it correctly as evidence. Constructive feedback on research papers makes a difference for effective information use over time.

2. Aptitude for the subject area. When students are interested in a topic, they retain more information of all types. This may cause problems in differentiating between common knowledge and information that needs a citation. Even though students may know unique information, that doesn't mean that a citation isn't necessary.

3. Reading levels. Students with language-based reading comprehension difficulties will need more instruction in this area.

4. Previous information literacy instruction. Instruction delivered by librarians about the use of sources consistently helps this process.

Students may have additional challenges with this when completing research because of a differing context of common knowledge.

• Students for whom English is not their first language

• Those who have been homeschooled for any period of time before entering your school

- Any students who represent dramatic socioeconomic disparities within the school population
- Those with language-based learning disabilities

Advice for Teachers: What Do Your Students Know?

Students are exposed to several types of knowledge during their academic careers.

- General common academic knowledge learned as a result of previous years in school: Examples: Shakespeare wrote during the Elizabethan period. The African Campaign was fought in Egypt and Libya during World War II.

- Details retained from previous school curriculum: When students have a high degree of interest in a topic, they often remember details learned from textbooks and secondary sources. This can cause confusion when it comes to using this information in research later. These students may believe the information is common knowledge because they know it; you may have a different opinion.

- Opinions from social media, news, and other information sources: There is a continual blending of fact and opinion. Social media and the 24-hour news cycle have permanently changed the delivery of factual information. It is no longer easy to determine fact from opinion.

- Hobbies and areas of personal interest.

- Popular culture: This can include sports, music, and current trends.

- Health information about themselves, friends, and family members.

- Current grade level or subject-area knowledge.

- Common knowledge of a community—school, home, religious.

- Common knowledge of the world at large such as current events.

An important purpose in research is to teach students how to use new secondary sources as evidence to support a thesis. At the beginning of the school year, let students know what you consider to be common knowledge—information that doesn't need a citation. It is better to not allow students to use your lecture notes, textbook, or class presentations as sources. This is information that is better used for studying for tests, quizzes, and other assignments. Most textbooks represent a compilation of subject-specific common knowledge. The textbook is meant for the course work, not for research. It will also be easier for you to recognize plagiarism from secondary sources, which are written in a different vocabulary than the textbook and your classroom materials.

You may want to require citations from your students for images, primary sources, and secondary sources (books, research databases, and web pages).

- If you have a difference of opinion with a student about whether information in a research assignment needs a citation, listening to the student's justification can give you insight into what the student considers to be common knowledge in your subject area. This is important especially for students who fall within the list of those who may have a different perspective on common knowledge.

- For research assignments that focus on well-known people, ask students to exclude basic biographical information. Instead, the focus should be on the pivotal events or relationships that characterized this individual's life.

Usually, the sources your students are using will be on one overall subject, but only part of the article or book will be applicable to the research paper topic. In other words, a research database article about the work of Sigmund Freud will likely mention many aspects of his work, while the topic of the research paper may be about the unconscious mind. While students are reading secondary sources for research, there are three options in the decision-making process for how to use each sentence. (1) The information is not related to the thesis and should be disregarded. Even though it is related to the topic, it is irrelevant. It may not be common knowledge, but it is still considered irrelevant. (2) The information is related to the thesis. It is specific and requires a citation. (3) The information may be related to the thesis but is common knowledge and should not be included in the paper.

A collaboration with a librarian can help your students learn the process of differentiating between common knowledge and information that must be cited. This is part of understanding information relevance. If you don't have time to incorporate this instruction during a regular school day, ask your librarian to do this instruction when you have a planned absence. While it is essential for the research process, this instruction is important enough to be done anytime during the school year.

Appendix I includes two lesson plans on this topic. The "Common Knowledge, Citable Information, or Irrelevant? Lesson Plan" is a sentence-level approach, with research database articles to determine ethical use of information. "Considering the Audience: Common Knowledge Questions" covers recognizing the audience when deciding whether to use a citation.

Class Examples

Read the examples. Decide which sentences are common knowledge, are irrelevant, or need a citation. Encourage students to discuss different opinions about this information.

Example 1

The well-publicized murder trial for acclaimed author James Yeager began in Baltimore County after six months of legal delays. On the second day, the judge asked a male jury member if he had any contact with the defendant's family. Another jury member saw him speaking to Yeager's mother at a food truck in front of the courthouse during lunch and reported it to the judge. Even though he denied it, the judge replaced him with an alternate juror. Based on the implications of this misconduct, Yeager's attorney was able to obtain a mistrial the following day.

The well-publicized murder trial of James Yeager began in Baltimore County after six months of legal delays. On the second day, the judge asked a male jury member if he had any contact with the defendant's family. Another jury member saw him speaking to Yeager's mother at a food truck in front of the courthouse during lunch and reported it to the judge. Even though he denied it, the judge replaced him with an alternate juror. Based on the implications of this misconduct, Yeager's attorney was able to obtain a mistrial the following day.

The sentences that are underlined once are not common knowledge. This is unique information that needs a citation. The first sentence is common knowledge if the audience is local to the trial. Otherwise, it is irrelevant. The sentence about the alternate juror is not as important as the fact that there was a mistrial based on the implication that the juror spoke to the defendant's family member. These two underlined sentences should be paraphrased.

Example 2

Technology mixed with serendipity can create an artist's career. The little-known artist from Cleveland, Markus Levine, surprised the art world by being asked to exhibit his painting, "Birds in Flight," at the new artist's section of the Museum of Modern Art. Levine's newfound popularity came from an accidental introduction to the museum's new assistant curator at a gallery opening in Brooklyn when visiting New York. He was able to show the assistant curator his work through his smartphone and website. His latest work, "Utopia," was just sold for double its $5,000.00 asking price.

Technology mixed with serendipity can create an artist's career. The little known artist from Cleveland, Markus Levine, surprised the art world by being asked to exhibit his painting, "Birds in Flight," at the new artist section of the Museum of Modern Art. Levine's newfound popularity came from an accidental introduction to the museum's new assistant curator at a gallery opening in Brooklyn when he was visiting the city. He was able to show the assistant curator his work through his smartphone and website. His latest work, "Utopia," was just sold for double its $5,000.00 asking price.

The sentences that are underlined are not common knowledge. The use of technology for many purposes is common knowledge, but the fact that Levine was able to show his work through his smartphone then arrange for a museum exhibit is a unique, specific incident. The fact that Levine is from Cleveland is unique information since it is considered outside of the "art world" of New York. The names of his paintings and the price are specific. The way he came about the exhibit at the Museum of Modern Art and the meeting of the curator is also unique information. All this information should be cited.

Example 3

The library science education process has changed dramatically since Melvil Dewey created the first library school at Columbia University in 1887. Future librarians now study complex, technology-driven topics such as data analytics, digital curation, and information infrastructure. The days when these students spent an entire course learning how to conduct a reference interview with library patrons are over. Reference questions are when people ask librarians for information such as where to find answers for homework questions or referrals to books or research databases for research. The Internet and the continued emergence of technology will continue to drive a new framework for how librarians work each day.

The library science education process has changed dramatically since Melvil Dewey created the first library school at Columbia University in 1887. Future librarians now study complex, technology-driven topics such as data analytics, digital curation, and information infrastructure. The days when students spent a lot of instructional time learning how to conduct in-person reference interviews in order to recommend books or other sources for library patrons are over because of the Internet. The Internet and the emergence of technology will continue to drive a new framework for how librarians work each day.

The sentences that are underlined are not common knowledge. Many people have heard of Melvil Dewey and know he lived a long time ago. The fact that Melvil Dewey created the first library school at Columbia University in 1887 is not information that most people know ("common knowledge"), but it is available readily with an Internet search. The next two sentences are unique information but wordy. These sentences should be paraphrased. The changes in the library school curriculum are unique knowledge and should be cited.

Advice for Students

Background knowledge is general information about the subject. You may already know it. The only place where background knowledge is appropriate to use is in the first few paragraphs of your paper. It might be useful for an introduction to the topic area. There is an explanation about common knowledge in Chapter 6. You always want the best, most specific information to cite in your paper. When reading secondary sources to (possibly) include in your research paper, you will need to determine whether the information is common knowledge, unique information that needs a citation, or information that is irrelevant. Irrelevant information may be unique (not common knowledge) but still not appropriate for your research.

Here are some examples for deciding whether information is common knowledge (no citation necessary) and information that needs to be cited. This is a judgment call on your part. You will need to be prepared to be wrong occasionally.

No Citation Required: Common Knowledge or Background Knowledge

- The information is from a class lecture or your textbook. You're writing a paper for this class. This can be considered background knowledge.

- The sentence is a very general statement. Example: The Vietnam War caused many long-lasting problems for veterans.

- You learned the information during a previous year of school. This type of information is now considered background knowledge. You should not reuse information from previous school years.

- General biographical information of well- known people or historical figures.

- Popular culture. Example: Paul McCartney and Ringo Starr are the remaining members of the Beatles who are still living.

- The information is known in your community, state, or region. Example: Olympic swimmer Missy Franklin went to Regis Jesuit High School in Denver, Colorado. This is common knowledge in the Denver and Aurora, Colorado, areas. It may not be common knowledge outside of the Denver area.

- It is a subject-area fact that can be found on the Internet in many places. The research paper is in this subject area. Example: Germany invaded Poland on September 1, 1939.

Needs a Citation: Not Common Knowledge

- A first-person account of an event from a news article.

- Research or survey data that has been created by you or others. This is often found in chart form in secondary sources. Lab results also fall into this category.

- Definitions with technical language or vocabulary.

- Detailed information from another subject area you use in a paper either as a direct quote or paraphrase. Example: In a history paper about suicide, you use these sentences: In all of Shakespeare's plays, there were thirteen suicides. Psychologist Michael Evans noted that suicide was very commonplace among the lower class in Elizabethan times.

- *Any* information from another subject area you use in a paper that you're unsure if the teacher knows or not.

- Information where specific numbers, weights, measurements, or quantities are mentioned. Example: Government reports note that during World War II, there were 7,500 American planes destroyed during all the fighting.

- An important person's exact words or opinion.

- The sentence contains a list of items. This is a sign that it should be paraphrased. Example: The school's football team suffered from numerous injuries, including a torn left-leg ligament, two broken ankles, a broken collarbone, and various hairline fractures.

- A specific term is noted in quotes within the sentence. Example: The beatnik poets changed how everyone viewed "text" because of the major changes in expression after World War II.

- The information provides a unique understanding of another issue or idea.
  Example: Dr. Jane Allen's research on women's issues throughout history during times of political upheaval is the basis for the position paper on protest marches presented by NOW during their March meeting.

- When you are reading biography research database articles, look for new or unique information such as key relationships, pivotal moment and events, and important quotes from this individual which you may not have heard before. This type of information should be paraphrased. Avoid or minimize basic biographical information about this person that is available through various sources through a basic Internet search.

- Information from news articles that are a firsthand account of an event.

REFERENCE

Shi, Ling. 2011. "Common Knowledge, Learning, and Citation Practices in University Writing." *National Council of Teachers of English* 45, no. 3 (February): 308–34. http://www.jstor.org/stable/40997768.

8

Digital Images

This chapter covers the use of digital images in presentations and projects created by students. There are different expectations for the ethical use of digital images than books, web pages, and research database articles. The term "digital image" means a photograph or other graphic representation that is appropriate for a student to use in a presentation for academic credit. It is another type of secondary source. Some images are "born digital." This means that the image has never been in print. An example is a photograph that is taken by a digital camera and uploaded to a website. Other images, such as the ones found in the formal digital collections discussed in this section, have once existed in print format.

All images are protected by copyright even if you don't see a copyright sign next to it. Legally, permission is necessary for the reuse of copyrighted work. Two important issues with the use of images in academic work are the creation of image citations to avoid plagiarism and copyright. If an image is used in a presentation without a citation, this is considered plagiarism.

Technically, without permission from the creator, it is also a copyright violation. It is also possible to cite an image and, without permission from the creator to use it, be in violation of copyright. There are legal consequences to using an image under copyright without permission. The only type of images where permission is not required is public domain images. These are images, often grouped in collections, where the copyright has expired or the creator of the image has allowed for it to be used without restriction.

Images are permitted to be used for academic purposes under the doctrine of Fair Use. You need to understand these guidelines, but this is a legal doctrine that the courts use to decide whether use of a copyrighted image is Fair Use. There are four factors. (1) The use must be for nonprofit educational purposes. (2) Factual works are more likely to support Fair Use than creative works. (3) The amount used of the copyrighted work—both in quality and quantity—is important. Using small portions is more likely to support Fair Use. (4) The effect of the use on the market value and overall value of the work (U.S. Copyright Office 2019).

ADVICE FOR TEACHERS ABOUT DIGITAL IMAGES

Digital images are an important type of intellectual property. While citing images can be considered a little more complicated, expecting students to cite images in presentations helps them understand the importance of respecting intellectual property rights across all information types. The only way to build competency is through consistent expectations.

Teachers should be conscious of the use of copyrighted work on online learning management systems, including digital images. The reuse of copyrighted work and posting it on the Internet represent multiple distributions, which could be misinterpreted as outside of educational Fair Use. While these systems are not available to the public, there is always the possibility of information being seen casually by others in private or public spaces or places where network connections are not secure. At the very least, it is important to carefully cite all secondary-source information including images on learning management systems.

If your students regularly use images from Google Images, this is a good time to collaborate with a librarian. Whether or not your students use a citation tool, a prerequisite for accurate digital image citations is competence with web page article citations. Google Images originate from websites. They will need to understand the idea that the image and web page article are two separate sources as well as the publication parts of the web page and image.

Requiring the source documentation of images is essential, even from the youngest students. Before your students are competent with online citation tools and web page article citations, a minimum requirement for citing should be to expect a URL under the image in the presentation. A slide at the end of the presentation with a list of the images should be mandatory; then you can expect full citations.

Some other ways to improve your students' use of digital images are as follows.

- Images should not be used in presentations for decorative purposes. The use of images in a presentation should add substantial meaning.

- Restricting your students' use of digital images to well-known digital collections that provide citations is a good option. These credible image collections are highly developed along different themes and easily searchable. There is a list at the end of this chapter.

- Ask your librarian to provide your students with an overview of digital image citations using your school's preferred citation tool.

- If you have your own website for teaching outside of your school's learning management system, do not post your students' presentations with digital images there.

- If it applies to your assignment, encourage your students to use their own digital photographs for presentations.

- Since so many digital collections feature historical artifacts like letters and memorabilia, encourage the use of these images as primary sources.

- If you believe you will reuse the same digital images over many school years in your teaching, contact the copyright holder for legal permission. You will find that many people will happily cooperate with the use of their work if you ask permission and provide attribution. The U.S. Copyright Office offers information on this topic: https://www.copyright.gov/circs/m10.pdf.

CATEGORIES OF DIGITAL IMAGES

Google Images

This has become one of most common places where students search for images. Google Images is an aggregator that searches for images on web pages all over the Internet. These images are compiled and organized into categories for searching. It does not provide citations or determine copyright status. To use the image, click through to the originating web page. This image should be considered a separate, specific type of source found on a web page, along with the web page article.

Images can be published in a variety of different ways. Some will have an image title and creator. Others will have no identifiable information at all. It is critical to remember that the web page article and the digital image are two separate sources on the website.

Titles are an important first consideration. Some digital images will have titles at the bottom horizontal edge of the image. This is most likely with news sources or publications. The image title may be stated as a descriptive sentence. Example: Penguins in the Antarctic Adapt to Global Warming. Other images will not have a title, and you will have to create one for the citation.

Example: An untitled image of a rock formation in Sedona, Arizona, can be titled "Sedona Rock Formation." The image of a large group of red rocks is with an article about the culture of Sedona, Arizona.

The image title should not be confused with the web page article title. To create the citation yourself or through an online citation tool, it is necessary to identify the web page article title and the website title. These are two separate, distinct sources. The web page article title is placed directly above the paragraphs of text for the article. The website title is usually at the top left of the web page, which describes the website in a general way.

Here's what you need to know about digital images you use from Google Images and other web pages.

- A web page article and image are normally near one another on a web page. The image is intended to enhance the information in the article. The article and the image each need a separate citation.

- The author of the web page article is *not* the creator of the image. If there is an author for the article but not for the image, do *not* use the article author as the image creator for the citation.

- Many images will not have an author/creator name listed with it.

- If there is no image title, you will need to create one.

- If there is no other date, the article publication date can be used as the publication date for the image.

- Images and web page articles are created by two different people, but the publisher is the same—the website.

- News and other publication-type websites are most likely to have an image that adds information to the article.

When deciding to use an image, complete a brief analysis. Here are questions to ask before using an online citation tool or citation guide:

- Is there a creator/author name listed with the image? Don't confuse the image creator with the author of the web page article.

- Check the image—does it have a title and creator listed? This is normally found on the bottom horizontal edge of the image.

- What is the publication date of the image? For undated images, you can use the date of publication for the accompanying article if available. If not, use the copyright date.

- What is the web page title? This is normally found at the top or top left of the web page.

- Who is the publisher? Check for this at the copyright sign at the bottom of the web page.

After this analysis, use a citation tool or the examples in this chapter to create a citation.

Digital Collections

Many high-quality digital image collections are available on the Internet. These collections make photographs, cartoons, maps, manuscripts, letters, postcards, and similar artifacts available for academic use. These digital collections offer a solid alternative to random Google searches for images. Some of these digital collections have a citation tool. In many cases, the copyright status of the image has already been determined. You still have the responsibility to determine if your use of the image merits Fair Use. The images found in these collections have often been in print or another format. You can also find searchable digital collections through major universities and presidential libraries. Here are a few of the best collections available:

New York Public Library Digital Collections (https://digitalcollections .nypl.org/): This diverse, extensive historical media collection covers an amazing array of subjects, including theater, historical events, popular culture, zoology, and architecture. It includes a citation tool. NYPL also has a strictly public domain collection that is searchable from a drop-down menu from the search box.

Library of Congress Digital Collections (https://www.loc.gov/collec tions/): The Library of Congress extensively documents the American experience. Each image has a citation and Rights and Access, which explains what is known about the copyright by the Library of Congress.

The Metropolitan Museum of Art Digital Collections (https://libmmma .contentdm.oclc.org): This collection features a wide collection of art, architecture, and rare books. A citation is not provided, but there is an explanation of the copyright status for each item.

Public domain images: Numerous public domain image websites can be found through an Internet search. One of the best is Wikimedia Commons (https://commons.wikimedia.org). This site includes all types of media files, including images, which are free of copyright restrictions. However, these images do need to be cited.

Creative Commons (https://creativecommons.org/share-your-work/licensing-types-examples/licensing-examples/): Creative Commons is a website that allows contributors to place their work for others to use through a Creative Commons license. There are various Creative Commons license options, but all require attribution. This gives an explanation of each type of Creative Commons license.

CITATIONS FOR DIGITAL IMAGES

The books for the three major citation styles do not directly address citations for images. Here are some examples.

Google Images

When you use an image from Google Images, your citation will be for a web page that "points" to the image instead of the article.

MLA Examples

Basic format

The underlined portions of the image citation example are the same as a citation for a web page.
Creator Last Name, First Name. *Title of Image.* Copyright Date. <u>Web Page Title, Year of Publication, URL. Accessed Day Month Year.</u>

Example 1—image with a creator name and image title

(1) Richards, Jeremy. (2) *Colony of Rockhopper Penguins.* (3) 2018. (4) *Lonely Planet,* (5) April 2018, (6) www.lonelyplanet.com/falkland-islands/travel-tips-and-articles/an-essential-guide-to-the-falkland-islands/40625c8c-8a11-5710-a052-1479d2755599. (7) Accessed 9 July 2018.

    (1)   Creator's Last Name, First Name.
    (2)   Title of image.
    (3)   Publication date.
    (4)   Title of the web page.
    (5)   Copyright date.
    (6)   URL for the image.
    (7)   Accessed Day Month Year.

Example 2—image without a creator name

(1) *Roman Fish Processing Factory.* (2) 2018. (3) *SmartNews,* (4) Smithsonian Institution, (5) www.smithsonianmag.com/smart-news/romans-may-have-hunted-whales-extinction-their-home-waters-180969605/. (6) Accessed 16 July 2018.

1. Image title.
2. Publication date.
3. Web page title (container).
4. Publisher.
5. URL for this image.
6. Accessed Day Month Year.

Example 3—image without a creator/author name or a title

In this case, you should create a basic title with no more than three or four words. Follow the citation model for example 2.

APA Examples

Example 1—a photograph from a web page with a creator name and title listed

(1) Richards, J. (2) (2018). (3) *Colony of rockhopper penguins* (4) [Photograph]. (5) Retrieved from https://www.lonelyplanet.com/falkland-islands/travel-tips-and-articles/an-essential-guide-to-the-falkland-islands/40625c8c-8a11-5710-a052-1479d2755599.

(1) Creator Last Name, First Initial.
(2) Publication date.
(3) Title of image.
(4) Type of image in [brackets].
(5) Retrieved from URL for the image.

Example 2—a photograph from a web page without a creator name

(1) *Labrador retriever* (2) [Photograph]. (3) (2018). (4) Retrieved from https://www.akc.org/dog-breeds/labrador-retriever/.

(1) Title of image.
(2) Type of image in [brackets].
(3) Publication date.
(4) Retrieved from URL for the image.

Chicago Author-Date Examples

Example 1—a photograph from a web page with a creator name and title listed.

(1) Richards, Jeremy. (2) 2018. (3) *Colony of Rockhopper Penguins.* (4) Photograph. (5) Lonely Planet. (6) April 2018. (7) Accessed February 23, 2019.(8)https://www.lonelyplanet.com/falkland-islands/travel-tips-and-

articles/an-essential-guide-to-the-falkland-islands/40625c8c-8a11-5710-a052-1479d2755599.

(1)   Creator's Last Name, First Name.
(2)   Publication year.
(3)   Title of image.
(4)   Type of image.
(5)   Web page title.
(6)   Publication date.
(7)   Accessed date.
(8)   URL for the image.

Example 2—a photograph from a web page without a creator name.

(1) Labrador Retriever. (2) 2018. (3) Photograph. (4) American Kennel Club. (5) Accessed February 23, 2019. (6) https://www.akc.org/dog-breeds/labrador-retriever/.

(1)   Title of image.
(2)   Publication year.
(3)   Type of image.
(4)   Website publisher.
(5)   Accessed date.
(6)   URL for the image.

Chicago Notes and Bibliography Examples

Example 1—a photograph from a web page with a creator name and title listed

(1) Richards, Jeremy. (2) *Colony of Rockhopper Penguins.* (3) Photograph. (4) Lonely Planet. (5) April 2018. (6) Accessed February 23, 2019. (7) https://www.lonelyplanet.com/falkland-islands/travel-tips-and-articles/an-essential-guide-to-the-falkland-islands/40625c8c-8a11-5710-a052-1479d2755599.

(1)   Creator's Last Name, First Name.
(2)   Title of image.
(3)   Type of image.
(4)   Web page title.
(5)   Publication date.
(6)   Accessed date.
(7)   URL for the image.

Example 2—a photograph from a web page without a creator name

(1) Labrador Retriever. (2) Photograph. (3) American Kennel Club. (4) Accessed February 23, 2019. (5) https://www.akc.org/dog-breeds/labrador-retriever/.

(1) Image title.
(2) Type of image.
(3) Website title.
(4) Accessed date.
(5) URL for the image.

ADVICE FOR LIBRARIANS ABOUT DIGITAL IMAGES

Your students will have the least amount of practice with digital images. One of the most challenging aspects of using Google Images is to show students that the digital image and the web page article are two different sources. It is difficult to create a correct image citation without competence with web page citations. Even if you can't provide classroom instruction in this area, it is worthwhile to create examples and materials for students and teachers which cover the following areas:

• Citation for a digital image with a creator listed and an image title

• Citation for a digital image without a creator but with an image title

• Citation for a digital image without a creator and without an image title

• Citation for a digital image with a creator but without an image title

These examples can be posted on the library's web page. The evaluation process for Google Images mentioned in a previous section is perfect for creating a screencast for students to view. Consider whether your students would benefit from a review of how to create an image in an online citation tool.

ADVICE FOR STUDENTS ABOUT DIGITAL IMAGES

When you use an online citation tool for digital images, use "born digital" or similar term for the type of source. Digital images are just like any other source. If your current teacher does not require you to cite digital images, be aware that other teachers may expect you to do so.

All digital images need to be cited in your academic work. The only exception is Microsoft Word and PowerPoint clip art. This does not need to be cited because it originates from a computer program.

REFERENCE

U.S. Copyright Office. "More on Fair Use." U.S. Copyright Office Fair Use Index. Last modified March 2019. Accessed April 2, 2019. https://www.copyright.gov/fair-use/more-info.html.

RESOURCES

Center for Media and Social Impact: http://cmsimpact.org/program/fair-use/. This organization from American University supports Fair Use, copyright, and intellectual property issues for different professions.

Fair Use: https://www.copyright.gov/fair-use/more-info.html. This information from the U.S. Copyright Office explains the criteria for Fair Use.

Library of Congress Copyright and Primary Sources for Teachers: http://www.loc .gov/teachers/usingprimarysources/copyright.html.

Reproduction of Copyrighted Works by Educators and Librarians: https://www .copyright.gov/circs/circ21.pdf. This article provides information about Fair Use.

Conclusion

The different types and quantities of information available for the average person on the Internet are staggering. This information has the potential to educate us in ways that weren't possible twenty years ago. This growth demands that we teach high school and college students the necessary skills to locate, evaluate, and ethically use this information. None of this is intuitive, even for digital natives. When teachers introduce plagiarism education in the classroom, it lays the groundwork for students to be more effective academic, personal, and professional information decision makers over the long term.

Citation tools and plagiarism checkers are not a substitute for educating students about the ethical use of information. Both are very useful and deserve a place in schools. Citation tools help students organize citations, allowing more time to focus on writing. Plagiarism checkers provide teachers with a relative indicator of plagiarism after the fact, allowing them to decide on further education for the student or appropriate penalties. Research shows that plagiarism education instruction works. These tools are not a substitute for teaching students paraphrasing, citation styles, and the differences between facts, opinions, and common knowledge, all necessary components for avoiding plagiarism *before* the paper is handed in for a grade.

Plagiarism education and information literacy instruction are naturally connected. Librarians, as information experts, should be at the center of this education process, either individually or in collaboration with teachers. When teachers collaborate with librarians for information literacy and plagiarism education, students gain awareness of how to locate the best information and use it ethically. This improves the quality of writing.

The reality is that some plagiarism will always be undetected. Copy and paste, in particular, cannot be prevented. Teaching effective paraphrasing and summarizing to students should be seen as essential, ethical information management skills that help students reduce plagiarism in research but also in homework assignments that require use of the Internet to complete.

Reducing plagiarism begins with awareness. Digital information will continue to be at the center of plagiarism problems in the future. We all need to understand, through a proactive educational process, that authors deserve our respect through the ethical use of information under every circumstance.

APPENDIX A

The Anatomy of a Web Page

- A1: The Anatomy of a Web Page Lesson Plan—All Citation Styles
- A2: Evaluating a Web Page for Academic Use

APPENDIX A1

The Anatomy of a Web Page Lesson Plan—All Citation Styles

Objectives: Web pages are dynamic sources without strict publication standards. As a result, each one requires analysis. Reviewing the parts of a typical web page reduces plagiarism and improves citations. It increases student accuracy with online citation tools.

As a result of this lesson, students will understand the following:

- How to identify authorship for a web page article
- The various titles found on a web page
- The role of a publisher for web pages and websites
- How to identify the publication date of a web page article
- When to use copyright date for the publication date

Delivery: Classroom discussion of vocabulary and parts of a web page with instruction and classwork. A librarian should deliver this instruction to students when possible. This is a valuable skill to review at the beginning of the school year. It should also be completed during the research process when web pages are used as sources. Provide students with feedback on the web page citation classwork with grade or during class.

Discussion: While students use web pages frequently, they may not fully understand how and why web pages are developed on the Internet. Emphasize the correct terminology. A website is a collection of web pages. A web page is what appears on the computer screen after searching using a web browser such as Google Chrome or Internet Explorer. Websites can have one web page or thousands, depending on the site. "Web page article" is the correct term to use for the article that students use as source.

Length of time: One class period.

Materials: If necessary, provide students a citation guide with the parts of a website during this instruction. This guide should also include the correct author and date formats for your citation style. The teacher needs to create a mock citation for students to complete for the classwork.

LESSON PLAN

Choose an appropriate web page connected to the subject area to use as a teaching example. For example, for a ninth-grade history class, a web page from PBS on Ancient Rome is appropriate. Project the web page on a screen for students. The goal is to take a "tour" of the parts of the web page and build a citation for the web page article.

As you discuss each part of the web page, build a citation on the board, beginning with the author. To understand the authorship and publication process, all parts of the web page should be discussed even if it is not part of the citation. This is a list of the individual parts of the web page, which should be covered in the classroom discussion.

- **Author:** For web pages, definitive authorship can be fleeting. Web page articles may have an author listed, or authorship may revert to an organization. The web page sources most likely to have a person as an author are newspapers and other dated online publications. If there is a person as an author, it is near the article title or, less likely, at the end of the article. Advise students that they should not go searching if it is not clearly stated near the article itself.

- **Web page article:** The web page article is the paragraphs of text on the web page. This is the source. Students read the web page article to find a relevant direct quote or sentences with enough importance to paraphrase.

- **Title of web page article:** This is located right above the article text. Let your students see that this is where the title fonts begin to change. The web page article title font will be larger than the article text font. It may also be a different-style font.

- **Web page title:** This is normally located above the article title and under the top navigation bar. It is a broader title, a "container" that sums up the content of this section of the website. This font will be larger than the article title. Not every web page will have an article title. Sometimes, the web page title and publisher are the same.

- **Publisher:** If your students are inexperienced researchers, discuss the concept of publisher. Many high school and college students do not read print newspapers or magazines regularly. Here are two points to mention:

  - The same publisher can create content in print and online.
  - Organizations and cultural institutions publish content on their websites.

- **Publication date, copyright date:** There are no standards for how dates are displayed on a web page. It may be listed as a year at the copyright sign or a full date near the article title for publications that publish very regularly.

- **Location:** Each web page has its own web address on the World Wide Web.

CLASSWORK

This skill needs to be reinforced through classwork. Students should create a citation for two different web pages. Alternative 1—Handout: Prepare two web page screenshots, one for each side of the paper. These screenshots should include part of the article and the top of the web page. This is where the information for the citation is located. Below the screenshot of the web page, create a mock citation where students "fill in the blanks" for the citation after analyzing the web page. For very inexperienced students, circle the parts of the web page on the screenshot, which are part of the citation with a computer pen if available, for matching with the blanks in the citation. For more experienced students who need a review, you will not need to circle the parts of the citation. Alternative 2: Provide students two web page links, and ask them to complete a citation using a citation guide.

RECOMMENDATIONS FOR CLASSWORK

MLA: One web page with an author; one without an author.

Chicago Notes and Bibliography: This exercise is an opportunity to practice both footnotes and citations for web pages. Use one web page without a fixed publication date. One web page should have an author and publication date.

Chicago Author-Date: Use one web page without a fixed publication date. One web page should have an author and publication date.

APA: One web page with an author and precise publication date (online newspaper or magazine). One web page without a person named as author or without a publication date.

APPENDIX A2

Evaluating a Web Page for Academic Use

Credible, authoritative web pages have specific, better-written information that is more difficult to plagiarize undetected. Students need to know the parts of a web page (see "The Anatomy of a Web Page Lesson Plan—All Citation Styles," Appendix A1), along with the characteristics of a web page appropriate for academic use. Here are some guidelines.

AUTHORSHIP AND CREDIBILITY

Look for an author's name near the title of the article. Even if none is listed, you should always be able to contact the company or organization that is responsible for the content on the site. Credible, authoritative websites want you to contact them with questions. There is normally an area noted as "Contact Us" or "About Us." It should be apparent that this information has been written by experts in the subject area. The term "expert" means a person or organization with a track record in the subject. This includes websites written by known academic, historical, and cultural institutions; universities; and prominent professionals. Major newspapers and magazines such as the *New York Times* and *Time* also have a long track record of credibility.

From *Combating Plagiarism: A Hands-On Guide for Librarians, Teachers, and Students* by Terry Darr. Santa Barbara, CA: Libraries Unlimited. Copyright © 2019.

CURRENCY

A credible, authoritative web page is current. Check for dates on the website near the article title and the copyright date. It should be recently updated. In this case, "current" means that the website has been updated within the last calendar year. For news and current events, "current" means as close as possible to the actual event.

OBJECTIVITY

The majority of the information on a credible web page should be factual and objective. If there is commentary or other opinions, this information should be clearly marked on the web page so there is no confusion.

LINKS

The links on a credible web page expand your knowledge on the topic. These links can be internal (on the same site) or external (other websites). There should not be any broken links. Ideally, once you read the article and click on related links, your knowledge should be comprehensive on the topic.

THE ROLE OF ADS

Except for the websites of major newspapers and magazines, web pages appropriate for academic use normally do not have any advertising. Web pages from known academic, historical, and cultural institutions; universities; and prominent professionals are self-supporting, so no advertising is necessary. The purpose of these web pages is to inform readers not to sell products or services. Major newspapers and magazines that are available online will often have advertising. This is normal since newspapers and magazines are published more frequently, with more content for a wider audience.

APPENDIX B

Identify the Parts of the Citation

- B1: Identify the Parts of the Citation Lesson Plan: All Citation Styles
- B2: Identify the Parts of the Citation Exercise: APA

  Identify the Parts of the Citation Answer Key: APA
- B3: Identify the Parts of the Citation Exercise: Chicago Author-Date

  Identify the Parts of the Citation Answer Key: Chicago Author-Date
- B4: Identify the Parts of the Citation Exercise: Chicago Notes and Bibliography

  Identify the Parts of the Citation Answer Key: Chicago Notes and Bibliography
- B5: Identify the Parts of the Citation Exercise: MLA

  Identify the Parts of the Citation Answer Key: MLA

APPENDIX B1

Identify the Parts of the Citation Lesson Plan: All Citation Styles

Objectives: Visual recognition skills for citations improve proofreading and the use of online citations tools. It helps students understand the type of source, authorship, and publication process, adding important context. This exercise has two objectives: (1) identify the type of source by seeing the citation and (2) identify the individual parts of the citation. This adds context to the source.

As a result of this lesson, students will understand the following:

- The visual, individual indicators of a book citation: author, title, publisher, and publication year

- The visual, individual indicators of a scholarly journal citation: author, article title, scholarly journal title, volume, issue number, and page range

- The visual, individual indicators of a web page article: author, article title, publisher, date of publication, and URL

Delivery: There are options for MLA, Chicago (Notes and Bibliography), Chicago (Author-Date), MLA, and APA. These citation questions can be projected on a screen for students to answer the questions verbally or provided on a handout. This can be delivered by a librarian or teacher. If this is delivered as a warm-up, the instructor should call on as many students as possible for answers. Students will begin to see the patterns in the citation style.

Length of time: Varies. Approximately fifteen minutes is necessary for a warm-up.

Source materials: The instructor should prepare citation examples appropriate for the resources most commonly used by students. A citation guide can be provided to students if necessary.

APPENDIX B2

Identify the Parts of the Citation Exercise: APA

Answer the questions about each citation.

1. Burleigh, M. (2008). *Blood and rage: A cultural history of terrorism.* New York, NY: Harper Perennial.

   a. What type of source is this? How do you know?

   b. Who is the author?

   c. What is *Blood and rage: A cultural history of terrorism*?

   d. What is "Harper Perennial"?

   e. What is the significance of 2008?

   f. What does "New York" mean in this citation?

2. Grant, R. (2016, September). Deep in the swamps, archaeologists are finding how fugitive slaves kept their freedom. *Smithsonian.* Retrieved from http://www.smithsonianmag.com/history/deep-swamps-archaeologists-fugitive-slaves-kept-freedom-180960122

   a. What type of source is this? How do you know?

   b. What is "(2016, September)"?

   c. Does this article have an author? How do you know?

    d.   What is the meaning of "Retrieved from http://www.smithson ianmag.com/history/deep-swamps-archaeologists-fugitive-slaves-kept-freedom-180960122"?

    e.   What is *Smithsonian* in this citation?

3.   Jones, S. (2018). Elvis Presley biography. Retrieved December 17, 2018, from Graceland: The Home of Elvis Presley website: https://www .graceland.com/biography

    a.   What type of source is this? How do you know?

    b.   Does this article have an author? How do you know?

    c.   What is the significance of 2018 in this citation?

    d.   What is "Elvis Presley biography"? Circle one.

        Article title   Web page title   Publisher

    e.   What is "Graceland: The Home of Elvis Presley"? Circle one.

        Publisher   Web page title   Article title

4.   Tate, J. (2004). My mother, my text: writing and remembering in Julia Alvarez's *In the name of Salome. Bilingual Review, 28*(1), 54+. Retrieved from http://link.galegroup.com/apps/doc/A164254177/LitRC?u=win5026&sid=LitRC&xid=2877752f.

    a.   What type of source is this? How do you know?

    b.   What is *Bilingual Review*?

    c.   Does this article have an author? How do you know?

    d.   Why does this citation have a URL? What does this URL tell you about the source?

    e.   When was this article originally published?

    f.   What is the title of the article?

5.   Yoder, J. (2009). The jungle (Upton Sinclair). In H. Bloom (Ed.), *Bloom's literary themes: The American dream* (pp. 97–107). New York, NY: Infobase.

    a.   What type of source is this? How do you know?

    b.   What does "In H. Bloom (Ed.)" mean?

    c.   What does "pp. 97–107" signify?

    d.   What is "The jungle (Upton Sinclair)"?

    e.   Who is the publisher?

    f.   What is the original source where this article originated?

    g.   Who wrote this article (chapter)?

6.   Etzioni, A. (2018). Apple: Good business, poor citizen? *Journal of Business Ethics, 151*(1), 1–11. doi:http://dx.doi.org/10.1007/s10551-016-3233-4.

   a.   What type of source is this? How do you know?
   b.   What does "2018" signify?
   c.   What does "vol. 151, no. 1" mean about this publication's age?
   d.   Does this article have an author? How do you know?
   e.   Is the *Journal of Business Ethics* a scholarly journal?
   f.   What is doi:http://dx.doi.org/10.1007/s10551-016-3233-4?

7.   Toni Morrison. (2016). In *Contemporary authors online.* Detroit, MI: Gale. Retrieved from http://link.galegroup.com/apps/doc/H1000070669/LitRC?u=win5026&sid=LitRC&xid=c76a7dfb.

   a.   What type of source is this? How do you know?
   b.   Where did the article "Toni Morrison" originate?
   c.   What is the name of the research database for this article?
   d.   Does this article have an author?
   e.   What does "2016" mean?

8.   Mack, D. (1993, June 17). Danger indoctrination: War on drugs? War on parents. *Wall Street Journal.* Retrieved from https://search.proquest.com/docview/398387030?accountid=41092.

   a.   What type of source is this? How do you know?
   b.   Why doesn't this URL point to the *Wall Street Journal*?

9.   Goffe, L. G. (2013, Aug.). The unfinished march. *New African*, 80–82. Retrieved from https://search.proquest.com/docview/1433264371?accountid=41092.

   a.   What type of source is this? How do you know?
   b.   What is *New African*?
   c.   How many pages is this article?
   d.   What does "Aug. 2013" mean?

10.   Gates, M. (2019). *The power of lift: How empowering women changes the world* [OverDrive].

   a.   What type of source is this? How do you know?
   b.   What are some other types of e-book editions you might use?

IDENTIFY THE PARTS OF THE CITATION
ANSWER KEY: APA

1. a. This is a print book. There is an author, an italicized title, and publisher.
    b. Burleigh, M. is the author.
    c. The title of a print book. For inexperienced researchers, this is a good time to discuss book subtitles.
    d. The publisher of the book.
    e. The year of publication.
    f. The location of the publisher.

2. a. This is a web page. You can tell from the URL and "Retrieved from" in the citation.
    b. "(2016, September)" is the year and month of publication for the article in *Smithsonian Magazine*.
    c. Yes. "Grant, R." is the author of the article. The name is at the beginning of the citation.
    d. "Retrieved from" means that this is a web page article.
    e. *Smithsonian* published this article.

3. a. It is a web page article. Website is mentioned in the citation.
    b. Yes. "S. Jones" is the author. The name is at the beginning of the citation.
    c. The year of publication (copyright date).
    d. Article title.
    e. Publisher and web page title.

4. a. This is a research database article. There are a scholarly journal title listed, *Bilingual Review*, and the volume/issue 28(1).
    b. *Bilingual Review* is a scholarly journal.
    c. Yes. "J. Tate" is the author. The name is at the beginning of the citation.
    d. Research databases are digital resources that have a URL.
    e. 2004. This is found next to the author's name.
    f. My mother, my text: writing and remembering in Julia Alvarez's In the name of Salome.

5. a. This is a chapter in an edited book. You can tell by the book title in the citation, the page range, and "H. Bloom (Ed.)," which means there is an editor.

    b. "H. Bloom" is the editor of the book, which follows his name, *Bloom's literary themes: The American dream.*

    c. This is the page range where this article (chapter) is found in the book.

    d. It is the article (chapter) title.

    e. Infobase.

    f. *Bloom's literary themes: The American dream.*

    g. Jon Yoder.

6. a. It is a research database article. You can tell because of the doi and the journal title—this shows it came from a journal.

    b. The year of publication.

    c. "Volume 151" means the publication has been in existence for 151 years. "No. 1" means this is the first issue of 2018.

    d. A. Etzioni. The author's name is at the beginning of the citation.

    e. Yes, this is a scholarly journal. You can tell by the "academic" title.

    f. doi:http://dx.doi.org/10.1007/s10551-016-3233-4 is the digital object identifier (doi) permanently assigned to this article, making it easier to locate on the Internet.

7. a. It is a research database article. You can tell by the URL.

    b. *Contemporary Authors Online.*

    c. From the URL, we can see that it is a Gale database.

    d. No. There is not an author's name listed at the beginning of the citation.

    e. The publication year.

8. a. Research database article. ProQuest is in the URL. The article originated from the *Wall Street Journal.*

    b. The article is found in *ProQuest*, not on the *Wall Street Journal* website. Research databases maintain articles for many years.

9. a. This is a research database article. You can tell because ProQuest is part of the URL.

    b. This is the publication where the article originated. *New African* is a monthly news magazine based in London. Encourage students to investigate unfamiliar publications.

    c.   Two pages.

    d.   This is the month this issue was published.

10.   a.   This is an e-book. There is no publisher listed, only OverDrive, a provider of e-books.

    b.   E-books are also available through Nook, Google Play, Kindle, and PDF versions from websites such as Project Gutenberg.

APPENDIX B3

Identify the Parts of the Citation Exercise: Chicago Author-Date

Answer the questions about each citation.

1. Burleigh, Michael. 2008. *Blood and Rage: A Cultural History of Terrorism*. New York: Harper.

   a. What type of source is this? How do you know?
   b. Who is the author?
   c. Which is *Blood and Rage: A Cultural History of Terrorism*?
   d. What is "Harper Perennial"?
   e. What is the significance of 2008?
   f. What does "New York" mean in this citation?

2. Grant, David. 2014. "Deep in the Swamps, Archaeologists are Finding How Fugitive Slaves Kept Their Freedom." *Smithsonian*. Last modified September 2014. Accessed December 17, 2018. http://www.smithsonianmag.com/history/deep-swamps-archaeologists-fugitive-slaves-kept-freedom-180960122.

   a. What type of source is this? How do you know?
   b. What does "Last modified September 2014" mean?
   c. What is the role of the *Smithsonian* in this article's publication?

From *Combating Plagiarism: A Hands-On Guide for Librarians, Teachers, and Students* by Terry Darr. Santa Barbara, CA: Libraries Unlimited. Copyright © 2019.

    d. Why is "http://www.smithsonianmag.com/history/deep-swamps-archaeologists-fugitive-slaves-kept-freedom-180960122" included in this citation?

    e. Why is *Smithsonian* included in this citation?

3. Jones, Stephen. 2014. "Elvis Presley Biography." Graceland: The Home of Elvis Presley. Last modified September 2014. Accessed December 17, 2018. https://www.graceland.com/biography.

    a. What type of source is this? How do you know?

    b. Does this article have an author?

    c. What is the significance of 2014 in this citation?

    d. What is "Elvis Presley Biography"? Circle one.

    Article title   Web page title   Publisher

    e. What is "Graceland: The Home of Elvis Presley?" Circle one.

    Publisher   Web page title   Article title

4. Tate, Julee. 2004. "My Mother, My Text: Writing and Remembering in Julia Alvarez's *In the Name of Salome*." *Bilingual Review* 28, no. 1: 54+. *Literature Resource Center*. http://link.galegroup.com/apps/doc/A164254177/LitRC?u=win5026&sid=LitRC&xid=2877752f.

    a. What type of source is this? How do you know?

    b. What is *Bilingual Review*?

    c. Is there an author? How do you know?

    d. What is *Literature Resource Center*?

    e. Why does this citation have a URL? What does it tell you about the source?

    f. When was this article originally published?

    g. What is the title of the article?

5. Yoder, Jon. 2009. "The Jungle (Upton Sinclair)." In *Bloom's Literary Themes: The American Dream*, edited by Harold Bloom, 97–107. New York: Infobase.

    a. What type of source is this? How do you know?

    b. What does "edited by Harold Bloom" mean?

    c. What does "In *Bloom's Literary Themes: The American Dream*" mean?

    d. What does "pp. 97–107" signify?

    e. What is "The Jungle (Upton Sinclair)"?

    f.   Who is the publisher?

    g.   Who wrote this article?

6.   Etzioni, Amitai. 2018. "Apple: Good Business, Poor Citizen?" *Journal of Business Ethics* 151, no. 1 (August): 1–11. doi:http://dx.doi.org/ 10.1007/s10551-016-3233-4. https://search.proquest.com/docview/ 2073960434?accountid=41092.

    a.   What type of source is this? How do you know?

    b.   What does "2018" signify?

    c.   What does "vol. 151, no. 1" mean about this publication's age?

    d.   Who wrote this article?

    e.   Is the *Journal of Business Ethics* a scholarly journal?

    f.   What is doi:http://dx.doi.org/10.1007/s10551-016-3233-4?

7.   "Toni Morrison." 2016. In *Contemporary Authors Online.* Detroit, MI: Gale. *Literature Resource Center.* http://link.galegroup.com/apps/ doc/H1000070669/LitRC?u=win5026&sid=LitRC&xid=c76a7dfb.

    a.   What type of source is this? How do you know?

    b.   Where did the article "Toni Morrison" originate?

    c.   What is the name of the research database for this article?

    d.   Does this article have an author?

    e.   What does "2016" mean?

8.   Mack, Dana. 1993. "Danger Indoctrination: War on Drugs? War on Parents." *Wall Street Journal,* June 17, 1993. https://search. proquest.com/docview/398387030?accountid=41092.

    a.   What type of source is this? How do you know?

    b.   What does "June 17, 1993" mean?

    c.   Why doesn't this URL point to the *Wall Street Journal*?

9.   Goffe, Leslie Gordon. 2013. "The Unfinished March." *New African* 47 no. 6 (Aug.): 80–82. https://search.proquest.com/docview/14332 64371?accountid=41092.

    a.   What type of source is this? How do you know?

    b.   What is *New African*?

    c.   How many pages is this article?

    d.   What does "Aug. 2013" mean?

10.   Gates, Melinda. 2019. *The Moment of Lift: How Empowering Women Changes the World.* New York: Flatiron Books. OverDrive.

    a.   What type of source is this? How do you know?

    b.   What are some other types of e-book editions you might use?

IDENTIFY THE PARTS OF THE CITATION ANSWER KEY: CHICAGO AUTHOR-DATE

1. a. This is a print book. There is an author, an italicized title, and publisher.
    b. Michael Burleigh is the author.
    c. The title of the book. For inexperienced researchers, this is a good time to discuss book subtitles.
    d. The publisher of the book.
    e. The publication year.
    f. The city of publication.

2. a. It is a web page. You can tell by the URL.
    b. This is the date of the publication.
    c. *Smithsonian* published this article.
    d. This is the URL of the article.

3. a. This is a web page article. You can tell by the URL.
    b. Yes, it is Stephen Jones. The author's name is at the beginning of the citation.
    c. It is the year of publication.
    d. Article title. You can tell because it is in quotation marks.
    e. It is the web page title and the publisher of the site.

4. a. It is an article from a research database. *Literature Resource Center*, a research database, is part of the citation.
    b. *Bilingual Review* is a scholarly journal.
    c. Yes. The name of "Julee Tate" is at the beginning of the citation.
    d. It is a research database.
    e. Research database articles are web-based resources, so they always have a URL.
    f. 2004.
    g. "My Mother, My Text: writing and remembering in Julia Alvarez's *In the Name of Salome*."

5. a. It is a chapter from a book. You can tell because the title is in quotation marks. There is a book title (in italics) within the citation, a visual clue that this is from a book.
    b. As the book editor, Harold Bloom compiled this chapter, along with others in the book.
    c. It is the title of the book where this chapter was published.
    d. The page range for this article (chapter).

  e. The title of the article (chapter).

  f. Infobase.

  g. Jon Yoder.

6. a. It is a research database article. You can tell by the doi and URL. There is also a journal name, *Journal of Business Ethics*, within the citation.

  b. The year of publication.

  c. The publication has been in existence for 151 years. This article is from the first issue of 2018.

  d. Amitai Etzioni.

  e. Yes. Encourage students to investigate unfamiliar publications.

  f. doi:http://dx.doi.org/10.1007/s10551-016-3233-4 is the digital object identifier (doi) permanently assigned to this article, making it easier to locate on the Internet.

7. a. It is a research database article about Toni Morrison. You can tell by *Literature Resource Center* in the citation.

  b. It originated in *Contemporary Authors Online*.

  c. *Literature Resource Center.*

  d. No. There is no author listed at the beginning of the citation.

  e. The year of publication.

8. a. It is a newspaper article from the *Wall Street Journal*.

  b. It is the exact date of publication.

  c. The article is found in ProQuest, not on the *Wall Street Journal* website. Research databases maintain articles for many years.

9. a. This is a research database article. You can tell because ProQuest is part of the URL.

  b. This is the publication where the article originated. *New African* is a monthly news magazine based in London. Encourage students to investigate unfamiliar publications.

  c. Two pages.

  d. The article was published in the August 2013 issue.

10. a. This is an e-book. OverDrive is a provider of e-books.

  b. E-books are also available through Nook, Go-ogle Play, Kindle, and PDF versions from websites such as Project Gutenberg.

APPENDIX B4

Identify the Parts of the Citation Exercise: Chicago Notes and Bibliography

1. Burleigh, Michael. *Blood and Rage: A Cultural History of Terrorism.* New York, NY: Harper Perennial. 2008.

   a. What type of source is this? How do you know?

   b. Who is the author?

   c. Which is *Blood and Rage: A Cultural History of Terrorism*?

   d. What is "Harper Perennial"?

   e. What is the significance of 2008?

   f. What does "New York" mean in this citation?

2. Grant, David. "Deep in the Swamps, Archaeologists are Finding How Fugitive Slaves Kept Their Freedom." *Smithsonian.* Last modified September 2014. Accessed December 17, 2018. http://www.smith sonianmag.com/history/deep-swamps-archaeologists-fugitive-slaves-kept-freedom-180960122.

   a. What type of source is this? How do you know?

   b. What does "Last modified September 2014" mean?

c.   What is the role of the *Smithsonian* in this article's publication?

d.   Why is "http://www.smithsonianmag.com/history/deep-swamps-archaeologists-fugitive-slaves-kept-freedom-180960122" included in this citation?

3.   Jones, Stephen. "Elvis Presley Biography." Graceland: The Home of Elvis Presley. Last modified September 2014. Accessed December 17, 2018. https://www.graceland.com/elvis/biography.aspx.

a.   What type of source is this? How do you know?

b.   Does this article have an author?

c.   What is the significance of 2018 in this citation?

d.   What is "Elvis Presley Biography"? Circle one.

   Article title   Web page title   Publisher

e.   What is "Graceland: The Home of Elvis Presley"? Circle one.

   Publisher   Web page title   Article title

4.   Tate, Julee. "My Mother, My Text: Writing and Remembering in Julia Alvarez's *In the Name of Salome*." *Bilingual Review* 28, no. 1 (2004): 54+. *Literature Resource Center* (accessed August 11, 2018). http://link.galegroup.com/apps/doc/A164254177/LitRC?u=win5026&sid=LitRC&xid=2877752f.

a.   What type of source is this? How do you know?

b.   What is *Bilingual Review*?

c.   Is there an author? How do you know?

d.   What is *Literature Resource Center*?

e.   Why does this citation have a URL? What does it tell you about the source?

f.   When was this article originally published?

g.   What is the title of the article?

5.   Yoder, Jon. "The Jungle (Upton Sinclair)." In *Bloom's Literary Themes: The American Dream*, edited by Harold Bloom, 97–107. New York, NY: Infobase, 2009.

a.   What type of source is this? How do you know?

b.   What does "edited by Harold Bloom" mean?

c.   What does "In *Bloom's Literary Themes: The American Dream*" mean?

d.   What does "pp. 97–107" signify?

e.   What is "The Jungle (Upton Sinclair)"?

f.   Who is the publisher?

g.   Who wrote this article?

6. Etzioni, Amitai. "Apple: Good Business, Poor Citizen?" *Journal of Business Ethics* 151, no. 1 (08, 2018): 1–11. doi:http://dx.doi.org/10.1007/s10551-016-32334 https://search.proquest.com/docview/2073960434?accountid=41092.

    a. What type of source is this? How do you know?
    b. What does "2018" signify?
    c. What does "vol. 151, no. 1" mean about this publication's age?
    d. Who wrote this article?
    e. Is the *Journal of Business Ethics* a scholarly journal?
    f. What is doi:http://dx.doi.org/10.1007/s10551-016-32334?

7. "Toni Morrison." In *Contemporary Authors Online.* Detroit, MI: Gale, 2016. *Literature Resource Center* (accessed December 15, 2018). http://link.galegroup.com/apps/doc/H1000070669/LitRC?u=win5026&sid=LitRC&xid=c76a7dfb.

    a. What type of source is this? How do you know?
    b. Where did the article "Toni Morrison" originate?
    c. What is the name of the research database for this article?
    d. Does this article have an author?
    e. What does "2016" mean?

8. Mack, Dana. "Danger Indoctrination: War on Drugs? War on Parents." *Wall Street Journal*, June 17, 1993. https://search.proquest.com/docview/398387030?accountid=41092.

    a. What type of source is this? How do you know?
    b. What does "June 17, 1993" mean?
    c. Why doesn't this URL point to the *Wall Street Journal*?

9. Goffe, Leslie Gordon. "The Unfinished March." *New African* 47 no. 6 (Aug. 2013): 80–82. https://search.proquest.com/docview/1433264371?accountid=41092.

    a. What type of source is this? How do you know?
    b. What is *New African*?
    c. How many pages is this article?
    d. What does "Aug. 2013" mean?

10. Gates, Melinda. *The Moment of Lift: How Empowering Women Changes the World.* New York, NY: Flatiron Books, 2019. OverDrive.

    a. What type of source is this? How do you know?
    b. What are some other types of e-book editions you might use?

IDENTIFY THE PARTS OF THE CITATION ANSWER KEY: CHICAGO NOTES AND BIBLIOGRAPHY

1. a. It is a print book. There is an author, an italicized title, and publisher.
    b. Michael Burleigh. His name is at the beginning of the citation.
    c. *Blood and Rage: A Cultural History of Terrorism.* For inexperienced researchers, this is a good time to discuss book subtitles.
    d. It is the publisher's name.
    e. It is the publication year.
    f. It is the location of the publisher.

2. a. It is a web page article. There is a URL in the citation.
    b. This is the publication date.
    c. *Smithsonian* published this article.
    d. This is the web address for this article on the Internet. It is the location.

3. a. This is a web page article biography of Elvis Presley. You can tell from the URL.
    b. Yes. The name of the author is at the beginning of the citation.
    c. It is the copyright (publication) date.
    d. Article title.
    e. Publisher and web page title.

4. a. It is a research database article from *Literature Resource Center.*
    b. *Bilingual Review* is a scholarly journal.
    c. Yes. The author's name is at the beginning of the citation.
    d. It is a research database.
    e. Research databases are web-based resources. Each article has an individual URL within the database itself.
    f. 2004.
    g. My Mother, My Text: Writing and Remembering in Julia Alvarez's *In the Name of Salome.*

5. a. It is a chapter from an edited book. There is a book title in italics (*Bloom's Literary Themes: The American Dream*) with an editor's name.
    b. Harold Bloom compiled the chapters and prepared the book for publication.
    c. It is the title of the book where the chapter originated.
    d. It is the page range for the article (chapter).

    e.   The title of the article (chapter).

    f.   Infobase.

    g.   Jon Yoder.

6. a.   It is a research database article. You can tell by the doi and the URL, which includes "ProQuest," a research database.

    b.   The publication year.

    c.   It has been publishing for 151 years. This is the first issue of 2018.

    d.   Amitai Etzioni. The author's name is at the beginning of the citation.

    e.   Yes.

    f.   doi:http://dx.doi.org/10.1007/s10551-016-3233-4 is the digital object identifier (doi) permanently assigned to this article, making it easier to locate on the Internet.

7. a.   It is a research database article. There is a research database name in the citation. The URL includes Gale, a publisher of research databases.

    b.   In another research database, *Contemporary Authors Online.*

    c.   *Literature Resource Center.*

    d.   No, the article is written *about* Toni Morrison. If there was an author, it would be stated in Last Name, First Name format.

    e.   This is the year the article was originally published in *Contemporary Authors Online.*

8. a.   It is a research database. *ProQuest*, the name of a research database, is in the URL.

    b.   It is the publication date of the article.

    c.   The article is from ProQuest, not directly from the *Wall Street Journal* website. Research databases maintain articles for many years.

9. a.   It is a research database article. ProQuest, the name of a research database, is in the URL.

    b.   This is the publication where the article originated. *New African* is a monthly news magazine based in London. Encourage students to investigate unfamiliar publications.

    c.   Two pages.

    d.   The month of publication for this article.

10. a.   This is an e-book. OverDrive is a provider of e-books.

    b.   E-books are also available through Nook, Google Play, Kindle, and PDF versions from websites such as Project Gutenberg.

APPENDIX B5

Identify the Parts of the Citation
Exercise: MLA

Answer the questions about each citation.

1. Burleigh, Michael. *Blood and Rage: A Cultural History of Terrorism.* Harper Perennial, 2008.

    a. What type of source is this? How do you know?

    b. What is "Harper Perennial"?

    c. What is the significance of 2008?

    d. Who is the author of this book?

    e. What is the title of this book?

2. Grant, David. "Deep in the Swamps, Archaeologists are Finding How Fugitive Slaves Kept Their Freedom." *Smithsonian*, Sept. 2016, www.smithsonianmag.com/history/deep-swamps-archaeologists-fugitive-slaves-kept-freedom-180960122. Accessed 17 Dec. 2018.

    a. What type of source is this? How do you know?

    b. What does "September 2016" mean?

    c. Does this article have an author?

d. Why is "http://www.smithsonianmag.com/history/deep-swamps-archaeologists-fugitive-slaves-kept-freedom-180960122" included in this citation?

e. What is *Smithsonian* in this citation?

3. Jones, Stephen. "Elvis Presley Biography." Graceland: The Home of Elvis Presley, 2018, https://www.graceland.com/elvis/biography.aspx.Accessed 14 Apr. 2018.

a. What type of source is this? How do you know?

b. Does this article have an author?

c. What is the significance of 2018 in this citation?

d. What is "Elvis Presley Biography"? Circle one.
Article title   Web page title   Publisher

e. What is "Graceland: The Home of Elvis Presley"? Circle one.
Publisher   Web page title   Article title

4. Tate, Julee. "My Mother, My Text: Writing and Remembering in Julia Alvarez's *In the Name of Salome*." *Bilingual Review*, vol. 28, no. 1, 2004, p. 54+. *Literature Resource Center*, http://link.galegroup.com/apps/doc/A164254177/LitRC?u=win5026&sid=LitRC&xid=2877752f. Accessed 11 Aug. 2018.

a. What type of source is this? How do you know?

b. What is *Bilingual Review*?

c. Is there an author? How do you know?

d. What is *Literature Resource Center*?

e. Why does this citation have a URL? What does it tell you about the source?

f. When was this article originally published?

g. What is the title of the article?

5. Yoder, Jon. "The Jungle (Upton Sinclair)." *Bloom's Literary Themes: The American Dream*, edited by Harold Bloom. Infobase Publishing, 2009. 97–107.

a. What type of source is this? How do you know?

b. What does "edited by Harold Bloom" mean?

c. What does "97–107" signify?

d. What is "The Jungle (Upton Sinclair)"?

e. Who is the publisher?

f. What is the original source where this article originated?

g. Who wrote this article (chapter)?

6. Etzioni, Amitai. "Apple: Good Business, Poor Citizen?" *Journal of Business Ethics*, vol. 151, no. 1, 2018, pp. 1–11. *ProQuest*, doi:http://dx.doi.org/10.1007/s10551-016-32334. https://search.proquest.com/docview/2073960434?accountid=4109.

   a. What type of source is this? How do you know?

   b. What does "2018" signify?

   c. What does "vol. 151, no. 1" mean about this publication's age?

   d. Who wrote this article?

   e. Is the *Journal of Business Ethics* a scholarly journal?

   f. What is doi:http://dx.doi.org/10.1007/s10551-016-32334?

7. "Toni Morrison." *Contemporary Authors Online*, Gale, 2016. *Literature Resource Center*, http://link.galegroup.com/apps/doc/H1000070669/LitRC?u=win5026&sid=LitRC&xid=c76a7dfb. Accessed 29 Sept. 2018.

   a. What type of source is this? How do you know?

   b. Where did the article "Toni Morrison" originate?

   c. What is the name of the research database for this article?

   d. Does this article have an author?

   e. What does "2016" mean?

8. Mack, Dana. "Danger Indoctrination: War on Drugs? War on Parents." *Wall Street Journal*, June 17, 1993, p. A10. *ProQuest*, https://search.proquest.com/docview/398387030?accountid=41092.

   a. What type of source is this? How do you know?

   b. Why does the page number note "A10"?

   c. Why doesn't this URL point to the *Wall Street Journal*?

9. Goffe, Leslie G. "The Unfinished March." *New African*, no. 531, Aug. 2013, pp. 80–82. *ProQuest*, https://search.proquest.com/docview/1433264371?accountid=41092.

   a. What type of source is this? How do you know?

   b. What is *New African*?

   c. How many pages is this article?

   d. What does "Aug. 2013" mean?

10. Gates, Melinda. *The Moment of Lift: How Empowering Women Changes the World*. OverDrive ed., Flatiron Books, 2019.

   a. What type of source is this? How do you know?

   b. What are some other types of e-book editions you might use?

IDENTIFY THE PARTS OF THE CITATION
ANSWER KEY: MLA

1. a. This is a print book. There is an author, an italicized title, and publisher.
    b. The book publisher.
    c. The year of publication.
    d. Michael Burleigh. The author's name is at the beginning of the citation.
    e. *Blood and Rage: A Cultural History of Terrorism.* For inexperienced researchers, this is a good time to discuss book subtitles.

2. a. It is a web page article. The URL and accessed date are visual clues.
    b. It is the month and year of publication for this article.
    c. No. The citation begins with the article title. There is no author listed at the beginning of the citation.
    d. This is the website address on the Internet where this article is located.
    e. *Smithsonian* published this article.

3. a. Web page article. The URL and accessed date are visual clues.
    b. Yes, Stephen Jones. It is at the beginning of the citation.
    c. Publication year.
    d. Article title.
    e. The website title and the publisher.

4. a. It is a research database article. There is a scholarly journal, *Bilingual Review,* and a research database name, *Literature Resource Center,* in the citation.
    a. It is a research database article.
    b. A scholarly journal title.
    c. Yes, Julee Tate. It is at the beginning of the citation.
    d. A research database. Research database titles are italicized in the citation.
    e. A research database is a digital resource with a URL.
    f. 2004.
    g. "My Mother, My Text: Writing and Remembering in Julia Alvarez's *In the Name of Salome.*"

5. a. This is a chapter (article) within a book, *Bloom's Literary Themes: The American Dream.* It has an editor in the citation. There is a book publisher listed.

b. Harold Bloom, as the editor, compiled chapters (articles) by different authors for this book.

c. This is the page range for the article, "The Jungle (Upton Sinclair)."

d. The title of the article (chapter).

e. Infobase Publishing.

f. *Bloom's Literary Themes: The American Dream.*

g. Jon Yoder.

6. a. It is a scholarly journal research database article. The "vol." and "no." in the citation show that this is a publication. The *Journal of Business Ethics* is a scholarly journal. *ProQuest*, a research database, is also in the citation.

b. The article was published in the journal during 2018.

c. "Volume 151" means the publication has been in existence for 151 years. "no. 1" means this is the first issue of 2018.

d. Amitai Etzioni. The author's name is at the beginning of the citation.

e. Yes. Encourage students to research unfamiliar publications.

f. doi:http://dx.doi.org/10.1007/s10551-016-3233-4 is the digital object identifier (doi) permanently assigned to this article, making it easier to locate on the Internet.

7. a. It is a research database article. You can tell because the citation mentions *Literature Resource Center.* Students should be able to visually recognize the titles of the library's research databases.

b. It was originally published in another database, *Contemporary Authors Online,* by the same publisher (Gale).

c. *Literature Resource Center.*

d. No. When a citation begins with a title in quotes, there is no listed author.

e. The date of publication.

8. a. It is a research database article. *ProQuest* is in the citation.

b. It is the original page the article appeared in the *Wall Street Journal.*

c. The article is found in *ProQuest*, not on the *Wall Street Journal* website. Research databases maintain articles for many years.

9. a. It is a research database article from ProQuest.

     b.   This is the publication where the article originated. *New African* is a monthly news magazine based in London. Encourage students to investigate unfamiliar publications.

     c.   Two pages.

     d.   It is the month of publication and year of publication.

10. a.   This is an e-book. There is no publisher listed, only OverDrive, a provider of e-books.

     b.   E-books are also available through Nook, Google Play, Kindle, and PDF versions from websites such as Project Gutenberg.

APPENDIX C

The Anatomy of a Research Database Article

APPENDIX C1

The Anatomy of a Research Database Article Lesson Plan: Information Literacy Option

Objectives: Information from research database articles is disconnected from the original source. Most students have never seen a scholarly journal or reference source in print, losing important context about the authorship and publication of this type of digital information. Many do not read print newspapers and magazines on a regular basis. The parameters of these sources are clearer once students understand the "anatomy" of a research database article. This lesson should be combined with research database searching skills during information literacy instruction.

As a result of this lesson, students will understand the following:

- The role of research database and research database articles as digital sources within the library

- The identification of authorship for a research database article by reading the available information

- How to identify the publication type from a research database article

- The basic publication cycle of a research database article

From *Combating Plagiarism: A Hands-On Guide for Librarians, Teachers, and Students* by Terry Darr. Santa Barbara, CA: Libraries Unlimited. Copyright © 2019.

Delivery: Librarians should deliver this lesson as part of information literacy instruction during a research assignment. There is no assessment or classwork.

Discussion: Students will have different understandings about publications. To gauge your class, here are two questions to ask your class. (1) Have you ever used a reference book? What type? For what reason? (2) Do you read the news or any magazines online or in print? Which ones? How often?

Materials: If available, bring print reference books, journals, and magazines to this class.

Once searching research databases has been explained to students, a typical research database article should be projected from the instructor's computer on a screen for students to see. Students should observe the instructor instead of following along on their own computer screen.

Lesson Plan

1. Depending on the research experience of your students, first review the location and log-in procedures to access your school's research databases along with any usernames and passwords for off-campus access.
2. Define a research database. Students may have some knowledge about research databases already depending on prior experience; the discussion should build on this. Here is a sample definition for inexperienced researchers. Research databases are an important part of the library's digital collection. Research databases are a type of digital "storage cabinet" of articles from various sources: reference books, specialized dictionaries, major newspapers, journals, magazines, scholarly publications. These sources have been scanned by the research database company and made digitally available in the database through a keyword search. Research databases allow you to have access to many more publications than those found on the Internet. Research databases often have access to decades of issues from publications that have been archived for use. A username and password are necessary for access. Review the life cycle of a research database article found in Chapter 6.
3. The instructor should search for a research database article that relates to the topics assigned to students. Open the article and isolate the publication information for the article. This is normally at the top of the page of the article. The purpose is to deliberately review the publication parts of a research database article for the location of this information and the individual elements, not create a citation.
4. Review the parts of the research database article chosen from the search process from the publication at the top of the article. Each research database will display publication information differently on

the article. This type of explanation is best completed in real time as part of normal information literacy instruction.

Here are some examples of how the publication information appears on different database articles. Pointing this information out to students allows them to consider the parenthetical citation (or footnote) and information context. This is not the citation. It is a listing of the publication information for the article. Note that volume number is the length of time the publication has been in existence; this is an indicator of reliability.

Example 1: Article from a publication

The publication information for this article in the research database *ProQuest* appears in this order on the article's publication page:

Alleva, Richard. **Commonweal; New York** Vol. 129, Iss. 1, (Jan 11, 2002): 21–22

Discussion: This publication information shows that there is an author which is important for the parenthetical citation or footnote. The article is from 2002, which may be too old depending on the topic. Vol. 129 means that this publication has been in existence for 129 years. This can be a sign of credibility. This is a short article, only two pages (21–22). There will be an author and page number in the parenthetical citation or footnote.

Example 2: Article from a reference source

For articles originating from reference sources such as Gale's *Student Resources in Context* or other similar research databases, the title of the article, the title of the reference book where the article originated, and the date of the publication are located near the top of the page. A volume number or edition number may also be included. Students should be able to recognize a reference book title after a few reviews. This is a typical example of the information available from an article:

California (article title)

UXL Encyclopedia of U.S. History. 2009

Discussion: There is no author listed, only the article title, reference book, and publication year. The article "California" was originally in a reference book, *UXL Encyclopedia of U.S. History*, which was published in 2009. There will not be an author in the parenthetical citation or footnote.

Example 3: Scholarly journal article

Scholarly journal articles are an important source for student research. This is the information found on an article in *JSTOR* on the article's cover page.

Not by Elizabeth Barrett Browning

Author: Aurelia Brooks Harlan

Source information: *PMLA*, Vol. 57, No. 2 (June 1942), pp. 582–585

Published by: Modern Language Association

Stable URL: https://www.jstor.org/stable/458795

Discussion: The article title is "Not by Elizabeth Barrett Browning." The author is listed as Aurelia Brooks Harlan. *PMLA* is the official publication of the Modern Language Association. Students should recognize this as a journal because it is italicized. "Vol. 57, No. 2" is another visual indicator of a journal that is published on a regular schedule. June 1942 is the publication date. The page number range of "pp. 582–585" shows the page range from the journal when it was in print. The author's name and a page number will be in the parenthetical citation or footnote.

Example 4: Newspaper article

This is typical of the information about a source found on an article in *ProQuest* from a major newspaper.

The Bard of Simple Things; For Poet Laureate Billy Collins, Writing Verse Is A Lot Like Breathing

Weeks, Linton. *The Washington Post*, Washington, DC. 28 Nov. 2001: C1

Discussion: This article was originally published on page C1 in the *Washington Post* on November 28, 2001. This type of pagination, C1, is usually not used in the citation. The title of this article, written by Linton Weeks is "The Bard of Simple Things; For Poet Laureate Billy Collins, Writing Verse is a Lot Like Breathing." This article is from a research database, but this is not noted in the basic publication information on the article itself. The parenthetical citation and footnote will have the author's name but not a page number.

Here are the main points to cover when discussing the anatomy of a research database article during information literacy instruction.

- **Authorship—who wrote it?:** Determining authorship is the most important step when reviewing a source. Authorship is an important visual signal to determine whether an author's name will need to be considered in the parenthetical citations and footnotes.

- **Type of publication:** Ask your students: what publication did this article come from? Is it from a reference book, a scholarly journal, a newspaper, or other publication? You may need to explain the different types of publications to your students. If possible, have print copies of these publications. Chapter 6 has lists of titles of typical reference books, journals, magazines, and newspapers.

- **Volume and issue number (vol. no.):** Students should be aware of the various dates in a publishing cycle.

- **Publication date:** Each citation style has its own date format. The publication date should be considered for relevance. Some research topics require recently published articles.

APPENDIX C2

The Anatomy of a Research Database Article Lesson Plan: Citation Visual Recognition Option

Objectives: Research databases, through a citation tool, create a full citation for articles without any context for the source itself. Except for major newspapers, these articles come from publications that the average student has not seen in print. The research database search process creates a results list from numerous journals and other sources, making it difficult to visualize the article's actual origin. Research database citation instruction, emphasizing authorship and publication, adds value to digital information, decreasing plagiarism. This instruction also develops relevance skills, so students better understand the type of source used for research. This also makes it easier to create a parenthetical citation and footnotes for these articles.

Materials: While there are examples of research database article citations in this lesson and throughout the book, other examples can be gained by searching a research database and using the citation tool.

As a result of this lesson, students will

- understand that using a research database means researching different types of publications, including reference book entries;

- visually discern the difference in the research database citations among magazines, scholarly journals, and reference books to better understand the source;

- accurately create a parenthetical citation or footnote from a full citation;

- better understand the publication cycle of research database articles.

Prerequisites: "The Anatomy of a Research Database" information literacy option should be presented first. That prerequisite lesson creates awareness of the publication details on different types of research database articles. Students should have significant research experience or be in the eleventh grade and above for this lesson.

Delivery: Students will need a thorough review of these examples. This instruction requires a separate class period. Librarians or teachers with significant research experience should lead this class.

Background information to present as part of this lesson:

- Entries from reference books and specialized encyclopedias are commonly presented as individual database articles. Encyclopedias are general information sources on one general topic, published as print books, often in multivolume sets. In multivolume sets, each volume (book) has a number (Vol. 5) or alphabetical range. Other reference books are published as one book with multiple entries on a subject area. If students have never used encyclopedias or reference books, these books can be shown to students in the library if available or on a website. Show students an example of this type of article in a research database, if necessary.

- You can provide a citation guide to students for the basics, such as article title formats, date variations, and guidelines for the use of italics.

- When a citation has a named person as author, that will be stated at the beginning of the citation. Beginning researchers benefit from a visual demonstration, which compares a citation with an author and a citation without an author.

- Book publisher names and scholarly journal titles are unfamiliar to many students. Instructors should review the names of typical publishers found in academic work.

READING THE RESEARCH DATABASE CITATION

Research database articles are presented out of context from the original source. For example, a research database article originally published in the *New York Times* is recognized as a "credible source" by the average high school student who has likely never read this newspaper in print. These citations are created through a citation tool within the database, requiring no input from students. "Reading" the citation also helps students make relevance decisions, making the different types of articles more recognizable. For example, students may need more general information on a topic, making a scholarly journal article too complex.

Here are the essential questions about a research database citation:

- Is there a named person listed as author? If an article is available to read, someone wrote it. However, there are many instances when the author is not listed with the article and the full citation. This is often because a team of writers work on content without one person named as the author. Determining authorship is important for determining the parenthetical citation or footnote.

- Does the citation have a page range? Page numbers are used primarily for scholarly journal articles in research databases, although reference source databases are now beginning to insert accurate page numbers in articles. The parenthetical citation will need a page number if the page numbers print out with the article.

- Is the article from a scholarly journal? Students should recognize the similar characteristics of scholarly journal titles.

- Is the article from a specialized encyclopedia or other reference book? A source of articles in research databases are entries (articles) scanned from specialized encyclopedias and reference books. If this is the case, the citation will have the name of the reference book in italics.

- Is the article from a newspaper or other accessible publications?

Full citations from research databases vary greatly depending on the publication cycle of the source. Review a few different types of full citations from research databases that students will typically use. Ask students the questions under each citation as your review it.

MLA Example—Citation 1: Newspaper or Other Dated Publication Article

Garner, Dwight. "A Poet Laureate Sends News from the End of Life." *The New York Times*, 30 July 2018, *Proquest*, https://search.proquest.com/docview/2078996327?accountid=41092.

1. Does this article have an author? How do you know? *There is a name at the beginning of the citation.*
2. Will you use a page number in your parenthetical citation? *No. There is no page number listed in the citation.*
3. What is the parenthetical citation? *(Garner).*

MLA Example—Citation 2: Scholarly Journal Article

Some research databases, such as *JSTOR*, predominantly feature scholarly journal articles. Scholarly journal articles will always have an author. Encourage students to look up titles if they are unsure if a publication is scholarly.

> Hopkins, John B., and Steven T. Kalinowski. "The Fate of Transported American Black Bears in Yosemite National Park." *Ursus*, vol. 24, no. 2, 2013, pp. 120–126. *JSTOR*, www.jstor.org/stable/24643807.

1. Does this article have an author? How do you know? *If an article has an author, that is one indicator of being a scholarly journal. The authors' names are at the beginning of the citation.*
2. What is *Ursus*? *It is a scholarly journal about bears. It is italicized in the citation, an indicator of a journal.*
3. Is this a scholarly journal? How do you know? *"Vol." and "no." are part of the citation. "Vol." (Volume) is the number of years the journal has published; "no." (issue number) is the number of issues this year. There is a page range. The journal name, Ursus, is italicized.*
4. If you quote a sentence from page 121 of the article, what is the parenthetical citation? *There are two authors. Both authors are in the parenthetical citation with the page number (Hopkins and Kalinowski 121).*

MLA Example—Citation 3: Reference Source Article

> "California." *Worldmark Encyclopedia of the States*, 8th ed., vol. 1, Gale, 2016, pp. 75–110. *Student Resources in Context*, http://link.gale group.com/apps/doc/CX3632200015/SUIC?u=win5026&sid=SUIC &xid=e6f94b6c. Accessed 3 Aug. 2018.

1. Does this article have an author? How do you know? *No. Show students that because the citation begins with the article title, "California," there is no author listed. If there was an author, there would be a Last Name, First Name at the beginning of the citation.*
2. What is "California"? This is the article title. *Article titles are in quotation marks.*
3. What is *Worldmark Encyclopedia of the States*? What does the term "encyclopedia" in the (book) title tell you about the book? *Students should be prompted to notice that* Worldmark Encyclopedia of the States *is italicized. The fact that the term "encyclopedia" is part of the title is a major clue that this is a book.*
4. What is the parenthetical citation? *Since this is an article from an encyclopedia, no page numbers are necessary. Use the title of the article in quotation marks for the parenthetical citation ("California").*

APA Example 1: Newspaper or Other Publication Article

Garner, D. (2018, April 30). A poet laureate sends news from the end of life. *The New York Times*. Retrieved from ProQuest database.

1. Why does the date in the citation include a year, month, and day? *Newspapers are published daily. This information should be part of the citation date.*
2. Will you use a page number in your parenthetical citation? *No. There is no page number listed in the citation.*
3. What is the parenthetical citation? *(Garner, 2018).*

APA Example 2: Scholarly Journal Article

Hopkins, J., & Kalinowski, S. (2013). The fate of transported American black bears in Yosemite National Park. *Ursus,* 24(2), 120–126. Retrieved from http://www.jstor.org/stable/24643807.

1. What is *Ursus*? How do you know? Ursus *is a scholarly journal for the study of bears.*
2. What are the alternatives for the parenthetical citation? *One choice is (Hopkins & Kalinowski, 2013, p. #). Another alternative is to use Hopkins and Kalinowski (2013) in the text of your sentence and place p. # at the end of the quote or paraphrase.*
3. What does "24(2)" mean? *Volume 24, issue 2. This means that the journal has been in circulation for 24 years. This is issue 2 of the 24th year of publication.*

APA Example 3: Reference Source Article

California. (2016). In *Worldmark Encyclopedia of the States* (8th ed., Vol. 1, pp. 75–110). Farmington Hills, MI: Gale. Retrieved from http://link.galegroup.com/apps/doc/CX3632200015/SUIC?u=win 5026&sid=SUIC&xid=e6f94b6c.

1. Does this article have an author? How do you know? *No. If there was an author, there would be a Last Name, First Initial at the beginning of the citation.*
2. What is "California"? *This is the article title.*
3. What is *Worldmark Encyclopedia of the States*? What does the term "encyclopedia" in the (book) title tell you about the book? *Students should be prompted to notice that* Worldmark Encyclopedia of the States *is italicized. The fact that the term "encyclopedia" is part of the title is a clue that this is a book.*
4. What is the parenthetical citation for this article? *("California," 2016)*

Chicago Notes and Bibliography Example 1: Newspaper or Other Dated Publication Article

Garner, Dwight. "A Poet Laureate Sends News from the End of Life." *The New York Times*, July 30, 2018. https://search.proquest.com/docview/2078996327?accountid=41092.

1. Why does this article have a month, day, and year for publication? The *New York Times is a daily newspaper. The specific date of publication was July 30, 2018, so this should be included in the citation.*
2. Does this article have an author? How do you know? *Yes. Dwight Garner. It is at the beginning of the citation.*
3. What is the footnote for this article?

    1.   Dwight Garner, "A Poet Laureate Sends News from the End of Life," *New York Times*, July 30, 2018, https://search.proquest.com/docview/2078996327?accountid=41092.

Chicago Notes and Bibliography Example 2: Scholarly Journal Article

Hopkins, John B., and Steven T. Kalinowski. "The Fate of Transported American Black Bears in Yosemite National Park." *Ursus* 24, no. 2 (2013): 120–26. http://www.jstor.org/stable/24643807.

1. Does this article have an author? How do you know? *It has two authors at the beginning of the citation.*
2. What is "The Fate of Transported American Black Bears in Yosemite National Park"? *This is the article title. Indicator: quotation marks.*
3. What is Ursus? *This is a scholarly journal dedicated to the study of bears. Indicator: the title is italicized.*
4. If you quoted from page 125 of this article, what is the footnote?

    1.   John B. Hopkins and Steven T. Kalinowski. "The Fate of Transported Black American Bears in Yosemite National Park." *Ursus* 24, no. 2 (2013): 125, http://www.jstor.org/stable/24643807.

Chicago Notes and Bibliography Example 3: Research Database Article—Reference Source

"California." In *Worldmark Encyclopedia of the States*, 8th ed., 75–110. Vol. 1. Farmington Hills, MI: Gale, 2016. *Student Resources in Context* (accessed August 3, 2018). http://link.galegroup.com/apps/doc/CX3632200015/SUIC?u=win5026&sid=SUIC&xid=e6f94b6c.

1. Does this article have an author? How do you know? *No. If there was an author, there would be a Last Name, First Name at the beginning of the citation.*

2. What is "California"? *This is the article title. Article titles are listed with quotation marks.*
3. What is *Worldmark Encyclopedia of the States*? What does the term "encyclopedia" in the (book) title tell you about the book? *Students should be prompted to notice that* Worldmark Encyclopedia of the States *is italicized. The fact that the term "encyclopedia" is part of the title is a clue that this is a book.*
4. What is the footnote for this citation?

> 1. "California," in *Worldmark Encyclopedia of the States*, 8th ed. (Farmington Hills, MI: Gale, 2016), 1: http://link.galegroup .com/apps/doc/CX3632200015/SUIC?u=win5026&sid=SUIC&xid= e6f94b6c.

Chicago Author-Date Example 1: Newspaper or Other Publication Article

Garner, Dwight. 2018. "A Poet Laureate Sends News from the End of Life." *New York Times*, July 30, 2018. https://search.proquest.com/ docview/2078996327?accountid=41092.

1. Why does this article have a month, day, and year for publication? *The* New York Times *is a daily newspaper. The specific date of publication was July 30, 2018, so this should be included in the citation.*
2. Does this article have an author? How do you know? *Yes. Dwight Garner. It is at the beginning of the citation.*
3. Why does this article have a URL to ProQuest instead of the *New York Times*? *The article is found in this database, as well as the* New York Times. *It has multiple homes.*

Chicago Author-Date Example 2: Scholarly Journal Article

Hopkins, John B., and Steven T. Kalinowski. 2013. "The Fate of Transported American Black Bears in Yosemite National Park." *Ursus* 24, no. 2 (2013): 120–26. http://www.jstor.org/stable/24643807.

1. Does this article have an author? How do you know? *It has two authors at the beginning of the citation.*
2. What is "The Fate of Transported American Black Bears in Yosemite National Park"? *This is the article title. Indicator: quotation marks.*
3. What is Ursus? *This is a scholarly journal dedicated to the study of bears. Indicator: the title is italicized.*
4. What is the parenthetical citation? *(Hopkins and Kalinowksi 2013, 125)*

Chicago Author-Date Example 3: Research Database Article—Reference Source

"California." 2016. In *Worldmark Encyclopedia of the States*, 8th ed., 75–110. Vol. 1. Farmington Hills, MI: Gale, 2016. *Student Resources In Context* (accessed August 3, 2018). http://link.galegroup.com/apps/doc/CX3632200015/SUIC?u=win5026&sid=SUIC&xid=e6f94b6c.

1. Does this article have an author? How do you know? *No. If there was an author, there would be a Last Name, First Name at the beginning of the citation.*

2. What is "California"? *This is the article title. Article titles are listed with quotation marks.*

3. What is *Worldmark Encyclopedia of the States*? What does the term "encyclopedia" in the (book) title tell you about the book? *Students should be prompted to notice that* Worldmark Encyclopedia of the States *is italicized. The fact that the term "encyclopedia" is part of the title is a clue that this is a book.*

4. What is the parenthetical citation? *("California" 2016)*

ADDITIONAL EXERCISE FOR STUDENTS: RECOGNIZING A CITATION FROM A SCHOLARLY JOURNAL

Group 1—MLA: Which citation is from a scholarly journal? *(a) and (c) are from scholarly journals.*

(a) Smith, Michael S. "Putting France in the Chandlerian Framework: France's 100 Largest Industrial Firms in 1913." *Business History Review*, vol. 72, no. 1, 1998, pp. 46–85. *ProQuest*, https://search.proquest.com/docview/274473863?accountid=41092.

(b) Durost, Becky, and Bruce Fish. "Frost, Robert." *Robert Frost*, Chelsea House, 2002. *Bloom's Literature*, online.infobase.com/Auth/Index?aid=106608&itemid=WE54&articleId=1584. Accessed 4 Aug. 2018.

(c) (This source is found through Google Scholar.)

   Howard, Rebecca. "Plagiarisms, Authorships, and the Academic Death Penalty." *College English* 57, no. 7 (1995): 788. https://surface.syr.edu/cgi/viewcontent.cgi?article=1002&context=wp. Accessed 21 Feb. 2019.

Group 2—MLA: Which citation is from a scholarly journal? *(b) and (d) are from a scholarly journal.*

(a) Dennhardt, Andrew J., and Todd Katzner. "Eagle." *World Book Advanced*, World Book, 2018, www.worldbookonline.com/advanced/article? id=ar171200. Accessed 4 Aug. 2018.

(b) Katchova, Ani L. and Robert Dinterman. "Evaluating Financial Stress and Performance of Beginning Farmers during the Agricultural Downturn." *Agricultural Finance Review*, vol. 78, no. 4, Oct. 2018, pp. 457–469. EBSCO*host*, doi:10.1108/AFR-08-2017-0074.

(c) Shumaker, Jeanette Roberts. *"Othello." The Facts on File Companion to Shakespeare*, Facts on File, 2012. *Bloom's Literature*, online.infobase.com/Auth/Index?aid=106608&itemid=WE54&articl eId=476450. Accessed 3 Aug. 2018.

(d) Potter, Lee A. "From Inconvenience to Inspiration." *The Science Teacher*, vol. 86, no. 1, 2018, pp. 60. *ProQuest*, https://search. proquest.com/docview/2081751346?accountid=41092.

Group 3—MLA: Which citation is from a reference book source?
(a) and (c) are from reference sources.

(a) "African American literature." *Britannica School*, Encyclopædia Britannica, 20 Sep. 2013. school.eb.com/levels/high/article/African-American-literature/343805. Accessed 21 Feb. 2019.

(b) Wood, Michelle Gaffner. "Negotiating the Geography of Mother-Daughter Relationships in Amy Tan's *The Joy Luck Club*." *The Midwest Quarterly*, vol. 54, no. 1, 2012, p. 82+. *Literature Resource Center*, http://link.galegroup.com/apps/doc/A306095523/LitRC?u =win5026&sid=LitRC&xid=f05cf77f. Accessed 21 Feb. 2019.

(c) "Iroquois." *International Encyclopedia of the Social Sciences*, edited by William A. Darity, Jr., 2nd ed., vol. 4, Macmillan Reference USA, 2008, pp. 151–152. *U.S. History in Context*, http://link.galegroup .com/apps/doc/CX3045301192/UHIC?u=win5026&sid=UHIC&xi d=c8e617fe. Accessed 21 Feb. 2019.

Group 1—APA: Which citation is from a scholarly journal? *(b) is from a scholarly journal.*

(a) Shumaker, J. R. (2012). *Othello*. In *The Facts on File Companion to Shakespeare*. New York: Facts on File. Retrieved August 3, 2018, from online.infobase.com/Auth/Index?aid=106608&itemid=WE54&articl eId=476450.

(b) Urgo, J. R. (1998). William Faulkner and the Drama of Meaning. *South Atlantic Review, 53*(2), 11–23. Retrieved from JSTOR database.

(c) Gregory, T. E. (1989). Byzantine Empire: History. In J. R. Strayer (Ed.), *Dictionary of the Middle Ages*. New York: Charles Scribner's Sons. Retrieved from http://link.galegroup.com/apps/doc/BT2353200490/ WHIC?u=win5026&sid=WHIC&xid=200471a6.

Group 2—APA: Which citation is from a scholarly journal? *(b) and (c) are from scholarly journals.*

(a) Drake. (2011). In *Contemporary Black Biography* (Vol. 86). Detroit: Gale. Retrieved from https://link.galegroup.com/apps/doc/K160 6005056/BIC?u=baltcntycpl&sid=BIC&xid=c5b45282.

(b) Smith, M. S. (1998). Putting France in the chandlerian framework: France's 100 largest industrial firms in 1913. *Business History Review, 72*(1), 46–85. Retrieved from https://search.proquest.com/ docview/274473863?accountid=41092.

(c) Masani, Z. (2017). The Battle of Hastings: The foundations of modern India were laid by the British governor-general, Warren Hastings. But he paid a heavy personal price. *History Today, 67*(11), 64–75.

(d) Twenty-First-Century G: The Great Gatsby as cultural icon. (2017). In *The Great Gatsby—F. Scott Fitzgerald, 2017 Edition*. Retrieved from Bloom's Literature database.

Group 3—APA: Which citation is from a reference source? *(a) and (c) are from reference sources.*

(a) African American literature. (2019). In *Encyclopædia Britannica*. Retrieved from https://school.eb.com/levels/high/article/African-American-literature/343805#232368.toc.

(b) Wood, M. G. (2012). Negotiating the geography of mother-daughter relationships in Amy Tan's The Joy Luck Club. *The Midwest Quarterly, 54*(1), 82+. Retrieved from http://link.galegroup.com/apps/ doc/A306095523/LitRC?u=win5026&sid=LitRC&xid=f05cf77f.

(c) Iroquois. (2008). In W. A. Darity, Jr. (Ed.), *International Encyclopedia of the Social Sciences* (2nd ed., Vol. 4, pp. 151–152). Detroit, MI: Macmillan Reference USA. Retrieved from http://link.galegroup.com/apps/doc/CX3045301192/UHIC?u=win5026&sid=UHIC&xid=c8e617fe.

Group 1—Chicago Notes and Bibliography: Which citation is from a scholarly journal? *(a) and (c) are from scholarly journals.*

(a) Urgo, Joseph R. "William Faulkner and the Drama of Meaning." *South Atlantic Review* 53, no. 2 (May 1998): 11–23. https://www.jstor .org/stable/3199910.

(b) Shumaker, Jeanette Roberts. *"Othello." The Facts On File Companion to Shakespeare*. Facts on File, 2012. Accessed August 3, 2018. online.infobase.com/Auth/Index?aid=106608&itemid=WE54&art icleId=476450.

(c) Katchova, Ani L., and Robert Dinterman. 2018. "Evaluating financial stress and performance of beginning farmers during the agricultural downturn." *Agricultural Finance Review* 78, no. 4: 457–469. *Business Source Premier,* EBSCO*host* (accessed August 4, 2018).

(d) Durost, Becky, and Bruce Fish. "Frost, Robert." *Robert Frost.* Chelsea House, 2002. Accessed August 4, 2018. online.infobase.com/Auth/ Index?aid=106608&itemid=WE54&articleId=1584.

Group 2—Chicago Notes and Bibliography: Which citation is from a scholarly journal? *(b) is from a scholarly journal.*

(a) "Drake." In *Contemporary Black Biography.* Vol. 86. Detroit: Gale, 2011. *Biography In Context* (accessed August 4, 2018). https://link .galegroup.com/apps/doc/K1606005056/BIC?u=baltcntycpl&sid= BIC&xid=c5b45282.

(b) Masani, Zareer. "The Battle of Hastings: The foundations of modern India were laid by the British governor-general, Warren Hastings. But he paid a heavy personal price." *History Today* 67, no. 11 (2017): 64–75. *History Reference Center,* EBSCO*host* accessed August 4, 2018).

(c) Vega, Robert D. "Library." In *World Book Advanced.* World Book, 2018. Last modified 2018. http://www.worldbookonline.com/advanced/ article?id=ar322340.

(d) Baker, Peter. "For Trump, the Reality Show Has Never Ended." *New York Times* (New York, NY), April 2, 2018, Politics. Accessed April 5, 2018. http://www.newyorktimes.com.

Group 3—Chicago Notes and Bibliography: Which citation is from a reference source? *(a) and (b) are reference sources.*

(a) *Britannica School,* s.v. "Chemical reaction," accessed February 21, 2019, https://school.eb.com/levels/high/article/chemical-reaction/ 110109.

(b) Gu, Ming Dong. "A Chinese Oedipus in Exile." *Literature and Psychology* 39, no. 1 (1993): 1–25. Quoted in *Short Story Criticism,* edited by Jelena O. Krstovic. Vol. 122. Detroit, MI: Gale, 2009. *Literature Resource Center* (accessed February 21, 2019). http://link.galegroup. com/apps/doc/H1420090801/LitRC?u=win5026&sid=LitRC&xid= 680bebfb.

(c) Schutt, Christopher A., Brandon Redding, Hui Cao, and Elias Michaelides. "The Illumination Characteristics of Operative Microscopes." *American Journal of Otolaryngology* 36, no. 3 (2015): 356–360. doi:http://dx.doi.org/10.1016/j.amjoto.2014.12.009. https://search. proquest.com/docview/1681969811?accountid=41092.

Group 1—Chicago Author-Date: Which citation is from a scholarly journal? *(a) and (c) are from scholarly journals.*

(a) Urgo, Joseph R. 1998. "William Faulkner and the Drama of Meaning." *South Atlantic Review* 53, no. 2 (May): 11–23. https://www.jstor .org/stable/3199910.

(b) Shumaker, Jeanette Roberts. 2012. *"Othello." The Facts On File Companion to Shakespeare.* Facts on File. Accessed August 3, 2018. online.infobase.com/Auth/Index?aid=106608&itemid=WE54&articleId=476450.

(c) Katchova, Ani L., and Robert Dinterman. 2018. "Evaluating Financial Stress and Performance of Beginning Farmers During the Agricultural Downturn." *Agricultural Finance Review* 78, no. 4: 457–469. *Business Source Premier,* EBSCO*host* (accessed August 4, 2018).

(d) Durost, Becky, and Bruce Fish. 2002. "Frost, Robert." *Robert Frost.* Chelsea House. Accessed August 4, 2018. online.infobase.com/Auth/Index?aid=106608&itemid=WE54&articleId=1584.

Group 2—Chicago Author-Date: Which citation is from a scholarly journal? *(b) is from a scholarly journal.*

(a) "Drake." 2011. In *Contemporary Black Biography.* Vol. 86. Detroit: Gale. *Biography In Context* (accessed August 4, 2018). https://link.galegroup.com/apps/doc/K1606005056/BIC?u=baltcntycpl&sid=BIC&xid=c5b45282.

(b) Masani, Zareer. 2017. "The Battle of Hastings: The foundations of modern India were laid by the British governor-general, Warren Hastings. But he paid a heavy personal price." *History Today* 67, no. 11: 64–75. *History Reference Center,* EBSCO*host* (accessed August 4, 2018).

(c) Vega, Robert D. "Library." In *World Book Advanced.* World Book, 2018. Last modified 2018. http://www.worldbookonline.com/advanced/article?id=ar322340.

(d) Baker, Peter. 2018. "For Trump, the Reality Show Has Never Ended." *New York Times,* April 2, 2018, Politics. Accessed April 5, 2018. http://www.newyorktimes.com.

Group 3—Chicago Author-Date: Which citation is from a reference source? *(a) and (b) are reference sources.*

(a) *Britannica School,* s.v. "Chemical reaction," accessed February 21, 2019, https://school.eb.com/levels/high/article/chemical-reaction/110109.

(b) Gu, Ming Dong. 1993. "A Chinese Oedipus in Exile." *Literature and Psychology* 39, no. 1: 1–25. Quoted in *Short Story Criticism,* edited by Jelena O. Krstovic. Vol. 122. Detroit, MI: Gale, 2009. *Literature Resource Center* (accessed February 21, 2019). http://link.galegroup.com/apps/doc/H1420090801/LitRC?u=win5026&sid=LitRC&xid=680bebfb.

(c) Schutt, Christopher A., Brandon Redding, Hui Cao, and Elias Michaelides. 2015. "The Illumination Characteristics of Operative Microscopes." *American Journal of Otolaryngology* 36, no. 3: 356–360. doi:http://dx.doi.org/10.1016/j.amjoto.2014.12.009. https://search.proquest.com/docview/1681969811?accountid=41092.

APPENDIX D

Can You Spot the Problems?
Citation Proofreading

215

APPENDIX D1

Can You Spot the Problems? Citation Proofreading Lesson Plan

Objectives: Along with avoiding accusations of plagiarism, students who learn to manage the details of citations are better able to manage more extensive research projects later. Books, web page articles, and research databases are the most frequently used sources for student research. Digital sources are abstract, presenting only through words on a computer screen and a citation. Proofreading helps students understand how the citation documents the author and publication process, adding to overall understanding of the source. This citation proofreading exercise also improves the accuracy of citations after the use of citation tools, which often have errors and variations.

As a result of this lesson, students will understand

- a complete citation for different source types;

- use of a citation guide to proofread citations;

- the correct order for the individual information parts in a citation;

- citations are an important representation of the source and should be sequenced correctly;

- more accurate use of an online citation tool through proofreading.

From *Combating Plagiarism: A Hands-On Guide for Librarians, Teachers, and Students* by Terry Darr. Santa Barbara, CA: Libraries Unlimited. Copyright © 2019.

Delivery: This is ideal for homework or classwork with a citation guide for inexperienced researchers. It can be completed as a warm-up exercise with experienced researchers with visual recognition skills without a citation guide. Since the available publication information for digital sources can vary, students should view the web page and research database articles on a computer to complete the exercise when possible.

Length of time: Varies. Approximately twenty minutes.

Materials: Additional citations can be changed around to create errors that need to be corrected in order to expand this exercise. Teachers can also use citation errors by students for additional proofreading practice.

APPENDIX D2

Can You Spot the Problems?
Exercise: APA

Make any corrections for the citations. There may be information that is missing, in the wrong place, or incorrect. Explain your corrections below.

1. Lewis, M. The Fifth Risk. New York, NY: W.W. Norton and Company.

   _____

   _____

2. Trueman, C. (2016, November 21). Supermarine Spitfire. Retrieved January 19, 2019, from The history learning site: http://www.historylearningsite.co.uk/world-war-two/world-war-two-in-western-europe/battle-of-britain/supermarine-spitfire/.

   _____

   _____

3. Riordan, R. (2017, August) *The trials of Apollo: the dark prophecy.* NY, NY.

   _____

   _____

4. Krakauer, J. (1999). *Into Thin Air.* New York: Anchor Books. Accessed 19 Jan. 2019.

   _____

   _____

5. Niestle, A. (2000). Neither sharks nor wolves: The men of nazi germany's U-boat arm, 1939–1945. The Journal of Military History, *64*(2), 587–589. https://search.proquest.com/docview/195614853?accountid=41092

6. Coleman, J. F. (2000). The battle of midway: Turning point in the pacific. All Hands, 20–33. Retrieved from https://search.proquest.com/docview/199402747?accountid=41092

7. Balko, R (2014 October). In defense of John Grisham. Washington Post, The Watch. Retrieved from https://www.washingtonpost.com/news/the-watch/wp/2014/10/16/in-defense-of-john-grisham/?utm_term=.e0f387841377

8. Franklin, Pierce. (2018). Retrieved January 16, 2019, from presidents: The White House website: http://www.whitehouse.gov/about-the-white-house/presidents/franklin-pierce/

9. Klass, P. (2019 February 18). Having anesthesia once as a baby does not cause Learning Disabilities, new research shows. Family. Retrieved February 19, 2019, from The New York Times website: https://www.nytimes.com/2019/02/18/well/family/one-exposure-to-anesthesia-in-children-does-not-cause-learning-disabilities-new-research-shows.html

10. U.s. primary energy consumption by source and section in 2017. (2017). Retrieved February 18, 2019, from Energy explained: Your Guide to Understanding Energy website: https://www.eia.gov/energyexplained/

CAN YOU SPOT THE PROBLEMS? ANSWER KEY: APA

1. Correct:
    Lewis, M. (2018). *The fifth risk*. New York, NY: W.W. Norton and Company.

    The publication year is missing. This should be placed after the author's name. The first word of the title is capitalized. The other title words are lowercase. The title is italicized.

2. Correct:
    Trueman, C. (2016, November 21). Supermarine Spitfire. Retrieved January 19, 2019, from The History Learning Site: http://www .historylearningsite.co.uk/world-war-two/world-war-two-in-western-europe/battle-of-britain/supermarine-spitfire/.

    "History Learning Site" is capitalized in its entirety as a website title. "Submarine Spitfire" is capitalized because it is a proper noun.

3. Correct:
    Riordan, R. (2017). *The trials of Apollo: The dark prophecy*. New York, NY: Hyperion Publishing.

    The period after the date and the book publisher is missing. All books have publishers so this should never be omitted from a book citation. There is only a publication year for books, so August should not be included. "The" should be capitalized because it is the first word after the colon in the title. "New York," the city of the publication, should not be abbreviated.

4. Correct:
    Krakauer, J. (1999). *Into thin air*. New York, NY: Anchor Books.

    There is no accessed date for print books. The citation should include the state of publication. Only the first major word of titles should be capitalized for a full citation.

5. Correct:
    Niestle, A. (2000). Neither sharks nor wolves: The men of Nazi Germany's U-boat arm, 1939–1945. *The Journal of Military History, 64*(2), 587–589. Retrieved from https://search.proquest .com/docview/195614853?accountid=41092

    "Nazi Germany" should be capitalized in the title because this is a proper noun. The "U" in "U-boat" should also be capitalized. "Retrieved from" should be in front of the URL of the research database. *The Journal of Military History* should be italicized because it is the title of a journal.

6. Correct:
    Coleman, J. F. (2000). The Battle of Midway: Turning point in the Pacific. *All Hands, 98*(2), 20–33. Retrieved from *ProQuest* database.

The volume number, 98, and the issue number, 2, are missing. Students need to look at the publication information carefully for research database articles. The availability of volume and issue number can vary. "The Battle of Midway" and "Pacific" are proper nouns, so these words should be capitalized. *All Hands* is the journal title so this should be italicized.

7. Correct:
    Balko, R. (2014, October 16). In defense of John Grisham. *Washington Post*, The Watch. Retrieved from https://www.washingtonpost .com/news/the-watch/wp/2014/10/16/in-defense-of-john-grisham/?utm_term=.e0f38784137.

Missing: Period after the author's first initial. *The Washington Post* is published daily, so there should be a (Year, Month Day) publication date in the parentheses. *Washington Post* should be italicized. Explain to students that The Watch is the section of the newspaper where this article is located.

8. Correct:
    Franklin Pierce. (2018). Retrieved January 21, 2019, from Presidents: White House website: http://www.whitehouse.gov/about-the-white-house/presidents/franklin-pierce/

This is a web page article about Franklin Pierce, a U.S. president. There should not be a comma between Franklin and Pierce. The "P" in "Presidents" should be capitalized because it is the name of the web page. You may have to explain to students that this article is written about Franklin Pierce, a president, not written by someone named "Franklin Pierce."

9. Correct:
    Klass, P. (2019, February 18). Having anesthesia once as a baby does not cause learning disabilities, new research shows. *The New York Times*, Family. Retrieved from https://www.nytimes. com/2019/02/18/well/family/one-exposure-to-anesthesia-in-children-does-not-cause-learning-disabilities-new-research-shows.html

"Learning disabled" should not be capitalized in the title. There should be a comma after "2019." "*The New York Times*" is italicized because it is the publication name and publisher. Family is the name of the section of the newspaper. Often the URL for web pages for newspaper articles can be very long. Teachers should decide whether students should use the full URL or an abbreviated version. In this case, using the URL www.newyorktimes.com would also be acceptable since the article is searchable from the main web page.

10. Correct:
     U.S. primary energy consumption by source and section in 2017. (2017). Retrieved February 18, 2019, from Energy Explained: Your Guide to Understanding Energy website: https://www.eia .gov/energyexplained/

The "S" is "U.S." should be capitalized since this is a proper noun. "Explained" should be capitalized since this is part of the website title.

APPENDIX D3

Can You Spot the Problems? Exercise: Chicago Author-Date

Make any corrections for the citations. There could be information that is missing, in the wrong place, or incorrect. Explain your corrections below.

1. The Fifth Risk. Lewis, Michael. New York: W.W. Norton and Company.

   _____

   _____

2. Trueman, Chris. Supermarine Spitfire. The History Learning Site. Last Modified 2018. Accessed 19 January 2019. www.history learningsite.co.uk/world-war-two/world-war-two-in-western-europe/battle-of-britain/supermarine-spitfire/.

   _____

   _____

3. Riordan, Rick. 2017. The Trials of Apollo: The Dark Prophecy. New York, NY: Hyperion Publishing, 2017.

   _____

   _____

4. Krakauer, Jon. *Into Thin Air.* New York, NY: Anchor Books, 1999. Accessed February 19, 2019.

_____

_____

5. Niestle, Axel. 2000. Neither Sharks nor Wolves: The Men of Nazi Germany's U-Boat Arm, 1939–1945. The Journal of Military History 64 (2): 587–589. https://search.proquest.com/docview/195614853?accountid=41092.

_____

_____

6. Coleman, John F. 2000. The Battle of Midway: Turning point in the pacific. All Hands, 06, 20–33.

_____

_____

7. Balko, Radley. In Defense of John Grisham. *The Washington Post,* October 2014, The Watch. Accessed February 24, 2019. https://www.washingtonpost.com/news/the-watch/wp/2014/10/16/in-defense-of-john-grisham/?utm_term=.e0f387841377.

_____

_____

8. The White House. *Franklin Pierce.* Presidents. Last modified 2018. Accessed February 19, 2019. http://www.whitehouse.gov/about-the-white-house/presidents/franklin-pierce/.

_____

_____

9. Klass, Perri. "Having Anesthesia Once as a Baby Does Not Cause Learning Disabilities, New Research Shows." The New York Times. Last modified Feb. 18, 2019. Accessed February 19, 2019. https://goo.gl/UoV3fT.

_____

_____

10. U.S. Energy Information Center. 2017. "U.S. Primary Energy Consumption by Source and Sector in 2017." Home—energy explained. Last modified 2017. Accessed February 19, 2019.

_____

_____

CAN YOU SPOT THE PROBLEMS? ANSWER KEY: CHICAGO AUTHOR-DATE

1. Correct:
   Lewis, Michael. 2018. *The Fifth Risk*. New York, NY: W.W. Norton and Company.

The publication year belongs after the author's name. The state of publication should be included after the city of publication. The author's name is always first in the citation.

2. Correct:
   Trueman, Chris. 2018. "Submarine Spitfire." History Learning Site. Last modified 2018. Accessed January 19, 2019. http://www .historylearningsite.co.uk/world-war-two/world-war-two-in-western-europe/battle-of-britain/supermarine-spitfire/.

The publication year belongs after the author's name. "Submarine Spitfire" needs quotation marks as the article title. "Modified" should be a lowercase "m." The accessed date and last modified date should be in Month Day, Year format.

3. Correct:
   Riordan, Rick. 2017. *The Trials of Apollo: The Dark Prophecy*. New York, NY: Hyperion Publishing.

The publication year should be after the author's name, not listed twice. The book title is italicized.

4. Correct:
   Krakauer, Jon. 1999. *Into Thin Air*. New York, NY: Anchor Books, 1999.

The year of publication should be after the author's name. Accessed dates are not used with print books.

5. Correct:
   Niestle, Axel. 2000. "Neither Sharks nor Wolves: The Men of Nazi Germany's U-Boat Arm, 1939–1945." *The Journal of Military History* 64 no. 2 (April): 587–589. https://search.proquest.com/docview/195614853?accountid=41092.

Article titles are in quotation marks. "*The Journal of Military History*" should be italicized. The issue number should be preceded by "no." The month (or season) of publication is missing.

6. Correct:
   Coleman, John F. 2000. "The Battle of Midway: Turning Point in the Pacific." *All Hands*, no. 998 (June): 20–33. https://search.proquest.com/docview/199402747?accountid=41092.

"June" should be used instead of "06." There should be a URL since a research database article is a digital source. All major words are capitalized in the article title. The article title needs quotation marks. The volume number is missing from the publication information found on the article, so only the issue number is included in the citation. For this source, students should view the article through *ProQuest* if possible.

7. Correct:
   Balko, Radley. 2014. "In Defense of John Grisham." *The Washington Post*, October 14, 2014, The Watch. Accessed February 24, 2019. https://www.washingtonpost.com/news/the-watch/wp/2014/10/16/in-defense-of-john-grisham/?utm_term=.e0f387841377.

The article title should have quotation marks. *The Washington Post* is published daily, so the day of publication should be included in the publication date. The publication year should be placed after the author's name. Explain to students that The Watch is the section of the newspaper where this article is located.

8. Correct:
   The White House. 2018. "Franklin Pierce." Presidents. Last modified 2018. Accessed February 19, 2019. http://www.whitehouse.gov/about-the-white-house/presidents/franklin-pierce/

"Franklin Pierce" should not be italicized—it needs quotation marks because it is the article title. The article title comes first in the citation. The year of publication should be after the article title. You may have to explain to students that this article is written about Franklin Pierce, a president, not written by someone named "Franklin Pierce."

9. Correct:
   Klass, Perri. 2019. "Having Anesthesia Once as a Baby Does Not Cause Learning Disabilities, New Research Shows." *The New York Times*. Last modified February 18, 2019. Accessed February 19, 2019. https://goo.gl/UoV3fT.

The year of publication should be after the author's name. "February" should not be abbreviated. Often the URL for web pages for newspaper articles can be very long. Teachers should decide whether to use the full

URL or an abbreviated version. In this case, using the URL www.newyork times.com would also be acceptable since the article is searchable from the main web page.

10. Correct:

    U.S. Energy Information Center. 2017. "U.S. Primary Energy Consumption by Source and Sector in 2017." Home—Energy Explained. Last modified 2017. Accessed February 19, 2019. http://www.eia.gov/energyexplained/index.php?page=coal_home.

The URL is missing. The first letter of the major words in the website title should be capitalized.

APPENDIX D4

Can You Spot the Problems? Exercise: Chicago Notes and Bibliography

Make any corrections for the citations. There could be information that is missing, in the wrong place, or incorrect. Explain your corrections below.

1. Lewis Michael. The Fifth Risk. New York: W.W. Norton and Company, 2018.

   _____

   _____

2. Trueman, Chris. "Supermarine Spitfire." The History Learning Site. Last modified 2018. Accessed January 19, 2019. "Supermarine Spitfire." The History Learning Site, 2018, www.historylearning-site.co.uk/world-war-two/world-war-two-in-western-europe/battle-of-britain/supermarine-spitfire/. Accessed 19 Jan. 2019.

   _____

   _____

3. Riordan, Rick. The Trials of Apollo: The Dark Prophecy. New York, NY: Hyperion Publishing, 2017. Accessed January 19, 2019.

   _____

   _____

4. Krakauer, Jon. *Into Thin Air.* New York, NY: Anchor Books, 1999. 75–77.

5. Niestle, Axel. 2000. "Neither Sharks nor Wolves: The Men of Nazi Germany's U-Boat Arm, 1939–1945." The Journal of Military History 64 (2): 587–589. https://search.proquest.com/docview/195614853?accountid=41092.

6. Coleman, John F. 2000. "The Battle of Midway: Turning Point in the Pacific." All Hands, 06, 20–33. https://search.proquest.com/docview/199402747?accountid=41092.

7. Balko Radley. In Defense of John Grisham. *The Washington Post,* October 2014, The Watch. Accessed February 24, 2019. https://www.washingtonpost.com/news/the-watch/wp/2014/10/16/in-defense-of-john-grisham/?utm_term=.e0f387841377.

8. The White House. *Franklin Pierce.* Presidents. Last modified 2018. Accessed February 19, 2019. http://www.whitehouse.gov/about-the-white-house/presidents/franklin-pierce/.

9. Klass, Perri. *"Having Anesthesia Once as a Baby Does Not Cause Learning Disabilities, New Research Shows."* The New York Times. Last modified Feb. 18. Accessed Feb. 19, 2019. https://goo.gl/UoV3fT.

10. "U.S. Primary Energy Consumption by Source and Sector in 2017." *Home—Energy Explained.* Last modified 2017. Accessed February 19, 2019. http://www.eia.gov/energyexplained/index.php?page=coal_home.

CAN YOU SPOT THE PROBLEMS? ANSWER KEY: CHICAGO NOTES AND BIBLIOGRAPHY

1. Correct:
   Lewis, Michael. *The Fifth Risk*. New York, NY: W.W. Norton and
       Company, 2018.

There is a comma between "Lewis" and "Michael." The state of publication, New York, should be included in the citation. Italicize the book title.

2. Correct:
   Trueman, Chris. "Submarine Spitfire." History Learning Site. Last
       modified November 16, 2018. Accessed January 19, 2019. http://
       www.historylearningsite.co.uk/world-war-two/world-war-two-
       in-western-europe/battle-of-britain/supermarine-spitfire/.

This is an example of repeated elements because of cut-and-paste errors with a citation tool. The last modified date should have a month and year. Accessed date is in the wrong place in the citation. It should be stated only once. This date should be in Month Day, Year format.

3. Correct:
   Riordan, Rick. *The Trials of Apollo: The Dark Prophecy*. New York,
       NY: Hyperion Publishing, 2017.

The full title should be italicized. There is no accessed date included in book citations.

4. Correct:
   Krakauer, Jon. *Into Thin Air*. New York, NY: Anchor Books, 1999.

Do not include a page range in the full citation unless the book is an anthology.

5. Correct:
   Niestle, Axel. "Neither Sharks nor Wolves: The Men of Nazi Germany's U-Boat Arm, 1939–1945." *The Journal of Military History*
       64, no. 2 (April 2000): 587–89. https://search.proquest.com/
       docview/195614853?accountid=41092.

The year of publication belongs after the issue number in Chicago Notes and Bibliography. *The Journal of Military History*, as a scholarly journal, should be italicized. Insert "no." before the issue number. The month (or season) of publication is missing.

6. Correct:
   Coleman, John F. "The Battle of Midway: Turning Point in the Pacific."
       All Hands 998 (June 2000): 20–33. https://search.proquest.
       com/docview/199402747?accountid=41092.

The date of publication does not belong after the author's name. Use "June" instead of "06" in parentheses. *All Hands* is the name of the journal, which should be italicized. There is no volume number listed in the publication information for this article, only the issue number. For this source, students should view the article through *ProQuest* if possible.

7. Correct:
   Balko, Radley. "In Defense of John Grisham." *The Washington Post,* October 14, 2014, The Watch. Accessed February 24, 2019. https://www.washingtonpost.com/news/the-watch/wp/2014/10/16/in-defense-of-john-grisham/?utm_term=.e0f387841377.

When author names are inverted, use a comma between last name and first name. All newspaper titles should be italicized. *The Washington Post* is a daily publication. The publication date needs to be in Month Day, Year format. Explain to students that The Watch is the section of the newspaper where this article is located. It also serves as the web page title.

8. Correct:
   The White House. "Franklin Pierce." Presidents. Last modified 2018. Accessed February 19, 2019. http://www.whitehouse.gov/about-the-white-house/presidents/franklin-pierce/.

Franklin Pierce should not be italicized—it needs quotation marks. You may have to explain to students that this article is written about Franklin Pierce, a president, not written by someone named "Franklin Pierce."

9. Correct:
   Klass, Perri. "Having Anesthesia Once as a Baby Does Not Cause Learning Disabilities, New Research Shows." *The New York Times.* Last modified February 18, 2019. Accessed February 19, 2019. https://goo.gl/UoV3fT.

Article titles are not italicized. There is never a case where italics and quotation marks should be used at the same time. Include the year for the last modified date. Months should not be abbreviated. Often the URL for web pages for newspaper articles can be very long. Teachers should decide whether to use the full URL or an abbreviated version. In this case, using the URL www.newyorktimes.com would also be acceptable since the article is searchable from the main web page.

10. Correct:
    U.S. Energy Information Center. "U.S. Primary Energy Consumption by Source and Sector in 2017." Home—Energy Explained. Last

modified 2017. Accessed February 19, 2019. http://www.eia.
gov/energyexplained/index.php?page=coal_home.

Since there is no named author, use the organization or sponsor of the
site to begin the citation. "Home—Energy Explained" should not be
italicized.

APPENDIX D5

Can You Spot the Problems?
Exercise: MLA

Make any corrections for the citations. There could be information that is missing, in the wrong place, or incorrect. Explain your corrections below.

1. Lewis, Michael. The Fifth Risk. W.W. Norton and Company 2018.

_____

_____

2. "Supermarine Spitfire." History Learning Site. Chris Trueman. 21 Nov. 2016. www.historylearningsite.co.uk. 11 Jan. 2019.

_____

_____

3. Riordan Rick. "The Trials of Apollo: the dark prophecy." Hyperion Publishing, 2017.

_____

_____

4. Krakauer, Jon. *Into Thin Air.* Anchor Books Accessed 13 Nov. 2018.

_____

_____

5. Niestle, Axel. Neither Sharks nor Wolves: The Men of Nazi Germany's U-Boat Arm, 1939–1945. The Journal of Military History, vol. 64, no. 2, 2000, pp. 587–589. ProQuest, https://search.proquest.com/docview/195614853?accountid=41092.

6. Coleman, John F "The Battle of Midway: Turning Point in the Pacific". *All Hands*, no. 998, 6, 2000, p. 20–33 *ProQuest*.

7. Balko, Radley. In Defense of John Grisham. *The Watch, The Washington Post*, Oct. 16, 2014, www.washingtonpost.com/news/the-watch/wp/2014/10/16/in-defense-of-john-grisham/?utm_term=.e0f387841377. Accessed 24 Feb. 2019.

8. Franklin Pierce. Presidents, *The White House*, 2018, www.whitehouse.gov/about-the-white-house/presidents/franklin-pierce/. Accessed 12 May 2018.

9. Klass, Perri. "Having anesthesia once as a baby does not cause learning disabilities, New Research Shows." Family, The New York Times, 18 Feb. 2019, goo.gl/nxxuPq. 19 Feb. 2019.

10. U.S. Primary Energy Consumption by Source and Sector in 2017." Home—Energy Explained, U.S. Energy Information Center, 21 Apr. 2017, www.eia.gov/energyexplained/index.php?page=coal_home. Accessed 5 June 2018.

CAN YOU SPOT THE PROBLEMS? ANSWER KEY: MLA

1. Correct:
   Lewis, Michael. *The Fifth Risk*. W.W. Norton and Company, 2018.

The book title should be italicized. There should be a comma after "Company."

2. Correct:
   Trueman, Chris. "Supermarine Spitfire." *The History Learning Site*, 2016,www.historylearningsite.co.uk/world-war-two/world-war-two-in-western-europe/battle-of-britain/supermarine-spitfire/. Accessed 19 Jan. 2019

The author's last name should be inverted. It should begin the citation. "The History Learning Site" should be italicized. "Accessed" should be typed before "19 Jan. 2019."

3. Correct:
   Riordan, Rick. *The Trials of Apollo: The Dark Prophecy*. Hyperion Publishing, 2017.

There is a comma between "Riordan" and "Rick." The first letter of all major words should be capitalized.

4. Correct:
   Krakauer, Jon. *Into Thin Air*. Anchor Books, 1999.

There is no accessed date for print books. The year of publication should come after the publisher in the citation.

5. Correct:
   Niestle, Axel. "Neither Sharks nor Wolves: The Men of Nazi Germany's U-Boat Arm, 1939–1945." *The Journal of Military History*, vol. 64, no. 2, 2000, pp. 587–589. *ProQuest*, https://search.proquest.com/docview/195614853?accountid=41092.

The article title should be in quotation marks. As a scholarly journal, *The Journal of Military History* should be italicized. *ProQuest* should be italicized.

6. Correct:
   Coleman, John F. "The Battle of Midway: Turning Point in the Pacific." *All Hands*, no. 998, June 2000, pp. 20–33. *ProQuest*, search.proquest.com/docview/199402747?accountid=41092. Accessed 21 June 2019.

The URL (or DOI) is missing from this research database article citation. The month of publication is missing. There should be a period after the "F" in the author's name. The period after "Pacific" in the article title should be within the closing quotation mark, not outside of it. There should be "pp. 20–33" instead of "p. 20–33" since these are multiple pages. This article is missing a volume number. Students should view the article in *ProQuest* if possible.

7.   Correct:
Balko, Radley. "In Defense of John Grisham." *The Watch*, The Washington Post, 16 Oct. 2014, www.washingtonpost.com/ news/the-watch/wp/2014/10/16/in-defense-of-john -grisham/?utm_term=.e0f387841377. Accessed 24 Feb. 2019.

The article title needs quotation marks. "The Washington Post" should not be italicized. In this citation, "The Washington Post" is the publisher. The publication date needs to be in Day Month Year format. Explain to students that The Watch is the section of the newspaper where this article is located.

8.   Correct:
"Franklin Pierce." *Presidents*, The White House, 2018, www.white house.gov/about-the-white-house/presidents/franklin-pierce/. Accessed 12 May 2018.

The article title should be in quotation marks. You may have to explain to students that this article is written about Franklin Pierce, a president, not written by someone named "Franklin Pierce." The web page title, *Presidents*, should be italicized. The White House is the publisher and should not be italicized.

9.   Correct:
Klass, Perri. "Having Anesthesia Once as a Baby Does Not Cause Learning Disabilities, New Research Shows." *Family*, The New York Times, 18 Feb. 2019, goo.gl/nxxuPq. Accessed 19 Feb. 2019.

All major words of a title should be capitalized. "Accessed" is missing— this belongs at the end before the last date. "Family" is italicized because it is the name of the website. Often the URL for web pages for newspaper articles can be very long. Teachers should decide whether to use the full URL or an abbreviated version as used in the above example. In this case, using the URL www.newyorktimes.com would also be acceptable since the article is searchable from the main web page.

10.   Correct:
"U.S. Primary Energy Consumption by Source and Sector in 2017." *Home—Energy Explained*, U.S. Energy Information Center, 21 Apr. 2017, www.eia.gov/energyexplained/index.php?page= coal_home.Accessed 5 June 2018.

"Home—Energy Explained" should be capitalized because it is the web page title. The article title should begin with a quotation mark. U.S. Information Center is the publisher.

APPENDIX E

Citation Guides

- E1: Citation Guide: APA
- E2: Citation Guide: Chicago Author-Date
- E3: Citation Guide: MLA

Citation guides are a very useful tool for helping students better understand sources, even if students use online citation tools. Librarians and teachers can decide how much information to provide students on a citation guide to add needed context for the ethical use of sources. Citation guides should be personalized for the assignment and learning needs of students.

Here are a few more uses for citation guides:

- Explaining citations for nonstandard sources.
- Presenting citation examples for a group of different types of sources for a specific assignment.
- Proofreading.
- An aid for students without Internet access at home or for students whose first language is not English.

For illustrative purposes, the citation guide examples in this section emphasize the proper use of parenthetical citations.

APPENDIX E1

Citation Guide: APA

PRINT BOOKS

Use the author's name as it is published on the book. The other citation information needed for books can be found on the publication page near the front of the book. If there is more than one publication year listed, use the most recent year for the citation. The year of publication will always be included with the author's last name in the parenthetical citation.

Basic format

Author Last Name, First Initial. (Year of Publication). *Title of book*. City of Publication, State of Publication: Publisher.

Example

Kershaw, A. (2013). *The liberator: One World War II soldier's 500-day odyssey from the beaches of Sicily to the Gates of Dachau*. New York, NY: Broadway Books.

Parenthetical Citation

Along with the author's last name and publication year, use the page number (p.) where you found the quote or paraphrase in the book for the parenthetical citation.

Basic format

(Author Last Name, Publication Year, p. #)

Example

(Kershaw, 2013, p. 78) should be placed at the end of your sentence with the quote or paraphrase. If you use Kershaw (2013) in your sentence, you can place (p. 78) at the end of the sentence.

WEB PAGE ARTICLES

Each web page requires analysis because information may be missing. Check to see if the web page article has an author. You will most often find this near the article title. In most cases, web pages do not have page numbers. Publication dates will vary on web pages. The year of publication will always be included in the parenthetical citation.

Example 1: Web page article without an author

Basic format

Article title. (Publication Date). Web page title. Retrieved from URL

Example

Michelle Obama. (2018). The White House. Retrieved from https://www.
whitehouse.gov/about-the-white-house/first-ladies/michelle-obama

Parenthetical Citation

Basic format

("Article Title," Publication Year)

Example

("Michelle Obama," 2018) is used because without an author, the article title is used within quotation marks, along with the publication year. Michelle Obama (the article title) is a proper noun, so capital letters are used. For other titles that are not proper nouns, the first letter in each major word of the title is capitalized for the parenthetical citation. Example: ("Immigrant Stories," 2019).

Example 2: Web page article with an author. The article in this example from CNN has a Year, Month Day publication date in the full citation because it is published daily. For the parenthetical citation, only use the publication year.

Basic format

Author Last Name, First Initial. (Publication Date). Title of article. Web page title. Retrieved from URL.

Example

Street, F. (2018, July 22). Meet Britain's real-life Iron Man. CNN Travel. Retrieved from https://www.cnn.com/travel/article/iron-man-richard-browning/index.html

Parenthetical Citation

Basic format

(Author Last Name, Publication Year)

Example

(Street, 2018) is used because there is an author. July 22 is not used in the parenthetical citation, only 2018.

RESEARCH DATABASE ARTICLES

Research databases produce an accurate full citation for articles that should be used on your References page. Use this citation instead of an online citation tool but check it for accuracy. The year of publication will always be included in the parenthetical citation.

Example 1: Scholarly research database articles always have an author and page numbers. The basic name format for the full citation is Author Last Name, First Initial. Second Initial. The author's name in this example is Shih-Chieh Chien. Use two initials for an author who publishes with a first name and middle (or second) name.

Full citation

Chien, S.C. (2014). Cultural constructions of plagiarism in student writing: Teachers' perceptions and responses. *Research in the Teaching of English, 49*(2), 120–140. Retrieved from JSTOR database.

Parenthetical Citation

Along with the author's last name and publication year, use the page number (p.) where you found the quote or paraphrase from the article for the parenthetical citation.

Basic format

(Author Last Name, Publication Year, p. #)

Example

(Chien, 2014, p. 122) should be placed at the end of your sentence with the quote or paraphrase. If you use Chien (2014) in your sentence with the quote or paraphrase, you can place (p. 122) at the end of the sentence.

Example 2: Research database article without an author. In this example, no page numbers are listed in the full citation for this source.

Full citation

Wells, S. (1979). William Shakespeare. In I. Scott-Kilvert (Ed.), *British Writers* (Vol. 1). New York: Charles Scribner's Sons. Retrieved from http://link.galegroup.com/apps/doc/H1479001386/LitRC?u=win50 26&sid=LitRC&xid=ea28ec40.

Parenthetical Citation

Basic format

(Author Last Name, Publication Year)

Example

(Wells, 1979) is used because there is an author. There are no page numbers in the full citation.

APPENDIX E2

Citation Guide: Chicago Author-Date

PRINT BOOKS

Use the author's name as it is published on the book. For authors who publish with a middle name or middle initial, this is placed after the author's first name. The other citation information needed for books can be found on the publication page near the front of the book. If there is more than one publication year listed, use the most recent year for the citation.

Basic format

Author Last Name, Author First Name. Publication Year. *Book Title*. City of Publication: Publisher.

Example

Bressler, Charles E. 2011. *Literary Criticism: An Introduction to Theory and Practice*. New York: Pearson.

Parenthetical Citation

Use the page number where you found the quote or paraphrase in the book for the parenthetical citation. The year of publication will always be included in the parenthetical citation.

Basic format

(Author Last Name Publication Year, Page Number)

Example

(Bressler 2011, 89) should be placed at the end of your sentence with the quote or paraphrase. If you use Bressler (2014) in your sentence with the quote or paraphrase, you can place (89) at the end of the sentence.

WEB PAGE ARTICLES

Each web page requires analysis because information may be missing. Check to see if the web page article has an author. You will often find this near the article title. If no name is listed, use the organization or owner of the site. In most cases, web pages do not have page numbers. The year of publication will always be included in the parenthetical citation.

Example 1: Web page article without an author. If there is no author's name listed with the article, use the organization who publishes the web page instead.

Basic format

Organization. Publication Year. "Article Title." Accessed Month Day, Year.

Example

NPR. 2018. "Rome's Subway Expansion Reveals Artifacts from the Ancient Past." Accessed July 22, 2018.

Parenthetical Citation

Basic format

(Organization Publication Year)

Example

(NPR 2018) is used because NPR is the organization responsible for the web page article. Web pages normally do not have page numbers.

Example 2: Web page article with an author

Basic format

Author Last Name, Author First Name. Publication Year. "Article Title." Accessed Month Day, Year. URL.

Example

Akapn, Nsikan. 2018. "The Arctic is Experiencing its Most Unprecedented Transition in History." Accessed December 11, 2018. https://www.pbs .org/newshour/science/the-arctic-is-experiencing-its-most -unprecedented-transition-in-history-heres-why.

Parenthetical Citation

Basic format

(Author Last Name Publication Year)

Example

(Akapn 2018) is used because there is an author.

RESEARCH DATABASE ARTICLES

Research databases produce an accurate full citation for articles that should be used in your Bibliography. Use this citation instead of an online citation tool. You still must check the citation for accuracy. The year of publication will always be included in the parenthetical citation.

Example 1: Research database article without an author and without page numbers. These citations will vary depending on the origin of the article.

"Franklin Delano Roosevelt." 2003. In *Presidential Administration Profiles for Students*, edited by Kelle S. Sisung and Gerda-Ann Raffaelle. Detroit, MI: Gale. *Student Resources in Context* (accessed June 11, 2019). http://link.galegroup.com/apps/doc/BT2304100033/SUIC?u =win5026&sid=SUIC&xid=1857f244.

Parenthetical Citation

Basic format

("Article Title," Publication Year)

Example

("Franklin Delano Roosevelt," 2003) is used because the full citation begins with the article title "Franklin Delano Roosevelt." No page numbers are listed.

Example 2: Research database article with an author but without page numbers

Benton, Richard P. 1994. "The Cask of Amontillado: Overview." In *Reference Guide to Short Fiction*, edited by Noelle Watson. Detroit, MI: St. James Press. *Literature Resource Center* (accessed February 20, 2019). http://link.galegroup.com/apps/doc/H1420006471/LitRC?u =win5026&sid=LitRC&xid=6bd96e4a.

Parenthetical Citation

Basic format

(Author Last Name Publication Year)

Example

(Benton 1994) is used because there is an author. There are no page numbers listed in the full citation.

Example 3: Research database article with an author and pagination

Example

Lupton, Julia Reinhard. 2014. "Birth Places: Shakespeare's Beliefs/Believing in Shakespeare." *Shakespeare Quarterly* 65, no. 4 (Winter): 399–420. https://search.proquest.com/docview/1665147860?account id=41092.

Parenthetical Citation

Use the page number where you found the quote or paraphrase in the article for the parenthetical citation.

Basic format

(Author Last Name Publication Year, Page Number)

Example

(Lupton 2014, 400) is used at the end of the sentence with the quote or paraphrase. If you include (Lupton 2014) in your sentence with the quote or paraphrase, you can place (400) at the end of the sentence.

APPENDIX E3

Citation Guide: MLA

PRINT BOOKS

Use the author's name as it is published on the book. For authors who publish with a middle name or middle initial, this is placed after the author's first name. The citation information for books can be found on the publication page at the front of the book. If more than one publication year is listed, use the most recent year for the citation.

Basic format

Author Last Name, First Name. *Title of Book*. Publisher, Year of Publication.

Example

Bryars, J. Pepper. *American Warfighter: Brotherhood, Survival, and Uncommon Valor in Iraq, 2003–2011*. Barnhill House, 2016.

Parenthetical Citation

Basic format

(Author Last Name Page Number)

Example

(Bryars 117) should be placed at the end of your sentence with the quote or paraphrase.

WEB PAGE ARTICLES

Each web page requires analysis because information may be missing. Check to see if the web page article has an author. You will often find this near the article title. If no name is listed, use the organization or owner of the site. In most cases, web pages do not have page numbers. Publication dates will vary on web pages.

Example 1: Web page article without an author

Basic format

"Article Title." *Web Page Title*, Publisher, Date of Publication, URL. Accessed Day Month Year.

Example

"Franklin Pierce." *Presidents*, The White House, 2018, www.whitehouse.gov/about-the-white-house/presidents/franklin-pierce/.   Accessed 12 May 2018.

Parenthetical Citation

Basic format

("Article Title")

Example

("Franklin Pierce") is used because no author is listed. The article title is used in quotation marks.

Example 2: Web page article with an author

Basic format

Author Last Name, Author First Name. "Article Title." Web Page Title, Publisher, Date of Publication, URL. Accessed Day Month Year.

Example

Brigham, Robert K. "Battlefield Vietnam: A Brief History." *PBS*, 2017. www.pbs.org/battlefieldvietnam/history/. Accessed 6 Apr. 2018.

Parenthetical Citation

Basic format

(Author Last Name)

Example

(Brigham) is used because an author is listed in the full citation. Web pages normally do not have page numbers.

RESEARCH DATABASE ARTICLES

Research databases produce an accurate full citation for articles that should be used on your Works Cited page. Use this citation instead of an online citation tool. Check the citation for accuracy. You will still need to determine the parenthetical citation. Page numbers should be included in the parenthetical citation for research database articles if page numbers print out with the article.

Example 1: Research database article without an author and without page numbers

Full citation

"Overview: "The Cask of Amontillado"." *Short Stories for Students*, edited by
      Ira Mark Milne, vol. 7, Gale, 2000. *Literature Resource Center*, http://
      link.galegroup.com/apps/doc/H1430004939/LitRC?u=win5026&sid
      =LitRC&xid=4e858d84. Accessed 27 July 2018.

Parenthetical Citation

Basic format

("Article Title")

Example

("Overview: "The Cask of Amontillado") is used because there is no author. The article title is used in quotation marks. No page numbers are listed in the full citation.

Example 2: Research database article with an author but without page numbers

Full citation

Wells, Stanley. "William Shakespeare." *British Writers*, edited by Ian Scott-
      Kilvert, vol. 1, Charles Scribner's Sons, 1979. *Literature Resource
      Center*, http://link.galegroup.com/apps/doc/H1479001386/LitRC?u
      =win5026&sid=LitRC&xid=ea28ec40. Accessed 27 July 2018.

Parenthetical Citation

Basic format

(Author Last Name)

Example

(Wells) is used because there is an author. No page numbers are listed in the full citation.

Example 3: Research database article with an author and page numbers. The page numbers will be on the article when you print it out.

Full citation

Willis, Lloyd. "Monstrous Ecology: John Steinbeck, Ecology, and American Cultural Politics." *The Journal of American Culture*, vol. 28, no. 4, Dec. 2005, pp. 357–67. *ProQuest*, search.proquest.com/docview/20 0610417/72BC25BA23AF4B12PQ/1?accountid=41092. Accessed 26 Sept. 2016.

Parenthetical Citation

Basic format

(Author Last Name Page Number)

Example

(Willis 359) is used because there is an author. There is a page range listed in the full citation.

APPENDIX F

Final Documentation Lists

APPENDIX F1

Final Documentation List

The list of citations at the end of a research paper can tell teachers quite a bit about student research. The most obvious use is to document every use of primary and secondary sources. This list is also a "snapshot" of the quality and quantity of sources used in the paper. The examples in the following pages are for Works Cited (MLA), Bibliography (Chicago Notes and Bibliography), and References (APA, Chicago Author-Date) lists. These examples should not be used in place of consulting the official citation guide but will provide teachers and librarians with a relative understanding of what to expect from students.

The Works Cited, Bibliography, and References pages have important points in common:

- One-inch margins are standard with a common font, such as Times New Roman 12.

- All citations should have a hanging indent.

- The citations should be alphabetized according to the author's last name (or the organization responsible for the content) or the first major word in the article title.

- Teachers: The individual parts of the citation should always be in the correct order, even if there are punctuation or other formatting errors

From *Combating Plagiarism: A Hands-On Guide for Librarians, Teachers, and Students* by Terry Darr. Santa Barbara, CA: Libraries Unlimited. Copyright © 2019.

in the citation. This order—author (if listed or organization responsible for the site), title, publication information—provides the most important information about the source. These elements also make it easier for you to check the source if you have any questions.

- The citations on the Works Cited, Bibliography, and References pages should all be on the same general subject area. There may be some variations. For example, a British literature paper on gender issues may include history sources on the politics of the time. Any glaring exceptions to this should be investigated.

- For web page articles, there is a direct correlation between the credibility and quality of the resource and the completeness of the citation. High-quality, credible web pages are more likely to have complete publication information, making it easier to complete the citation accurately.

- The *types* of sources should follow the research paper requirements. For example, if the paper requires the use of books and research database articles, there should not be any web page or social media citations.

- The expected number of sources should be specified by the assignment. Any papers that use significantly more or less sources should be reviewed more carefully.

- The citation tool within research databases should be used for these articles instead of an online citation tool for accuracy. Visually, research database article citations will have a very consistent look because of the use of the citation tool. These will also be the longest of any citations. Students should be expected to review these citations for accuracy.

- The citations should not have any elements that are repeated within the citation. For example, the URL should not appear twice in a citation. This may indicate the improper use of a citation tool.

- Any capitalization errors, font inconsistencies, or missing elements from the copy and paste of citations from citation tools should be corrected by students during the rough draft stage.

- All research database article and web page citations should include a URL.

The examples pages show a typical Works Cited, Bibliography, and References page for a research paper on monarch butterflies.

APPENDIX F2

References Page Example: APA

REFERENCES

Boyd-Barrett, C. (2019, January 8). Monarch butterfly numbers plummet 86% in California. *USA Today*, p. 1A. Retrieved from http://link .galegroup.com/apps/doc/A568762839/SUIC?u=win5026&sid=SUI C&xid=46b116d6

Halpern, S. (2011). *Four wings and a prayer: Caught in the mystery of the monarch butterfly*. New York, NY: Vintage Books.

Migration and overwintering. (2018). Retrieved February 1, 2019, from United States Department of Agriculture website: https://www.fs.fed .us/wildflowers/pollinators/Monarch_Butterfly/migration/

Solensky, M. J., & Oberhauser, K. S. (2004). *The monarch butterfly: Biology and conservation*. Devon, England: Comstock Publishing.

Wells, C. N. (2010). An ecological field lab for tracking monarch butter-flies & their parasites. *The American Biology Teacher, 72*(6), 339–344. Retrieved from https://search.proquest.com/docview/75128757 3?accountid=41092

FORMATTING THE REFERENCES PAGE

• The page number is at the top right of the References page. It is a new page and the last page of the paper.

- Each citation is double spaced, with a double space between each citation.

- The font should be Times New Roman 12.

- The first letter of the title is capitalized, as is the first letter of the first word after the colon for a subtitle.

- If there is no author name listed, the article title should be used without quotation marks.

- Web page citations from frequently updated publications (newspapers, magazines, other journals) should be in the (Year, Month Day) format for (Year, Month) depending on the publication frequency.

APPENDIX F3

References Page Example: Chicago Author-Date

REFERENCES (OR WORKS CITED)

Boyd-Barrett, Claudia. 2019. "Monarch Butterfly Numbers Plummet 86% in California." *USA Today*, January 8, 2019. *Student Resources in Context.* http://link.galegroup.com/apps/doc/A568762839/SUIC?u =win5026&sid=SUIC&xid=46b116d6.

Halpern, Sue. 2011. *Four Wings and a Prayer: Caught in the Mystery of the Monarch Butterfly*. New York, NY: Vintage Books.

Solensky, Michelle J., and Karen S. Oberhauser. 2004. *The Monarch Butterfly: Biology and Conservation*. Devon, England: Comstock Publishing.

United States Department of Agriculture. 2018. "Migration and Overwintering." Forest Service. Last modified 2018. Accessed February 1, 2019. https://www.fs.fed.us/wildflowers/pollinators/Monarch_Bu tterfly/migration/.

Wells, Carrie N. 2010. "An Ecological Field Lab for Tracking Monarch Butterflies and Their Parasites." *The American Biology Teacher* 72 (6) (August):339–344. https://search.proquest.com/docview/751287573 ?accountid=41092.

FORMATTING THE REFERENCES (OR WORKS CITED) PAGE

- The instructor should decide if this page should be References or Works Cited. Both are permissible.

- The page number is at the top right of the References page. It is a new page and the last page of the paper.

- Each citation is single spaced, with a single space between each citation.

- Accessed date is used for web page citations when there is no known publication date.

APPENDIX F4

Bibliography Example: Chicago Notes and Bibliography

BIBLIOGRAPHY

Boyd-Barrett, Claudia. "Monarch Butterfly Numbers Plummet 86% in California." *USA Today*, January 8, 2019, 1A. *Student Resources in Context.* http://link.galegroup.com/apps/doc/A568762839/SUIC?u=win5026&sid=SUIC&xid=46b116d6.

Halpern, Sue. *Four Wings and a Prayer: Caught in the Mystery of the Monarch Butterfly.* New York, NY: Vintage Books, 2011.

Solensky, Michelle J., and Karen S. Oberhauser. *The Monarch Butterfly: Biology and Conservation.* Devon, England: Comstock Publishing, 2004.

United States Department of Agriculture. "Migration and Overwintering." Forest Service. Last modified 2018. Accessed February 1, 2019. https://www.fs.fed.us/wildflowers/pollinators/Monarch_Butterfly/migration/.

Wells, Carrie N. "An Ecological Field Lab for Tracking Monarch Butterflies & their Parasites." *The American Biology Teacher* 72, no. 6 (August 2010): 339–344. https://search.proquest.com/docview/751287573?accountid=41092.

FORMATTING THE BIBLIOGRAPHY

- Each citation is single spaced. There is a single space between each citation.

- The bibliography is the last page of the paper. It is a new page. The page number is in the top right corner.

- Research database articles should have a volume number, issue number, and page range. The publication month (or season) should be in parentheses before the publication year. The availability of this information can vary slightly.

APPENDIX F5

Works Cited Page Example: MLA

WORKS CITED

Boyd-Barrett, Claudia. "Monarch Butterfly Numbers Plummet 86% in California." *USA Today*, 8 Jan. 2019, *Student Resources in Context*, http://link.galegroup.com/apps/doc/A568762839/SUIC?u=win502 6&sid=SUIC&xid=46b116d6. Accessed 1 Feb. 2019.

Halpern, Sue. *Four Wings and a Prayer: Caught in the Mystery of the Monarch Butterfly*. Vintage Books, 2011.

"Migration and Overwintering." *Forest Service*, United States Department of Agriculture, 2018. https://www.fs.fed.us/wildflowers/pollinators/Monarch_Butterfly/migration/. Accessed 1 Feb. 2019.

Solensky, Michelle J., and Karen S. Oberhauser. *The Monarch Butterfly: Biology and Conservation*. Comstock Publishing, 2004.

Wells, Carrie N. "An Ecological Field Lab for Tracking Monarch Butterflies & their Parasites." *The American Biology Teacher*, vol. 72, no. 6, 2010, pp. 339–344. *ProQuest*, https://search.proquest.com/docview/751287573?accountid=41092. Accessed 1 Feb. 2019.

FORMATTING THE WORKS CITED PAGE

- The last name and page number are at the top right of the Works Cited page. It is the last page of the paper.

- Each citation is double spaced, with a double space between each citation.

APPENDIX G

General Citation Style Reviews

APPENDIX G1

General Citation Style Review Lesson Plan

Objectives: Visual recognition of correct citation formatting conventions helps students proofread more effectively. It also helps to add important context to digital resources.

Delivery: Librarians, who are familiar with citations, should deliver this lesson when possible. This type of general warm-up of citation conventions is appropriate for students new to research and experienced students who need a review before research begins.

As a result of this lesson, students will understand the following:

- Author and editor formats

- Title formats: capitalization, quotation marks, italics

- The process for creating a hanging indent

- Date formats

- Publisher name recognition

- The placement of quotes within the text of a research paper

Warm-up questions should be projected onto the screen from the instructor's computer. The questions can be adapted and repeated depending on student competence, with this warm-up and performance with academic assignments requiring citations.

Source materials: Questions for the warm-up can be developed from student responses from these baseline questions or errors on previous work products. Instructors and librarians can discuss areas of particular need with students.

Length of time: Ten to fifteen minutes at the beginning of class during the research paper process.

APPENDIX G2

General Citation Style Review Exercise: APA

1. Why doesn't this source have an author?

   Mason, J. D. (Ed.). (1989). *Poems of Phillis Wheatley.* Chapel Hill, NC: University of North Carolina Press.

2. What is the correct way to write an author's name, Keith Robinson, in a citation on the References page?

   a. Robinson, Keith
   b. Keith Robinson
   c. Robinson, K.

3. Where can the author's name be found on a web page article?

   a. At the top navigation bar on the web page
   b. Near the title of the article
   c. At the end of the article

4. Which date is correct for the date of a newspaper article citation?

   a. (October 9, 2017)
   b. (2017, October 9)
   c. (2017)

5. How should an article title be stated in a citation?

    a. "The rain forests in Brazil"
    b. "The Rain Forests in Brazil"
    c. The rain forests in Brazil

6. Which one of these is a publisher?

    a. The New York Times
    b. Scholastic
    c. Smithsonian Institution

7. How do you do a hanging indent for your Bibliography?

    Grant, R. (2016, September). Deep in the Swamps, Archaeologists are Finding How Fugitive Slaves Kept Their Freedom. Smithsonian. Retrieved from http://www.smithsonianmag.com/history/deep-swamps-archaeologists-fugitive-slaves-kept-freedom-180960122

8. What is the correct title format for an e-book in a citation?

    a. Jane Eyre
    b. *Pride and prejudice*
    c. "Crime and punishment"
    d. "*The professor*"

9. Correct the capitalization of these book titles used in the text of your paper.

    a. Before we were yours
    b. The end of World War II: a Prisoner of war perspective
    c. Worth Dying for
    d. War On Peace: The End Of Diplomacy And The Decline of American Influence

10. Which one is correct? This is from a book written by John Kelly in 2018. The quote is from page 15.

    a. John Kelly (2018), explained, "The two murders took place less than one mile apart, making it urgent for the police to canvas the area carefully. (p. 15)
    b. "The two murders took place less than one mile apart, making it urgent for the police to canvas the area carefully" (Kelly, 2018, 15).
    c. "The two murders took place less than one mile apart, making it urgent for the police to canvas the area carefully" (Kelly, 2018).

GENERAL CITATION STYLE REVIEW ANSWER KEY: APA

1. This is an edited book of poems by Phillis Wheatley. Phillis Wheatley is deceased. Often, editors will compile works of authors such as this and republish them.
2. The answer is (c).
3. The answers are (b) and (c). If a web page article has a named author, it is usually found near the article title (this is most common in online newspapers and other current publications) or at the end of the article. You can show a web page for demonstration purposes to help with this question. This question reinforces the idea that if there is a named author for a web page article, it is apparent—no excessive searching is necessary.
4. The answer is (b). Newspaper articles are published daily, so these sources will have the most specific dates possible in Year, Month Day format.
5. The answer is (c). "Brazil" is capitalized because it is a proper noun.
6. All of these are publishers. Each one publishes online and print content.

7. • Highlight the citation.
    • Click on Paragraph.
    • Change Special to Hanging.
    • Change Line Spacing to Double.
    • Click OK.

8. The answer is (b).
9. When titles are found in the text of the paper for APA, all major words are capitalized.

    a. Before We Were Yours
    b. The End of World War II: A Prisoner of War Perspective
    c. Worth Dying For
    d. War on Peace: The End of Diplomacy and the Decline of American Influence

10. (a) This is incorrect. There is a missing quotation mark at the end.
    (b) Incorrect. The "p." is missing before the 15.
    (c) This is incorrect. The page number, p. 15, is missing.

APPENDIX G3

General Citation Style Review Exercise: Chicago Author-Date

1. Why doesn't this source have an author?

    Mason, Julian D., ed. 1989. *Poems of Phillis Wheatley*. Chapel Hill, NC: The University of North Carolina Press.

2. What is the correct way to write an author's name, Keith Robinson, on the Bibliography page?

    a. Robinson, Keith
    b. Keith Robinson
    c. Robinson, K.

3. Where can the author's name be found on a web page article?

    a. At the top navigation bar on the web page
    b. Near the title of the article
    c. At the end of the article

4. Which publication date is correct in Author-Date format for a newspaper article citation on your References page?

    a. October 9, 2017

    b.   9, October, 2017

    c.   9 Oct. 2017

5.   How should an article title be stated in a citation?

    a.   "The Brazilian Rain Forest"

    b.   The Brazilian Rain Forest

    c.   *The Brazilian Rain Forest*

6.   Which one of these is a publisher?

    a.   The New York Times

    b.   Scholastic

    c.   Smithsonian Institution

7.   How do you do a hanging indent for your Bibliography?

Grant, Richard. 2016. "Deep in the Swamps, Archaeologists are Finding How Fugitive Slaves Kept Their Freedom." *Smithsonian Magazine*, September 2016. http://www.smithsonianmag.com/swamps.

8.   What is the correct title format for an e-book?

    a.   Jane Eyre

    b.   *Pride and Prejudice*

    c.   "Crime and Punishment"

    d.   *"The Professor"*

9.   Correct the capitalization of these book titles.

    a.   Before we were yours

    b.   The end of World War II: a Prisoner of war perspective

    c.   Worth Dying for

    d.   War On Peace: The End Of Diplomacy And The Decline of American Influence

10.   Which one is correct? This is a quote from page 15 from a print book written by John Kelly in 2018.

    a.   "The two murders took place less than one mile apart, making it urgent for the police to canvas the area carefully (Kelly 15).

    b.   Kelly said, "The two murders took place less than one mile apart, making it urgent for the police to canvas the area carefully" (2018, 15).

    c.   "The two murders took place less than one mile apart, making it urgent for the police to canvas the area carefully" (Kelly 2018, 15).

GENERAL CITATION STYLE REVIEW ANSWER KEY:
CHICAGO AUTHOR-DATE

1. It is an edited book of the poems of Phillis Wheatley. Editors often compile the works of authors and publish them in book format. Julian D. Mason is the editor.

2. Author Last Name, First Name format is used.

3. The answer is (b) and (c). If a web page article has a named author, it is usually found near the article title (this is most common in online newspapers and other current publications) or at the end of the article. You can show a web page for demonstration purposes to help with this question. This question reinforces the idea that if there is a named author for a web page article, it is apparent—no excessive searching is necessary.

4. The answer is (a). Newspapers are generally published daily.

5. Article titles are in quotes.

6. All of these are publishers. Each one publishes online and print content.

7. • Highlight the citation.
   • Click on Paragraph.
   • Change Special to Hanging.
   • Change Line Spacing to Single.
   • Click OK.

8. The answer is (b). The title format for e-books and print books is the same.

9. All of the major words of a book title should be capitalized.
   a. Before We Were Yours
   b. The End of World War II: A Prisoner of War Perspective
   c. Worth Dying For
   d. War on Peace: The End of Diplomacy and the Decline of American Influence

10. (a) This is incorrect. The closing quotation mark is missing. The year of publication is missing.
    (b) This is correct. Using the author's name in the text before the quote is an option.
    (c) This is correct.

APPENDIX G4

General Citation Style Review Exercise: Chicago Notes and Bibliography

1. Why doesn't this book footnote have an author listed?

    1. Julian D. Mason, ed., *The Poems of Phillis Wheatley* (Chapel Hill, NC: The University of North Carolina Press, 1989), 64.

2. What is the correct way to write an author's name, Keith Robinson, on the Bibliography page?

    a. Robinson, Keith
    b. Keith Robinson
    c. Robinson, K.

3. Where can the author's name be found on a web page article?

    a. At the top navigation bar on the web page
    b. Near the title of the article
    c. At the end of the article

4. Which date is correct in Chicago Notes and Bibliography format for a newspaper article citation?

    a. October 9, 2017

    b.   9, October, 2017

    c.   9 Oct. 2017

5.   How should an article title be stated in a citation?

    a.   "The Brazilian Rain Forest"

    b.   The Brazilian Rain Forest

    c.   *The Brazilian Rain Forest*

6.   Which one of these is a publisher?

    a.   The New York Times

    b.   Scholastic

    c.   Smithsonian Institution

7.   How do you do a hanging indent for your Bibliography?

Grant, David. "Deep in the Swamps, Archaeologists are Finding How Fugitive Slaves Kept Their Freedom." Smithsonian. Last modified September 2014. Accessed December 17, 2018. http://www.smith sonianmag.com/history/deep-swamps-archaeologists-fugitive-slaves-kept-freedom-180960122.

8.   What is the correct title format for an e-book?

    a.   Jane Eyre

    b.   *Pride and Prejudice*

    c.   "Crime and Punishment"

    d.   *"The Professor"*

9.   Correct the capitalization of these book titles.

    a.   Before we were yours

    b.   The end of World War II: a Prisoner of war perspective

    c.   Worth Dying for

    d.   War On Peace: The End Of Diplomacy And The Decline of American Influence

10.   Where do you check for the publication information of a print book?

11.   This quote is from page 15 from a book, *A History of Violent Crime in Baltimore, 1965–2015*, by John Kelly which was published in 2015. "The two murders took place less than one mile apart, making it urgent for the police to canvas the area carefully." Which footnote is correct?

    a.   [1]John Kelly, *A History of Violent Crime in Baltimore, 1965–2015* (Baltimore: Johns Hopkins University Press, 2015), 15.

b. [1]John Kelly, A History of Violent Crime in Baltimore, 1965–2015 (Baltimore: Johns Hopkins University Press, 2015).

c. [1]Kelly, John. *A History of Violent Crime in Baltimore, 1965–2015* (Baltimore: Johns Hopkins University Press, 2015), 15.

GENERAL CITATION STYLE REVIEW ANSWER KEY: CHICAGO NOTES AND BIBLIOGRAPHY

1. It is an edited book of the poems of Phillis Wheatley. Editors often compile the works of authors and publish them in book format. Julian D. Mason is the editor.
2. Author Last Name, First Name format is used.
3. The answer is (b) and (c). If a web page article has a named author, it is usually found near the article title (this is most common in online newspapers and other current publications) or at the end of the article. You can show a web page for demonstration purposes to help with this question. This question reinforces the idea that if there is a named author for a web page article, it is apparent—no excessive searching is necessary.
4. The answer is (a). Publication dates in a citation are in Month Day, Year format.
5. Articles are in quotation marks.
6. All of these are publishers.
7. • Highlight the citation.
    • Click on Paragraph.
    • Change Special to Hanging.
    • Change Line Spacing to Single.
    • Click OK.
8. The answer is (b). The title for e-books and print books is italicized.
9. All of the major words of a book title should be capitalized
    a. Before We Were Yours
    b. The End of World War II: A Prisoner of War Perspective
    c. Worth Dying For
    d. War on Peace: The End of Diplomacy and the Decline of American Influence
10. The publication information is found on one of the first few pages in the front of the book. While the author and title are on the cover, the publication page has the publication date and publisher information. The same is true for e-books.
11. The correct answer is (a). (b) is incorrect because the book title is not italicized. Since this connects to a quote, a page number should be included in the footnote. (c) is incorrect because the author's name should not be inverted in the footnote.

APPENDIX G5

General Citation Style Review
Exercise: MLA

1. Why doesn't this book have an author listed in the citation?

   Mason, Julian D., ed. *The Poems of Phillis Wheatley.* The University of North Carolina Press, 1989.

2. What is the correct way to write an author's name, Keith Robinson, on the Works Cited page?

   a. Robinson, Keith
   b. Keith Robinson
   c. Robinson, K.

3. Where can the author's name be found on a web page article?

   a. At the top navigation bar on the web page
   b. Near the title of the article
   c. At the end of the article

4. Which date is correct in MLA format?

   a. October 9, 2017
   b. 9, October, 2017
   c. 9 Oct. 2017

5. How should an article title be stated in a citation?

   a. "The Brazilian Rain Forest"

   b. The Brazilian Rain Forest

   c. *The Brazilian Rain Forest*

6. Which one of these is a publisher?

   a. The New York Times

   b. Scholastic

   c. Smithsonian Institution

   d. CNN

7. How do you do a hanging indent for your Works Cited page?
   Grant, Richard. "Deep in the Swamps, Archaeologists are Finding How Fugitive Slaves Kept Their Freedom." *History*, Smithsonian, Sept. 2016. www.smithsonianmag.com. Accessed 9 Sept. 2016.

8. Which is the correct title format for an e-book?

   a. Jane Eyre

   b. *Pride and Prejudice*

   c. "Crime and Punishment"

   d. *"The Professor"*

9. Correct the capitalization of these book titles.

   a. Before we were yours

   b. The end of World War II: a Prisoner of war perspective

   c. Worth Dying for

   d. War On Peace: The End Of Diplomacy And The Decline of American Influence

10. Where do you check for the publication information for a print book?

11. Which one is correct? This is from a print book written by John Kelly in 2018.

   a. "The two murders took place less than one mile apart, making it urgent for the police to canvas the area carefully. (Kelly 18)

   b. "The two murders took place less than one mile apart, making it urgent for the police to canvas the area carefully" (Kelly 18).

   c. "The two murders took place less than one mile apart, making it urgent for the police to canvas the area carefully" (Kelly, 18).

GENERAL CITATION STYLE REVIEW ANSWER KEY: MLA

1. It is an edited book of the poems of Phillis Wheatley. Editors often compile the works of authors and publish them in book format. Julian D. Mason is the editor.

2. Author Last Name, First Name format is used.

3. (b) and (c). If a web page article has a named author, it is usually found near the article title (this is most common in online newspapers and other current publications) or at the end of the article. You can show a web page for demonstration purposes to help with this question. This question reinforces the idea that if there is a named author for a web page article, it is apparent—no excessive searching is necessary.

4. Review the Day Month Year format with students. No punctuation except for the period after the month abbreviation should be used in MLA format.

5. (a). Article titles are in quotes.

6. All of these are publishers. Each one publishes online and print content.

7. • Highlight the citation.
   • Click on Paragraph.
   • Change Special to Hanging.
   • Change Line Spacing to Double.
   • Click OK.

8. (b). The title format for e-books and print books is the same. It should be italicized.

9. All of the major words of a book title should be capitalized.
   a. Before We Were Yours
   b. The End of World War II: A Prisoner of War Perspective
   c. Worth Dying For
   d. War on Peace: The End of Diplomacy and the Decline of American Influence

10. The publication information is found on one of the first few pages in the front of the book. While the author and title are on the cover, the publication page has the publication date and publisher information. The same is true for e-books.

11. (a) This is incorrect. The closing quotation mark is missing.
    (b) This is correct.
    (c) This is incorrect. There is no comma after the author's last name in the parenthetical citation.

APPENDIX H

Explaining Plagiarism

- H1: Plagiarism Definition Discussion for Students: Lesson Plan
- H2: Plagiarism Definition Handout for Students

APPENDIX H1

Plagiarism Definition Discussion for Students: Lesson Plan

Objectives: Digital sources require a detailed discussion of plagiarism. Honor agreements and basic definitions are insufficient for students to understand the meaning of plagiarism. Since there is no standard plagiarism education curriculum in schools today, a discussion with ample opportunity to ask questions is essential for students. Plagiarism should be discussed without any differences between unintentional and intentional plagiarism. Plagiarism is actually very definitive. The challenge for teachers and school administrators is to decide how to handle it when it occurs.

Teachers can distribute one or two copies of this plagiarism definition to students. It should also be posted on the teacher's learning management system. Depending on the students, one copy should be maintained by the students for reference. If you think it is necessary, the second copy can be signed, dated, and returned to you at the end of the discussion. This verifies that the student attended the discussion.

The tone of the discussion facilitators should be firm and definitive. This is not creating a culture of fear. The purpose of this discussion is to objectively review the behaviors that you will consider plagiarism without threats. Encourage questions and comments from students to clear up any misunderstandings. A definitive, firm tone lays the groundwork to eliminate excessive excuses and justifications. For schools with a moral or religious mission, these elements should be included in the discussion.

Ideally, this discussion should be facilitated by a teacher and librarian before a research project. A librarian can provide expertise and support. The librarian should post this information on the library's website for students and teachers. Since so much of avoiding plagiarism is closely tied to citations and understanding sources, the librarian can answer questions and provide models for these elements in this definition. It also establishes the librarian as someone who can answer these types of questions during the research process.

Facilitator discussion suggestions for each point are listed in italics. This explanation should be adapted depending on the needs of your students. This can be adapted as a remediation discussion for students who have plagiarized.

PLAGIARISM DEFINED

To steal and pass off the words and/or ideas of others as one's own. *This includes words and ideas from books, web pages, research database articles, and anything else you find on the Internet. What you read on the Internet is not free for the taking. No matter what, there's an author, and it needs to be cited. You don't have the right to ever use anyone else's words and ideas without a citation, especially since avoiding plagiarism is just a skill set. Even using one sentence someone else wrote without citing it is plagiarism.*
All of these are considered plagiarism:

- Turning in someone else's work as your own. *This means that you don't reuse papers or projects of your own, your siblings, cousins, or anyone else you know. This includes parts of someone else's work, including your own. Do not purchase research papers on the Internet or pay anyone to do a paper for you.*

- Copying words or ideas from someone else without giving credit. *When you copy someone else's words or ideas, you are stealing. Words and ideas can't be held in your hand, but they can still be stolen.*

- Failure to put a quotation (of original words and phrases, direct quotes) in quotation marks. *There are writers, authors, and scholars who are working daily on research and presenting it out in the world. They deserve credit for their original ideas. When you use quotation marks and a citation, you have given them credit in your paper. If you don't use quotation marks when you should, you are falsely claiming that the sentences are yours. It doesn't matter whether you forgot or not. (Depending on the research experience of students, demonstrate how a quotation should look on the board.)*

- Giving any incorrect information about the source of the information. *The librarian should lead this part of the discussion.*

  - Making up sources in entirety. *If you are in a situation where you have lost a source, stop by the library for help with this. Intentionally making up a source is considered plagiarism.*

  - Making up any part of a citation. This includes any information about the page numbers, authorship, publisher, or date of publication. *This is fraud.*

- Incorrect paraphrasing—changing words but copying the sentence structure of a source even if you give credit. This includes summarizing ideas in any way without citing the source. *Good paraphrasing means being aware of the author's original sentence structure. Your paraphrase should maintain the author's main idea or point of view but be in your own words. (Teachers should plan for micro-paraphrasing instruction for students.) When you paraphrase or summarize someone else's work, it's no different than a direct quote—it needs a citation.*

- Copying so many words or ideas from a source that it makes up a majority of your work, whether you give credit or not. *Your analysis should make up the majority of the paper. When you copy too much from other sources, this is plagiarism because you have used that source's structure.*

- Using words and passages you don't understand and can't explain. *Information from a source is meant to support your thesis. If you use words and passages from a source that you don't understand or can't explain, there is no real basis to your paper.*

- Copying and pasting passages from electronic sources without placing the passages in quotes and properly citing the source. *You should print out web pages and research database articles, not copy and paste. It takes only a few minutes to type a quote or paraphrase into your paper with a citation. The greater the amount of text copied from a source, the higher the possibility that you will plagiarize.*

APPENDIX H2

Plagiarism Definition Handout for Students

PLAGIARISM DEFINED

To steal and pass off the words and/or ideas of others as one's own. **All of these are considered plagiarism:**

- Turning in someone else's work as your own.

- Copying words or ideas from someone else without giving credit.

- Failure to put a quotation (of original words and phrases, direct quotes) in quotation marks.

- Giving any incorrect information about the source of the information.

- Incorrect paraphrasing—changing words but copying the sentence structure of a source even if you give credit. This includes summarizing ideas in any way without citing the source.

- Copying so many words or ideas from a source that it makes up a majority of your work, whether you give credit or not.

- Using words and passages you don't understand and can't explain.

- Copying and pasting passages from electronic sources without placing the passages in quotes and properly citing the source.

From *Combating Plagiarism: A Hands-On Guide for Librarians, Teachers, and Students* by Terry Darr. Santa Barbara, CA: Libraries Unlimited. Copyright © 2019.

APPENDIX H2

Plagiarism Definition Handout for Students

PLAGIARISM DEFINED

APPENDIX I

Common Knowledge

- I1: Considering the Audience: Common Knowledge Questions
- I2: Common Knowledge, Citable Information, or Irrelevant? Lesson Plan

APPENDIX I1

Considering the Audience: Common Knowledge Questions

Objectives: The audience and topic for a research paper need to be considered when deciding whether information is common knowledge or needs a citation. Students can practice this important judgment call by analyzing sentences that are typical information for the school community. This includes the people, situations, and the information students have studied. These questions should be changed to reflect your community situation and priorities. Students should answer if the sentence is common knowledge or if it needs a citation. The instructor should change the audience context during the discussion.

As a result of this instruction,

- students will be able to consider the audience when deciding whether information is common knowledge;

- students will be able to consider the topic of the paper as a factor in whether information needs a citation.

Delivery: These questions can be delivered as a warm-up or classwork by a teacher or librarian. The instructor should prepare five to ten questions about topics that are common for the school community. These questions should be projected from a computer on a screen for students. Differences of opinion and discussion are encouraged for this exercise.

From *Combating Plagiarism: A Hands-On Guide for Librarians, Teachers, and Students* by Terry Darr. Santa Barbara, CA: Libraries Unlimited. Copyright © 2019.

Length of time: Ten to fifteen minutes, depending on the number of questions.

SAMPLE QUESTIONS

These sample questions are typical for a private high school. Create similar questions for your school culture.

1. Ben Rubeor is the head lacrosse coach at Loyola Blakefield.

    Discussion: Within the school community, this is common knowledge that does not need a citation. Rubeor would not need to be identified as a lacrosse coach. It is already known. If this information is used in a publication about regional or national lacrosse in secondary schools, it would likely be stated as "Loyola Blakefield Lacrosse Head Coach Ben Rubeor," which identifies him, so a citation is unnecessary.

2. Germany invaded Poland on September 1, 1939.

    Discussion: This falls under the category of subject-area common knowledge for history. This information is found in many different Internet and print sources about World War II. It does not need a citation for a history research paper about World War II. However, if this sentence is used in another subject area, it may need a citation. For example, for a literature paper that tracks changes in the works of writers through historical events, it should be considered for a citation.

    Note to instructors: You may find that students are uncomfortable not citing this sentence because it includes a date. Explain that this type of information which is stated in multiple places with a basic Internet search does not need a citation.

3. In his book *The Greatest Generation*, Tom Brokaw believes that the women at home were the true heroes of World War II.

    Discussion: This sentence needs a citation in all situations. It is a paraphrased opinion by the author, Tom Brokaw.

4. Shakespeare was the greatest writer of the Elizabethan period.

    Discussion: This is an opinion shared throughout history about Shakespeare. It is known by people with a high school education. If this sentence was copied exactly from a source by an author who is a Shakespeare expert, it should have quotation marks around it with a citation.

5. The latest statistics show that tuition for private high schools on the East Coast has increased by 15% since 2010.

> Discussion: While people who are associated with private schools may have some knowledge of this, the exact percentage means that this sentence needs a citation in all situations. The exact percentage of tuition increase across all schools is not common knowledge.

6. The character of Beowulf is the basis for the superheroes depicted by Marvel Comics.

> Discussion: This is an opinion that should be cited by a direct quote for all audiences.

7. Even after a serious head injury from the Taliban, Malala Yousafzai and her father have continued to advocate for the education of girls in the Middle East.

> Discussion: This is well-known information. It is common knowledge for all audiences.

8. San Francisco was the backdrop for the social commentary of Beat poets like Jack Kerouac, Lawrence Ferlinghetti, and Gregory Corso.

> Discussion: For students studying the Beat poets, this is common knowledge. However, for a paper that discusses overall social changes in the United States, this should be considered for a citation because it mentions San Francisco.

9. Rosa Parks attended the Montgomery Industrial School for Girls.

> Discussion: This is not common knowledge about Rosa Parks. However, it is readily available through Internet searches and reference books about Rosa Parks's life. For a history paper on Rosa Parks's contribution to the civil rights movement, this would probably not be important enough to mention. However, it should be cited in a paper about the role of industrial schools in American history.

10. A principle of Jesuit education for boys is the formation of "Men for Others."

> Discussion: If this sentence is used for a research paper at a Jesuit school, no citation is necessary. This is common knowledge within this educational community. For all other uses of this information, a citation will be necessary.

APPENDIX 12

Common Knowledge, Citable Information, or Irrelevant? Lesson Plan

Objectives: Does this need a citation? This question is central for avoiding plagiarism while choosing information while reading secondary sources.

As a result of this lesson, students will understand

- better recognition of common knowledge, citable, and irrelevant information during the secondary-source reading process.

Delivery: The subject-area teacher or librarian can deliver this lesson. It can be completed during the research process or any time during the school year. For teachers, it offers an opportunity to refine the type of information preferred for direct quotes and paraphrases. The instructor should prepare a paragraph from a website or research database article to project for the class to see. During the class discussion, note the sentences with different colors for citable, common knowledge, or irrelevant. There are two other delivery alternatives. Copies of a research database article can be distributed to students to use a highlighter for the different sentence types while the teacher leads the discussion. This can be completed on the students' computers if they have access to technology where they can use a computer pen to write on a document.

A basic research prompt should be developed for discussion purposes. Research database articles from the subject area should be the first choice.

After students read the paragraph, the instructor should lead a discussion of each sentence to determine whether it is common knowledge, citable, or irrelevant to the research prompt. This process helps reading comprehension skills for secondary sources and the ability to recognize specific information that can serve as evidence for the research paper.

INFORMATION CATEGORIES

Citable: This is a sentence that contains specific information that is not previously known. It is directly connected to the topic or thesis statement.

Common knowledge: The information is connected to the topic but general or already known.

Irrelevant: The information may not be common knowledge, but it does not have a connection to the thesis statement.

Alternatively, this can also be completed as a homework or classwork assignment after a brief explanation from the instructor. More advanced students will not need a lengthy classroom explanation. The sentences should be highlighted or marked in three different colors to signify irrelevant, common knowledge, or citable.

Length of time: One class period or less, depending on the number of sentences.

Discussion: Students will likely have a difference of opinion about the classification of the sentences. This type of discussion should be encouraged as part of the learning process.

Materials: The instructor should choose a paragraph from a subject-specific research database article and decide on the best delivery method. Ask students to bring three different-colored pens or highlighters to this lesson if copies of a research database article will be distributed.

Example. This is from a research database article about Barack Obama.

"Barack Obama." *Contemporary Black Biography*, vol. 74, Gale, 2009. *World History in Context*, http://link.galegroup.com/apps/doc/K1606004418/UHIC?u=win5026&xid=2b4b0d61. Accessed 24 Feb. 2018.

The instructor should use different colors to underline sentences as citable, irrelevant, or common knowledge. For this example, a citable sentence is underlined once. Common knowledge is underlined twice. Irrelevant information is not underlined. The writing prompt is Barack Obama's Legislative Agenda.

Obama passed up job offers from Chicago's top law firms to practice civil rights law with the small public-interest law office Miner,

Barnhill & Galland and to lecture on constitutional law at the University of Chicago, holding the latter position until he ran for the U.S. Senate in 2004. He jumped into politics by chairing a voter-registration drive that helped carry the state of Illinois for Democratic presidential candidate Bill Clinton in 1992. As his political ambitions became more compelling, Obama turned down a chance to apply for a tenure-track professorship at the University of Chicago. Instead, when an Illinois State Senate seat in his home South Side district became open in 1996, he ran and was elected. In the Illinois Senate, Obama was noted for his role in developing legislation to curb racial profiling and a bill that mandated the videotaping of police interrogations carried out in death-penalty cases. (underscore added)

Explanation

Obama passed up job offers from Chicago's top law firms to practice civil rights law with the small public-interest law office Miner, Barnhill & Galland and to lecture on constitutional law at the University of Chicago, holding the latter position until he ran for the U.S. Senate in 2004.

While the name of the law firm that employed Obama before he ran for Senate is not common knowledge, in light of his other accomplishments, it is unlikely to be important enough to mention in a research paper. It is considered irrelevant.

He jumped into politics by chairing a voter-registration drive that helped carry the state of Illinois for Democratic presidential candidate Bill Clinton in 1992.

This is a judgment call. The specificity of the voter registration drive and the relationship with Bill Clinton mean that this should probably be cited. However, this information is available through various reference and Internet sources.

As his political ambitions became more compelling, Obama turned down a chance to apply for a tenure-track professorship at the University of Chicago.

This is irrelevant in the context of Obama's entire political career.

Instead, when an Illinois State Senate seat in his home South Side district became open in 1996, he ran and was elected.

This information is common knowledge. It can be found in many sources.

In the Illinois Senate, Obama was noted for his role in developing legislation to curb racial profiling and a bill that mandated the videotaping of police interrogations carried out in death-penalty cases.

This relates directly to the topic. It is specific and should be cited.

Glossary

Academic integrity
The education process operates with the understanding that students will do academic work honestly without cheating or plagiarism.

Accessed
"Accessed" is used at the end of MLA citations for digital resources. It is the last date you viewed the material. Accessed is also used for Chicago style with digital sources where no date of publication is available.

Annotations
Annotations are made on a secondary source during the research process. Annotations are notes that help to understand and use the source. Some online citation tools allow you to annotate your citations.

Anthology
A book, prepared by an editor, where multiple authors have contributed individual chapters, stories, or poems. When you cite sources from an anthology, note the author and title of the work you are using from the book. Most course textbooks are considered anthologies.

Attribution
The process of giving credit to the author through a citation or footnote.

Author
The individual or group who wrote the information.

Author-Date system
In the *Chicago* Author-Date citation style, the parenthetical citation emphasizes the author's last name and the year of publication. The year of publication is listed after the author's name in the full citation.

Bibliography
This is a list of the all the sources used for a research paper, presentation, or other project. It includes sources cited and those that were consulted but not cited. The *Chicago Manual of Style* uses a Bibliography for an alphabetized list of sources.

Block quote
A block quote is used for longer quotations in your paper, generally over four lines. Quotation marks are not used. Block quotes should be used sparingly to avoid plagiarism. See Chapter 6 for more information.

Born digital
Resources that have never been in print format. The source was created digitally and is viewed through a computer only. An example is a photograph taken by a digital camera and posted on a website.

***Chicago Manual of Style* (also known as Turabian)**
Currently in its seventeenth edition, this citation style uses Notes (footnotes and endnotes) and Bibliography or the Author-Date system to document sources used in a research.

Citation
A full citation lists the author, title, publisher, date of publication, and location for a source used in a research project. In-text citations are placed within the text of the paper for MLA, APA, and Chicago Author-Date where there are direct quotes or paraphrases. Full citations are placed on your Works Cited, References, or Bibliography page.

Citation tools
Citation tools are online resources that assist in writing citations. The user types in information about the parts of a source into various boxes to create the citation.

Common knowledge
Information that is widely known without having to look it up ("everyone knows it"). For more information, see Chapter 7.

Copy and paste
This is a very common cause of plagiarism. Using the tools within Word processing program, lines of text from a digital resource such as a web page or research database article are copied and pasted onto a new document.

Copyright
The author or creator of a work has the right to decide how the work is used and by whom. The length of copyright is the life of the author plus seventy years. A copyright symbol does not have to be put on the work for copyright protection to be in effect. The U.S. Copyright Office defines copyright as "a form of protection provided by the laws of the United States for 'original works of authorship,' including literary, dramatic, musical, architectural, cartographic, choreographic, pantomimic, pictorial, graphic, sculptural, and audiovisual creations" (Circular One-Copyright Basics 2017).

Copyright year
The year when the original work was created in a fixed format.

Copyright-free images
Images that do not have any copyright restrictions. These images can be used without permission for academic and commercial purposes. These are also known as public domain images.

Creative Commons license
A digital copyright method for authors and other creators to allow others to use their work in different ways with attribution. For more information, see https://creativecommons.org/licenses.

Digital images
Images that are stored through the Internet as a part of an individual website, image aggregator site, or other digital database of images.

Digital sources, digital resources
Sources only available using a computer. Examples—web pages, images, research database articles, e-books, videos.

Direct quotes
Sentences are copied from a source exactly as they appear in the source and placed in the paper using quotation marks or a block quote.

DOI (digital object identifier)
This is a permanently assigned string of numbers and letters that identify an article on the Internet. Many research databases use a DOI instead of a URL. It is found with the other publication information for the article. Usually, citation tools automatically include the DOI if the article has one. For more information, see https://www.apastyle.org/learn/faqs/what-is-doi and https://www.doi.org/.

E-books
E-books are digital versions of books that are available for reading through a web browser or reading app. Some e-books are an alternative version of print books. Other e-books are "born digital" and have been published only in e-book format.

Editor
Editors are responsible for reviewing articles and other content before it is printed or made available online on websites. They also compile chapters by different authors to be published in a book. An editor does not normally write any of the content.

Encyclopedia
A multivolume set of books, often broken down into alphabetical order ranges (A–C, D–F) with individual alphabetical entries. Some encyclopedias cover all types of knowledge. Others may be on a more specific subject area. Most encyclopedias are now digitally available through libraries.

Endnotes (notes)
In Chicago style, the notes are listed at the end of each chapter or the end of the entire work.

Fact
Information that cannot be disputed. It is proven and well known. Facts generally do not need to be cited.

Fair Use
According to the U.S. Copyright Office, Fair Use is a legal doctrine that promotes freedom of expression by permitting "the unlicensed use of copyright-protected works in certain circumstances." Fair Use is a reason why copyrighted works can be used without permission of the author for academic purposes.

Footnotes (Notes)
In the Chicago Notes and Bibliography citation style, footnotes provide information about a source mentioned in the text of the paper. The footnotes are placed at the bottom of the page or at the end of a chapter (Notes). The notes are numbered in the paper with a superscript to correspond with the text of the paper.

Full text
For research database articles, the full text version is the entire article, along with an abstract.

Google Images
Google Images is an aggregator of images from all over the Internet. It makes the images from millions of web pages available to you in one web search. For more information, see Chapter 8 that discusses the ethical use of digital images.

Hanging indent
A hanging indent keeps your citations organized and separated from one another. In Microsoft Word, begin the process with left justification of the citation on your document.
- Highlight the citation.
- Right click and choose Paragraph.
- On the next window, change the Spacing (according to the citation style) and then change Special to Hanging.
- Click OK.

Honor policies
Guidelines schools develop to manage incidents of cheating, plagiarism, and other issues of academic dishonesty. Honor policies normally list the acceptable behaviors for how students should handle different types of academic work.

Idea
A concept that has not been fully realized in a set format. See Chapter 7 for more information.

Information management
To avoid plagiarism, good information management practices are important.
- Creating a draft Works Cited, References, or Bibliography page where you add sources as you research and adjust through the process.
- Printing out all digital sources for highlighting and annotations when possible. Use of Microsoft Word OneNote and maintaining web page resources in the Favorites in your web browser can also be used if you do not wish to print.
- Checking that each full citation has a corresponding parenthetical citation/footnote when you proofread your paper.

Information synthesis
The process of reading and evaluating information from various sources—primary and secondary—and using it effectively with your own ideas to write a research paper or other project.

Intellectual property

According to the World Intellectual Property Organization, (http://www.wipo.int/about-ip/en/), "Intellectual property refers to creation of the mind such as inventions; literary and artistic works; designs; and symbols, names and images used in commerce."

In-text citation (parenthetical citation)

These are interchangeable terms. In-text citations document the use of secondary sources in a research paper or other project for MLA, APA, and the Author-Date style for Chicago. It marks the place, normally at the end of the sentence, where a direct quote or paraphrase has been used in a research project.

Issue number

Magazines and scholarly journals have issue numbers as part of their publication process. The issue number is the number of issues published in a year. See Chapter 6 for more information.

Journal

A journal is a printed, often research-based publication geared toward professionals in a field. It is a type of magazine. The articles in the journal are then made available to you through research databases.

Keyword

Keywords are words terms, and phrases that specifically describe information research needs. A keyword is typed in the search box of digital resources to access articles and other sources.

Location

Every resource is placed in a specific location where it is available for access. For web pages, the location is the URL. For print books, it is the call number where the book is located on the shelf in the library. For research database articles, the first location is the journal or reference source where the information was originally published. The second location is the research database.

Magazine

Magazines are print publications that are made widely available for purchase or subscription to the public. The subject area normally has a wide appeal for readers. *Time* magazine, *The New Yorker*, and *Vogue* are examples of magazines.

Overciting

When too many citations are used, it gives the appearance that too much has been borrowed from the source or that quotes have been used to "piece" the paper together. A general guideline is one or two citations for each page of the paper.

Pagination

This is a more formal term for page numbers. If a source has a page number, it needs to be used in a parenthetical citation or footnote. See Chapter 6 for guidelines about which sources have page numbers.

Paraphrasing (micro-paraphrasing)
Restating secondary-source information in your own words with a citation. See Chapter 2 for more information about this process.

Parenthetical citation (in-text citation)
See in-text citation.

Peer review
This is part of the editorial process when an article is submitted for publication in a scholarly journal. To publish information of the highest quality, editors will send articles submitted for publication to professionals in the same field to review. The comments of these "peer reviewers" are used as the basis for any changes to the article.

Periodical
A printed magazine, scholarly journal, or other publication such as a newspaper that is published on a set schedule. This can be daily, weekly, monthly, quarterly, or by the season.

Plagiarism, intentional
Using the words and ideas of others without crediting the source on purpose. This can mean copy and paste of sentences or an entire paragraph with or without crediting the source or incorrect paraphrasing. Intentional plagiarism can also include the purchase of a research paper from another person or from a website.

Plagiarism, unintentional
Plagiarism that has been committed accidentally, usually because of a lack of knowledge or experience. The penalties for unintentional plagiarism are normally the same as those for intentional plagiarism.

Proofreading
A thorough review of a research paper or other project which includes the placement and use of sources.

Public domain
Information sources (including images) that were created in the United States before 1923. You can copy, modify, or distribute the image without permission.

Publication date
The date the source was published. Publication dates can vary. For more information, see Chapter 6.

Publication page
For books, the publication page is found within the first few pages at the front of the book. It contains important information for the citation such as the year of publication, publisher name, and the publisher's city and state.

Publisher
The publisher is a company that is responsible for making a book or other information available for readers, either digitally or in print.

Recycling fraud
Reuse of previously completed academic work. This is a type of plagiarism. One of the tenets of academic integrity is that each academic assignment is newly completed.

Reference book
A book that is consulted for information purposes, not read cover to cover. It is normally on one general topic area with alphabetical entries.

References list
For Chicago Author-Date style, the References list is the sources you have cited and consulted for the research paper. For APA format, it is an alphabetical, double-spaced list of all the sources used in your research paper. For more information, see Chapter 6.

Relevant (relevance)
Information that can be used as evidence to support a claim in a research paper through a direct quote or paraphrase.

Research database article (research databases)
Research databases are subscription-based secondary sources through a school or public library. These articles are originally from a wide range of publications and made available digitally for research.

Research process
Depending on the subject area and the teacher, the research process takes different paths. Some of the common elements are choosing a topic, thesis, background knowledge, outline, research, and use of secondary sources, and citations.

Scholarly journal
A scholarly journal publishes research-based articles from a professional group. For example, *The Journal of the American Medical Association* publishes research articles for the medical community. *English Journal* publishes article for middle school and high school English teachers. Research databases make these articles available through your library.

Superscript number
In the Chicago Notes and Bibliography citation style, a superscript number is placed at the end of a quote or paraphrase, which corresponds to a footnote.

Turabian
See *Chicago Manual of Style*.

Volume number
Magazines and scholarly journals will have a volume number. This is the number of years the publication has circulated. For example, volume fifty-four means the publication has been in existence for fifty-four years. It is abbreviated in full citations as "vol."

Web page
A single web page within a larger website. A web page, with an article, is considered a source.

Web page article
The information written on a topic that appears on a web page in article format. This is the paragraphs of text you will use as a source for your paper from a web page.

Web page article title
The title directly above the web page article's paragraphs of text. It sums up the paragraphs listed beneath it.

Web page title
A title that is normally found at the top or top left of the web page. It is a broader title that encompasses the subject of the information on the web page.

Website
A collection of web pages, normally on one general topic.

Works Cited page (MLA format)
This is an alphabetical list of all the sources you cited in the text of your paper or project. This is necessary for PowerPoint, posters, and other projects that require research. For more information, see chapter 6.

Works Consulted page
An alphabetical list of all the sources cited and consulted (but not used) in a research paper. Students should not create a formal Works Consulted page unless requested by a teacher.

REFERENCES

Circular 1: Copyright Basics. 2018. Washington, DC: U.S. Copyright Office. Accessed February 27, 2019. https://www.copyright.gov/circs/circ01.pdf.

U.S. Copyright Office. 2018. "More Information on Fair Use." Copyright.gov. Last modified December 2018. Accessed February 27, 2019. https://www.copy right.gov/fair-use/more-info.html.

RESOURCES

Fair Use (https://www.copyright.gov/fair-use/more-info.html): This is a legal definition of Fair Use.

United States Copyright Office (https://www.copyright.gov/help/faq/defini tions.html).

United States Patent and Trademarks Office (https://www.uspto.gov): This site has legal information about intellectual property, patents, and trademarks.

Index

About the Author

Terry Darr is library director at Loyola Blakefield, an independent college preparatory school for boys in grades six through twelve. She teaches more than 200 information literacy classes each school year. The past ten years have taught her how to design instruction that works for her students. She is a regular book reviewer for the American Library Association and *Library Quarterly*. Darr has presented on plagiarism education and micro-paraphrasing in the Maryland and DC areas.